Blacks at the Net

Sports and Entertainment
Steven A. Riess, *Series Editor*

Other titles in Sports and Entertainment

BLACKS | at the Net

Black Achievement in the History of Tennis

VOLUME 1

Sundiata Djata

Syracuse University Press

Library of Congress Cataloging-in-Publication Data
Djata, Sundiata A.
Blacks at the net : Black achievement in the history of tennis,
volume 1 / Sundiata Djata.— 1st ed.
p. cm.— (Sports and entertainment)
Includes bibliographical references and index.
ISBN 0-8156-0818-7 (volume 1 : alk. paper)
1. Tennis—History   2. African American tennis
players—History.   I. Title.   II. Series.
GV992.D53 2005
796.342089'96073—dc22
2005025794

Manufactured in the United States of America

To Idella Maria Perkins Madison Djata,
whose favorite players are
Yannick Noah, Gustavo Kuerten, Martina Navratilova,
Lori McNeil, Pete Sampras, and Mary Jo Fernandez

Sundiata Djata studies and teaches African history, African American history, Caribbean history, Latin American history, and U.S. sport history, and has received degrees from the University of Illinois, Urbana-Champaign; Oklahoma City University; Morgan State University; and the University of Massachusetts. Djata is the author of *The Bamana by the Niger: Kingdom, Jihad, and Colonization, 1712–1920* and has written articles on black music history, the Brazilian Naval Revolt of 1910, blacks and advertising, and the construction of black sexuality.

Contents

Illustrations

Acknowledgments

MANY PEOPLE have been helpful in the completion of this manuscript. I thank Aubrey Battee, the recipient of the University Research Apprenticeship Program at Northern Illinois University, who was instrumental in most phases of this research. Pontus Hiort, historian and former professional tennis player on the satellite tour, made invaluable suggestions during the countless hours of discussing various issues. Makan B. Keita, Patrick Royer, Jinaki Wilson, and Sarah A. Ward were gracious enough to work as field liaisons.

I extend a special thanks to Ronald Agenor, touring professional, for his insights and encouragement. I fondly appreciate the hospitality of Mary L. Perkins, who provided lodging while I conducted interviews in her area. Branch Curington was particularly helpful in providing historical photographs. Many others have been helpful in various ways, including Keith Allen, Leslie Allen-Selmore, Andre Christopher, Carlos Fleming, Serah Hyde, Marcus Freeman (editor of *B T Magazine*), Nancy Wingfield, Gabe Logan, Lewellyn Ferguson, and Garth Gittens.

Others who have provided support in one way or another include Arnold Houston, a media relations specialist at Tuskegee University; Nick Cheales at Information Sport England; Leslie Slocum, head of the Reference and Library Division of the British Information Services; Reggie Belgrave, Tournament Committee chairperson at Rochdale

Racquet Club; and Annette Atherton, information officer of the Lawn Tennis Association (England). I am also grateful to Juliet E. K. Walker, Charles C. Stewart, and Glenn Phillips, who have continued to be my mentors. And I particularly appreciate the cooperation of the many people I interviewed.

Caveats

FOR A BETTER UNDERSTANDING, it is important to explain the usage of certain terms and the limitations of this work. The terms *black, white,* and *yellow* denote the three major "racial" categories. I do not use *Asian* because I wish to maintain consistency in terminology and because *Asian* denotes geography, not race. However, I use *race* in this study only as a socioeconomic and political construct because it is within this context that racism, discrimination, and stereotypical thinking were created and have thrived. In addition, I use the term *Aborigine* (Australia) owing to the popular usage in the existing literature.

It is also important to comment on the phrase *black community*. The popular phrase has often suggested homogeneous thinking among a people. However, no one personality, ideology, or goal describes all black people. Dwight A. McBride, English professor and editor, maintains that "Too often African American cultural critique posits an essential black community that serves as a point of departure of commentary. In other cases it assumes a kind of monolith when it calls upon the term *black community* at all."[1] I have used the phrase in the plural form to represent various types of communities among blacks. The distinction is especially important because this work covers not only blacks in the United States, who have been incorrectly seen as the representative of a whole, but blacks in other countries.

This work excludes the discussion of being black and homosexual in tennis because of the lack of sufficient data available on the subject. The general antigay sentiment in tennis has been evidenced by the treatment of and comments about Martina Navratilova, Amelie Mauresmo, and professional women athletes in general. There has been no "openly gay" black tennis player who can be used to determine just how tennis establishments have responded to that person and the issue as a whole. Considering the widespread homophobia in black communities, it would be interesting to see how blacks respond to a black, homosexual athlete as a heroic figure. Furthermore, just because black, gay individuals have achieved great professional heights does not mean that everyone in the black community has held them in high esteem. For example, the treatment of Bayard Rustin, James Baldwin, and others has demonstrated the levels of homophobia among blacks. The omission of the topic from this work is no indication that the issue is unimportant. I discuss occasions when male tennis players have had their masculinity questioned. However, such comments have generally been based on the view of tennis as a "sissy sport" rather than on specific suspicions regarding a player's sexual orientation. The irony of viewing tennis as a "feminine" sport has been that female tennis players have constantly had their femininity, even their sexual orientation, questioned. Women of all "races" have been subjected to stereotypical, discriminatory perceptions just for participating in sporting activities.

Introduction

IN 1892, the Associated Cycling Clubs concluded that "They would not tolerate colored riders as members";[1] this action effectively barred blacks from the league in the Illinois division. The following year it was announced that the annual United States Tennis Association (USTA) tennis tournament in Chicago was opened "to all comers."[2]

These examples reveal the complexities in sports as it deals with race. Black participation in tennis has had a long tradition, clouded by obscurity, racism, and genderism. Nevertheless, great stories have emerged.

The major purpose of this study is to provide a historical outline of black participation in tennis, highlighting some historic personalities and the matches they played. Beginning with the formation of early black clubs in the nineteenth-century United States and the emergence of professional black tennis players, who rose to the top ranks of the sport in the twentieth century, I explore the development of the black tennis professional. Moreover, focusing on the players who have competed on the minor professional circuits not only reveals a greater number of blacks who have played professional tennis, but also provides some insights to the obstacles they have faced.

Although most professional black players have come from the United States, this study includes some discussion of tennis in several African and Caribbean nations as well as in France, Australia, and England, although a forthcoming second volume will have more to say on the subject.

I compare and contrast athletes and circumstances from other sports with those in tennis to highlight general trends in sports and to determine to what degree black tennis players have shared similar experiences. An uncompromising look at the racism that has confronted these players provides a nuanced picture of the particular pressures and challenges they have faced, including the expectation that they must represent a race.

This study is based largely on various sources, including personal and published interviews, life writings, newspaper articles, and tennis publications. There is no monographic literature on blacks in tennis. More recently, biographical works have been published on a few individuals in the sport. It is imperative that the rich history of blacks' participation in tennis, spanning more than a century, is preserved. This work is not intended to be the final word on blacks in tennis; instead, I hope that it will create discussions and promote additional historical scholarship on all levels of the sport. Tennis has traveled a rocky road from a time when the best-known tennis clubs were "exclusive," barring admission to all but a self-selected group of wealthy white players. Looking back from the vantage point of the new millennium, I aim to show how black tennis players have changed the face of the game.

Blacks at the Net

1

The American Tennis Association
and the Early Years

THE CREATION OF TENNIS in its original form has been a disputed issue. It has been argued that the term came from the name of an ancient city in the Nile Delta: Tanis (as the Greeks called it) or Tinnis (as Arabs called it). Fine linens were manufactured in Tinnis, and early balls used for tennis were made of linen. People of Tinnis played a game using this ball and a crude racket. Other historians cite Homer's mentioning that Nausicaa, daughter of King Alcinous of Phaeacia, played a game of handball with her maidens, and they believe that tennis derived from this game.

Robert W. Henderson advanced the argument that ancient Egyptians devised a ball game that is an antecedent of the modern tennis game.[1] Malcolm D. Whitman credits Arabs with creating the game and claims that cloth used for tennis balls in medieval times were made in Tinnis in the Nile Delta.[2] However, Heiner Gillmeister argues that Egyptologists have been unable to find evidence of a ball game described as a fertility rite and that the medieval cloth-manufacturing monopoly was founded in Flanders in northern Europe.[3] According to one sport historian, tennis and other sports are "merely vestigial remains of religious rites of ancient times."[4]

Although it is clear how modern tennis was introduced in modern Africa, the Caribbean, and Australia, historians have debated who brought the sport to the United States. At least three people have been

1

given credit for introducing the sport here. James Dwight and Fred Sears played the game in August 1874 in Nahant, Massachusetts, near Boston. Others argue that Mary Ewing Outerbridge brought the sport from Bermuda to Staten Island, New York, in February 1874. Martha Summerhayes, however, claims that Emma Wilkins Bailey played tennis at Camp Apache in the Arizona Territory in 1874.[5] Another source maintains that Major Harry Gem founded "the first lawn tennis club in the world" at Leamington in 1872 and served as its first president. In a letter, he claimed that he and a friend, J. B. A. Pereira, played "such a game" in 1860. Gem never claimed to have invented the game, but he has been given credit for doing just that.[6] In any event, Major Walter Wingfield, a retired British army officer first marketed the game. He applied for a patent for a version of tennis called Spairistike, Greek for "ball game," on February 23, 1874, in England.[7]

The first U.S. tennis championship tournament was held in 1881 at the Casino Club in Newport, Rhode Island. "Fewer than 50 spectators, all wealthy vacationers who resided in their splendid stone 'cottages' during the summer, milled around the court." The players "sported white flannels, long-sleeved shirts, and neckties, though they exchanged their bowlers for striped caps when playing." Twenty-two players from wealthy families vied for the title, using the rules of the All England Croquet and Lawn Tennis Club in Wimbledon. Richard D. "Dickey" Sears, age nineteen, won the tournament.[8]

Because the written history of the sport has focused on specific individuals and organizations involved in early play, it is unclear why blacks were attracted to the game in the first place. Missing are the cultural and social processes that brought blacks to the sport around the late 1880s. Paralleling other aspects of developing American culture, blacks played tennis as they did other sports they saw whites or Aborigines play. For instance, boxing had attracted blacks as early as the late eighteenth century; planters sometimes promoted boxing bouts among slaves, and blacks themselves sponsored prizefights in New York City. In antebellum New Orleans, blacks played raquette, a game resembling lacrosse, possibly borrowed from the Choctaw people.

After the Civil War, blacks quickly adapted to baseball, which became the most popular team sport of urban blacks.[9]

Three developments in tennis occurred very rapidly for blacks. First, a number of blacks were playing the game by the 1890s. Second, racial segregation in tennis was also set by that time. Finally, even among blacks, tennis was very much a pursuit of the upper classes. When the United States Lawn Tennis Association (USLTA) was formed in 1881, the organization followed the racial and class rules of the society. Private clubs were not just for the elites, but for white elites. In addition, there was the lack of sufficient public facilities for black players, so some wealthy black families had tennis courts constructed in their yards.

By 1900, the ultrarich in America had adopted tennis, yachting, polo, fox hunting, and golf, "pursuits whose cost put them out of reach of ordinary Americans." The rich used sport as a means of "establishing social exclusiveness and prestige," and set it in "distinctive environments shaped for their pursuits." Adapting the customs of the British elites, they quickly brought tennis and golf into vogue. This exclusionary attitude existed among wealthy women, particularly in tennis, "evidently [prized for] its social effects as much as [for] its hygienic benefits." According to Elizabeth C. Barney, "The enjoyment of tennis revolved around the 'social intercourse' at the club house." The country club was the "most repeated form, and lavish clubhouses designed by leading architectural firms served as centers of social interchange as well as focal points of golf and tennis." Within this context, the compound at Newport, Rhode Island, was constructed. Players in the tournament "came from the ranks of social fashion."[10] This image of tennis survived into the new millennium, although with some exceptions.

Faculty members at Tuskegee Institute in Alabama began to promote tennis at the school in 1890 after seeing the game played in the North.[11] In addition, black players from eastern cities participated in local tournaments, and, according to record, the first tournament with black players was held in 1898 in Philadelphia, sponsored by the Chautauqua Tennis Club.[12] The black players and sponsors of these local tournaments founded the most important tennis organization for blacks, the American Tennis Association (ATA).[13]

Although some blacks played tennis by the close of the nineteenth century, little is known about the best players of this period, in contrast to black players in some other sports whose names have survived. For instance, Marshall W. "Major" Taylor was the U.S. sprint champion in bicycling in 1898; Peter Jackson, the "Black Prince of the Ring," was a heavyweight boxer at the turn of the century; and Isaac Murphy rode three Kentucky Derby winners in the 1880s. By World War I, blacks were pushed out of professional horse racing and bicycle races, although they continued to box. However, they were denied entry into professional tennis from the beginning.

Because of racial segregation, the ATA was formed on November 30, 1916, in Washington, D.C. It was at a tournament in New York City in 1916 that the idea was conceived to form a national association. After a meeting between members of the Association Tennis Club of Washington, D.C., and the Monumental Tennis Club of Baltimore, letters were mailed to all known black tennis clubs in the United States. In New York City, a permanent organization was formed, officers and a executive committee were elected, and a committee was appointed to draft a constitution.[14] H. Stanton McCard was elected the ATA's first president.

The Monumental Tennis Club hosted the first national championship in 1917 at Druid Hill Park in Baltimore, Maryland.[15] Only three events were played: men's singles, won by Tally Holmes; women's singles, won by Lucy Slowe; and men's doubles, won by Tally Holmes and Sylvester Smith.

On August 21, 1926, Dr. Ivson Hoage,[16] Gerald F. Norman, Kinckle Jones, Laurence C. Dancy, Loaura V. Junior, Lester B. Granger, Richard Hudlin, and Dr. W. H. A. Barrett executed a certificate of incorporation for the ATA and filed it in the office of the New Jersey secretary of state on September 1, 1926.[17] Although blacks were denied the opportunity to play in USTA events, the ATA had no rules that prevented whites from playing in its sponsored tournaments.

The black clubs on the East Coast were not the only clubs open to blacks formed in the early twentieth century. The West Louisville Tennis Club was organized in the early 1920s at Chickasaw Park in Louisville, Kentucky, because blacks were not permitted to play tennis in other inner-city facilities.

By 1926, tennis had become more popular in the United States. At the U.S. National Tennis Championships, more than seven thousand fans "gathered in the steel and concrete stadium of the West Side Tennis Club."[18] The sport was still associated, however, with the "English upper classes and rich Americans who played on their estates or in their exclusive clubs." Although it was not considered a manly sport, a "few brave men" played, perhaps owing to its "popularity among the upper classes in England."[19]

During the 1937 National Championships, the ATA approved an educational and goodwill tour of a team composed of its highest-ranking players to play at colleges and high schools. This tour was under the direction of the ATA's Intercollegiate Committee. In 1938, it visited twenty-one colleges and eight high schools, offering talks, lectures on keeping fit, and demonstrations between members of the team and local stars of promise.[20]

By 1939, 150 black tennis clubs existed, with twenty-eight thousand players. In addition, there were thirty-five sectional and state tournaments, leading to the ATA National Championships tournament.[21] For example, the Tuskegee Club, composed of Tuskegee faculty and U.S. Veteran's Hospital employees, became affiliated with the ATA in 1930 and hosted the fifteenth ATA National Championships in 1931.

Although the ATA was a much welcomed and much needed organization for black tennis players, those black players who played tennis at white colleges "had the best exposure to serious, high level tennis" because they were "recipients of skilled coaching and intense competition, and they enjoyed the use of modern facilities."[22] Black athletes who participated in other sports at white colleges have been far more visible, however, in the annals of history than have black tennis players in similar circumstances. For example, blacks in track programs of major white universities received more press. Eddie Tolan at Michigan,

Howard P. Drew at the University of Southern California (USC), Sol Butler at Dubuque University, Ned Gourdin of Harvard, as well as De-Hart Hubbard, Pete White, and Roy Morse made remarkable gains in track. Early in the century, John B. Taylor at the University of Pennsylvania was the first black to excel in broad jumping. In football, the top black athletes included Fritz Pollard, Paul Robeson, and Duke Slater.[23]

At the same time, however, blacks were also playing tennis at predominately white institutions. For instance, Richard Hudlin was the captain of the University of Chicago tennis team and the first black captain in the Big Ten colleges. Douglas Turner of Illinois was the runner-up for the Big Ten Championship in 1930; Reginald Weir was the team captain at City College of New York for three years; and Tom Walker Sr. played at West Virginia State College.

A tennis tradition was also developing at black colleges. After tennis became popular at Tuskegee, coaches and interested parties at other institutions promoted tennis in surrounding communities. Emmitt J. Scott, S. E. Courtney, Warren Loggan, and E. T. Atvell at Tuskegee Institute; Charles Cook of Howard University; and Thomas Jefferson of Lincoln University were leading black collegians. The Annual Southern Tennis Championship was inaugurated in 1930 and was played on Tuskegee Institute's clay courts. In addition, the Twenty-fourth U.S. Infantry Invitation Tournament began in 1930. Despite the claim that black players at predominately white colleges had better exposure to tennis at a higher level, a player from a black college, Nathaniel Jackson of Tuskegee, defeated Reginald Weir in 1932 and 1933 for the Williams Cup.

Tuskegee and Wilberforce University in Ohio had the top tennis players in the 1930 Intercollegiate Championships. The competition was depicted as showcasing "a speedy and dazzling brand of tennis. The Netters of Wilberforce University, Wilberforce, Ohio, carried away the honors in the intercollegiate tournament."[24] James Trouman and Ernest Ashe of Wilberforce faced each other in the men's singles final, Trouman winning 2-6, 6-2, 6-4. They also won the doubles title, defeating Emanuel McDuffle and Clarence Smith of Tuskegee. Laura

Demery of Clark University defeated Elmira Fannin of Tuskegee Institute, then she and partner Almeta Hill defeated Charlotte Fannin and Elmira Fannin in the women's doubles final. Thirty-four players from nine colleges participated in the tournament.

At Tuskegee, the first tennis court was constructed in 1890 in front of the Academic Building, and two others were built near "the Oaks," the home of Booker T. Washington. Other courts were constructed behind the Oaks when those in front were discontinued. However, the court considered the "cradle of Tuskegee tennis" was built in 1900 between First and Second Emery, the dormitories for young men. Initially, there were no facilities for student players, and only the women who played well were allowed to enjoy the privileges of the tennis club. E. Davidson Washington, Booker T. Washington's son, and C. G. Kelly formed the first tennis club in 1909. The popularity of tennis grew at Tuskegee owing to the efforts of people such as G. W. A. Scott, who coached summer school teachers, until World War I, when interest waned. After the war, the tennis "spirit revived" under Coach Cleve L. Abbott, "who has probably done more than any one person to promote tennis development at Tuskegee Institute."[25] Three additional courts were built on Washington Field and two behind Douglas Hall for women players. Another was added near the John A. Andrew Memorial Hospital for the benefit of doctors and nurses. The popularity of tennis at Tuskegee continued to grow, and additional courts were constructed in 1928.

Two sisters, Margaret and Roumania Peters, helped to establish tennis even more firmly at Tuskegee in the 1930s. Their mother encouraged Margaret to wait until Roumania graduated from high school so that they could attend Tuskegee together. Athletic administrator Cleveland Leigh Abbott offered them full scholarships. Known as "Pete" and "Repeat," the sisters were a powerhouse in doubles, winning fourteen ATA tournament titles. In addition, Roumania won the ATA national singles titles in 1944 and 1946, defeating Althea Gibson in the final of the latter tournament. At the time, the sisters had to pay for their equipment and traveling expenses. They played exhibition matches for English royalty, and movie stars posed with them for publicity pictures. The sisters graduated in 1941 with degrees in physical education.[26]

Reginald Weir and Gerald Norman Jr. were two of the earliest players to challenge the USLTA's racist policy in 1929 when they paid the one dollar entry fee for the USLTA Junior Indoor Championships in New York. When they were refused spots in the draw, the National Association for the Advancement of Colored People (NAACP) filed a formal grievance in hopes of forcing the USLTA to "*publicly* defend its racist stance and thereby open itself up to tremendous criticism."[27] Weir had success, however, on the ATA circuit by winning the national singles title five times from 1931 to 1942. The USLTA eventually rewarded Weir a high eastern ranking. Years later, he captured its National Seniors Indoor title, becoming the first black man to win an official USLTA championship in 1956. However, the first black known to win a USLTA title was Lorraine Williams of Chicago, who won the girls' singles in 1954.[28]

Some of these early black tennis players participated in other sports. For example, Eyre Saitch, who won a 1926 ATA men's singles title, was a member of the New York Renaissance basketball team, and Isadora Channels of Chicago, a net rusher who won four ATA titles in the 1920s, played for the Chicago Romas basketball team. Ora Washington, who won eight ATA national singles titles between 1929 and 1937, played for a basketball team sponsored by the *Philadelphia Tribune,* a black-owned newspaper.

Blacks in the collegiate ranks and those who played recreational tennis convened at the ATA Nationals. For instance, in 1957 the ATA National Championships tournament was held at Central State College in Wilberforce, Ohio. One observer remarked, "The caliber is improving year by year, several of its members having numerous victories to their credit in major competition all over the world. This too is tennis."[29]

• • •

Although many public courts were constructed during the Roosevelt administration, tennis was still an expensive sport, which limited the professional development of black players. In addition, formal instruction was not readily available to them, so that many players had to teach themselves. This was the case with Jimmie McDaniel, who watched the best white players and then practiced in front of a mirror.

Although McDaniel won three consecutive ATA National Championships from 1939 to 1941 and another in 1946, he received greater publicity when he played a famous white tennis champion, the great Don Budge, on July 29, 1940, in New York City on the courts of the Cosmopolitan Tennis Club, an affiliate of the ATA. The exhibition was organized by Wilson Sporting Goods, for which Budge had signed a deal to do promotional work. The president of the company "recognized a public relations opportunity when he saw it." [30] Al Laney of the *New York Herald Tribune* wrote, "Donald Budge, the greatest tennis player of the day, performed an important service yesterday for the good of the game that has made him a celebrity and a moderately wealthy man before one of the most interesting groups that he has encountered in his compartively [*sic*] long tennis life." [31]

A red carpet was rolled out for Budge when he arrived at the club. The event was held in a black venue, and the match was of great interest to blacks; the stands were full, and others watched from windows and fire escapes of nearby buildings. Still others stood outside the club on the street to listen to the score on the address system. Budge and McDaniel played in front of a crowd that numbered almost two thousand. [32] A local paper reported, "The color line was erased, at least temporarily, for the first time in [the] history of major American Tennis yesterday. Don Budge, [the] greatest tennis player in the world, encountered Jimmy McDaniel, Negro National Singles Champion, defeating him, 6-1 and 6-2." [33]

One explanation for the one-sided match was that McDaniel was a hard-court specialist, a serve-volleyer from California, who was out "of his element on the slow clay courts of the Cosmopolitan Club." [34] Budge, in contrast, was skillful on both clay and grass, proving it by winning the Grand Slam (see glossary) in 1938. Laney analyzed Budge's and McDaniel's games:

Budge played at something approaching his best game and they marveled that such things could be done with a tennis racket.

Jimmy McDaniel, the Negro Champion, also marveled and was beaten quite easily, 6-1, 6-2, because he was unable on such an occasion to play his best game. But he was good enough to put an edge on Budge's game so that those who saw could judge properly of its greatness.[35]

McDaniel got lost on the way to the club and arrived minutes before the starting time. He recalled, "I remember getting thoroughly waxed. He hit a backhand so hard it dug a hole in the clay. I turned around and I said to my coach, 'What do I do with that, coach?' but he acted like he never saw me. Budge just killed me. It was like going from the bush leagues to the majors."[36]

Despite the one-sided match, Laney warned, "It is not quite fair to McDaniel or to Negro tennis in general to judge by this one match. McDaniel did not play well at all and it is impossible to say how good a player he is." He explained that McDaniel was playing before a black audience against a major champion and was quite nervous, "so nervous he could not make his shots." Laney determined that McDaniel was a good player and that it was likely "he could hold his own against the current crop of white players if he were able to play a few tournaments in which they competed."[37] After the singles match, Budge and Reginald Weir, former ATA national champion, played a doubles match against McDaniel and Richard Cohen, the holders of the ATA national doubles title.

McDaniel had to rely on Budge's spirit to play a black man in front of a black audience, away from white tennis venues. The Cosmopolitan Tennis Club was the leading black tennis club in the nation, with members including prominent New York City doctors, lawyers, merchants, college professors, as well as famous black athletes and "just ordinary people."[38] From Laney's description, tennis was played by the black elite in the community, although it is unclear what he meant by "ordinary people" or just how many of these ordinary people were members at the club.

Jimmie McDaniel was a black tennis superstar, and his match

against Budge in 1940 propelled him into tennis history for a brief moment. Even so, segregation prevented him and other black players of the period from competing in the upper echelon of tennis, thereby denying them a potential place in the record books. One writer commented in 1979, "It's been 40 years since Jimmie McDaniel was at the peak of his game. Time has passed him by. No famous camps bear his name. No dinners have been held in his honor. No one much remembers any more." In his prime, McDaniel dominated the black tennis circuit. Between 1939 and 1941, he won thirty-eight of the forty-three tournaments he entered. McDaniel's serve was his weapon; "he could serve gullets, or kick a topspin delivery in either direction."[39] As Laney argued, however, although McDaniel could serve hard, his second serve was faulty.

McDaniel's father, Willis McDaniel, was a professional baseball player in the Negro Leagues. Jimmie played various sports and was an outstanding baseball and softball player. Sometimes, he played an entire volleyball team by himself and won. His athletic abilities brought him the Southern California scholastic high-jump title, and he was a sprinter as well.

The elder McDaniel moved his family from Alabama to Los Angeles, where he worked as a railroad porter. Historians have given less attention to blacks' migration to the West than to their northern migration, even though their migration to the West dates back to the earliest move to the "frontier." Black workers entered the factories and shipyards, a process called the "proletarianization" of the black workforce.[40] Blacks' migration during World War II, however, occurred within a "larger white influx into the region," and resentment did not apply exclusively to blacks. Nevertheless, race became "a powerful component of that opposition."[41]

After Willis McDaniel's death, his wife, Ruby, had to care for seven children by working as a domestic.[42] Meanwhile, Jimmie started playing tennis in elementary school, hitting against a backboard and practicing on the school's one dirt court, but he did not try out for the Manual Arts High School tennis team until his senior year. Once on the team, he led the school to the league championship.

He frequented Exposition Park[43] to play anyone who would play with him, sometimes including seasoned black players such as Hugo Dandrige or Lefty Johnson. His opponents were in general white, however. He continued to play despite the warnings from his older brother, Al, that there was no future in tennis and that he was wasting his time.

Even though Jimmie had no lessons, never had a coach, and never played in a junior tournament, he faced Bobby Riggs, the top junior player in the country, in a high school match, where he exhibited his talent in a losing cause, 7-5, 13-11. A year later Riggs won the men's singles title in the U.S. National Clay Court Championships while McDaniel was in a reform school in northern California, serving a sentence for statutory rape.

Manual Arts had a predominately white student body, and an eighteen-year-old Jimmie got a fifteen-year-old white girl pregnant. As a result, he was sentenced to a year in the reformatory and spent another year outside of Southern California. *World Tennis* writer Barry Meadow noted more than forty years later that if the girl had been black and the boy white, the matter would have been dropped.[44] During these two years, McDaniel stopped playing tennis.

When he returned to Los Angeles, he started playing tennis again and won the black Pacific Coast title, defeating James "Slick" Stocks, the top black player in California for a decade. However, McDaniel's track accomplishments gained him a track scholarship at Xavier during one of Ralph Metcalfe's recruiting trips to the West Coast. At this time, the twenty-two-year-old McDaniel began to practice with Richard "Dick" Cohen, who had won the National Black Intercollegiate tennis title in 1938. They later played doubles together. Soon McDaniel began to focus on tennis instead of on track. Xavier sponsored a summer tour for the top players on the black college circuit, which included Tuskegee, Prairie View, and Hampton. Teammate William "Wild Bill" Johnson wrote of McDaniel, "Not long after Jimmie's arrival he was No. 1 with the standings falling [in] order behind him. He's really a great guy, a beautiful person."[45]

When McDaniel played the New York Open, he faced Reggie Weir.

Weir was the captain of the tennis team at City College and had beaten some of the top eastern white collegians. When Weir faced McDaniel, the latter won only four games. Later, McDaniel defeated Weir to win his first ATA national title.

McDaniel returned to Los Angeles to work at Lockheed Aircraft plant in Burbank during the World War II years. Meanwhile, he married and had five children. Although barred from most of the sectional events, he played tennis on weekends and in city-run tournaments. In 1959, he stopped playing tennis and began playing golf. When he told his friend Ted Stoglin, a leading black tennis player in the 1930s, of the switch, the latter did not believe McDaniel. After years away from the court, though, McDaniel began playing tennis again. He explained, "I looked in the mirror one day and saw big, fat guy. I said, 'That's not me.' So I went out and started working on the backboard. I found I could still move, although I had slowed up. And I could still hit the ball."[46]

He began teaching tennis when he retired from Lockheed. Times had changed, and the clubs that had barred him prior to World War II permitted him to play the senior circuit. In 1979, he was ranked number 18 nationally in the "sixty and overs." Even though he was permitted to play in these venues after all those years, he still sensed that he was unwelcome.

In the late 1970s, McDaniel taught tennis to mostly upper-income, middle-aged whites. None of the up-and-coming black youngsters that practiced nearby took lessons from him. To the young hotshots, McDaniel was just "a tired old relic of an era long gone, and best forgotten." When he told a young hard-hitting player, Delroy Reid, that Reid could not "just bang, bang, bang against these youngsters. . . . They can bang, bang, bang just like you," Reid was unimpressed and answered, "I'll bang 'em off the court, man." McDaniel admitted that the black tennis community had pretty much ignored him: "All they have to do is look back before Oscar Johnson and see who was doing the tennis. I don't care if they honor me. But maybe, maybe they could just acknowledge me."[47]

McDaniel was not the only black player in California in the 1930s.

In Los Angeles, Joe Wright, father of singers Darlene Love and Edna Wright, was a great tennis player. However, when he moved from Port Arthur, Texas, he had no racket with which to play, but wanting to play, he attempted to steal a "five-dollar model" at a sporting goods store located a few blocks from his house. The owner approached him with a shotgun, fired at him, and the bullet grazed him. Wright played not only tennis, but also golf. In her autobiography, Love explains, "He would think nothing of rising at 5 A.M. and getting on the course before most of the other golfers arrived." Her father affirmed, "There's no law that says I can't. Call the cops." Although his presence "raised a few eyebrows," no one bothered him.[48]

• • •

In 1953, Oscar Johnson became the fourth black player to play in the USLTA National Championships at Forest Hills. Johnson had a list of accomplishments besides becoming the first black player to win a USLTA-affiliated national event in Los Angeles in 1948. He won the Pacific Coast Junior Championships from 1946 to 1948 in singles and doubles, and he captured the 1950 ATA national singles title. He was awarded the Lt. Joseph R. Hunt Sportsmanship Award in 1956 during the Los Angeles Metropolitan Championships. Moreover, he led his high school, Thomas Jefferson, to the Southern League title. Brice Taylor, former USC football player who started his tennis team with athletes who had never played the game, served as Johnson's coach.

In 1948, when Johnson was eighteen years old, he applied to the USLTA National Junior Indoor Championships in St. Louis, but was denied entry when he appeared at the tournament site and USLTA officials discovered he was black. Johnson recalled, "The tournament director looked at me and said, 'You won't play here.' "[49] Richard Hudlin, former University of Chicago team captain, and Frank Summers, a black attorney from East St. Louis, accompanied Johnson. Anticipating the problem, they had sent a telegram to the New York USLTA office, insisting that Johnson be admitted because he had won a national championship. The officials readmitted Johnson, who eventually lost to Tony Trabert in the quarterfinals.[50] About the players Johnson commented, "Strangely enough, I had no trouble at all with any of the players. In fact, a guy from Texas asked me to be his doubles partner, and we reached the semifinals."[51]

Johnson was also a self-taught player and, like McDaniel, had learned by watching other players. He explained, "With some of these schools we'd play against, I figured that some of these guys were taking lessons, so I would watch the number-one player . . . and I'd copy what I saw . . . sometimes I'd jot it down and then I'd go home and practice in front of the mirror. I did that for three years, cause we didn't have any coaching."[52] When Johnson finally played in the USLTA National Championships at Forest Hills in 1953, Althea Gibson and two black men had already competed there.

Arthur Ashe argued that the best black tennis players in the United States "waited with the same sense of urgency after World War II as did the Negro League World [baseball] players."[53] However, there were differences. For example, baseball was the national pastime of the masses, whereas tennis was associated with the upper socioeconomic classes. Baseball games were played at public stadiums, but tennis tournaments were generally held at private clubs.

In 1950, Dr. Sylvester B. Smith, ATA president; Arthur E. Francis, assistant executive secretary; and Bertram L. Baker, executive secretary, held conferences with Dr. S. Ellsworth Davenport Jr. and Alrick H. Man Jr., who represented the USLTA. The latter wanted to accept qualified black players in USLTA tournaments. Although the conferences were held in private, Alice Marble wrote an editorial about them in *American Lawn Tennis Magazine*.[54] Althea Gibson was accepted for the U.S. National Clay Court Championships, the Eastern Grass Court Championships, and the USLTA National Championships at Forest Hills. For the first time that year, a black player participated in the USLTA National Championships.

George Stewart, who won the men's singles at the ATA National Championships seven times, and Reginald Weir were the first black men to play in the USLTA National Championships at Forest Hills in 1952. Playing for South Carolina State, Stewart was the first black to participate in a National Collegiate Athletic Association (NCAA) Tennis Championships. Weir, however, was the first black to compete in a

USLTA national tournament in 1948, losing in the second round to the number 1 seed and eventual champion Bill Talbert. A journalist described the history-making event in these terms:

> The dull routine of making a tennis draw, usually nothing more than a prosaic process of pulling names out of a hat or cup, proved to be anything but that yesterday. . . .
>
> The proceedings hardly had got under way at the offices of the United States Lawn Tennis Association when the name of Dr. Reginald Weir of New York turned up. Operations came to an immediate halt. History was in the making.[55]

Weir had competed in the Metropolitan and Eastern Indoor Championships in New York for several years. In fact, he had advanced to the semifinals in the Eastern Championships. Alrick H. Man Jr., chair of the National Indoor Championships Committee and captain of the Davis Cup team, told the press that "Dr. Weir in sending in his entry had expressed the hope that it would be accepted but stated that he did not intend to make an issue of it if it was rejected." Man chose his language carefully, considering the possible impact of Weir's entry: "We thought in view of his showing in the Eastern championships that he should be permitted to play. This does not mean that we are speaking officially for the U.S.L.T.A. or that we are establishing a precedent to be followed necessarily in other tournaments. It is simply a decision of this group."[56]

There were other players of note during the early years. Jerry Alleyne was an amateur tennis player in the 1930s and won national championships in several Latin American countries. He was one of the first black men to compete in the U.S. National Tennis Championships. Despite a serious motorcycle accident in 1955, he continued to play amateur tennis. At age thirty-seven, he made the third round of the U.S. Nationals at Forest Hills in 1958.[57]

Vernon Morgan started playing tennis at age sixteen at the Cosmopolitan Tennis Club in New York. One of his major wins was the 1956 New York State American Tennis Association Championships, defeating Billy Davis in the final. Morgan was a great grass-court player, whereas most top black players had experience only on clay courts. He also played at the City College of New York and at Tennessee Agricultural and Industrial College. At the latter, he played with Bob Ryland and Billy Davis.

Althea Gibson was the biggest name in tennis in the 1950s, but other blacks were also participating in tournament tennis, although many of their successes were within the confines of the ATA and black college circuits. Even though blacks were not playing at white country clubs, *World Tennis* magazine on rare occasions featured news items about blacks in tennis. For example, in 1957 the magazine published a photo of models who styled tennis outfits at a fashion parade at an ATA party in honor of Althea Gibson before her departure to England to play at Wimbledon.[58] More than twenty-seven hundred players entered in the 1956 Detroit News Novice Tournament. Marlene Everson took the first place trophy and got her photo in an issue of *World Tennis*.[59] In addition, the Western Wightman Cup winners in 1957 included two black women, Darnella Everson and Gwen McEvans, part of the four-woman "Hamtramck" group, headed by Jean Hoxie.[60]

The other major development in the 1950s centered around Bob Ryland, who made his professional debut at the Cleveland Arena in 1958.[61] Ryland, the ATA champion in 1956 and 1957, was a member of the Jack Marsh's pro-circuit troop, which also included Richard Gonzales and Lew Hoad. Marsh told Sarah Allen, mother of pro Leslie Allen-Selmore, that he wanted to bring a black player to his World Pro Championships in Cleveland, and Allen suggested Ryland. Marsh had decided that he would add a black player despite the consequences, and Ryland made $300 for his appearance.[62]

Ryland began playing tennis at age nine,[63] learning from his father, who was a teaching professional in Chicago. In order to perfect his game, Ryland practiced six hours per day, six days a week. As a child, he dreamed of being number 1 in the world. He played at Tilden Tech High School, an integrated school, where he helped win three city championships. Ironically, the championships were held on the public courts where blacks normally were forbidden to play. In 1939, the young Ryland won the Illinois State High School Championship and the ATA Junior Championship.

In 1944, he played a "historic" mixed-doubles match with two white women, Alice Marble and Mary Hartwick, and the scene was similar to the Budge-McDaniel exhibition. According to Ryland, "I was seeded No. 1 in the ATA, so they sent me down from the army. It was really groundbreaking, but there was no opposition [to the match] because it was played in Harlem. As long as you were playing in that neighborhood, you were OK." [64]

After a stint in the army, Ryland played two years at Wayne University (now Wayne State) and was one of the first two blacks to complete in the NCAA Tennis Championships in 1946. He has been inducted into the Wayne State Hall of Fame for his accomplishments.

He left Wayne University in 1946 to go to California, which was viewed as a mecca of hard-court tennis. He worked nights at the post office and played tennis during the day with Jimmie McDaniel, Oscar Johnson, Earthna Jacquet, and Pancho Gonzales in the public parks in Los Angeles. [65]

When living in the Bronx, Ryland was on the eastern team of the United States Professional Lawn Tennis Association (USPLTA), which won the Divisional Team Championships in Allentown, Pennsylvania, in 1964. Other members of the team were Bill Lufler, Robin Willner, and Mickey Phillips. After seeing Ryland play at the U.S. National Championships at Forest Hills, a twelve-year-old Arthur Ashe followed him around and told him that he wanted to play like him. Moreover, he coached professionals such as Harold Solomon and Leslie Allen, as well as celebrities Bill Cosby, Barbara Streisand, and Mary McFadden.

Ryland rebounded after a bout with cancer in 1997. He continued to play doubles and on the senior tour at age eighty and to teach tennis to children in Harlem.

• • •

Others became instrumental in blacks' progress in tennis by coaching. Dr. Robert Walter Johnson played a crucial role in the development of black tennis in the United States. Working with some of the best tennis talent for several decades, he was committed to integrating young black players into the tennis mainstream. His father, Jerry Johnson, was an astute businessman from Norfolk, Virginia, who worked for the John L. Roper Lumber Company, taking contracts that most others avoided. The company eventually gave him a home located in a white neighborhood. Robert Johnson had many jobs, including working at the Plymouth Box Panel Company at age fifteen and as a waiter in Virginia Beach during the summer at age eighteen. However, his father trained him to be an accountant. Before developing an interest in tennis, he was a college athlete. He played as a half-back for Lincoln University in the early 1920s and was called "Whirlwind" because of his lively broken-field running and high-scoring achievements, which included eight touchdowns in one game. He also played baseball and organized and coached a basketball team for the Omega Psi Phi fraternity. After graduating, he coached football, basketball, and baseball at Virginia Seminary College. At football practices, he'd play with the second team and reserves against the starting varsity and won in every practice.[66] To earn money for medical school, he worked as a Grand Central Station redcap. He was thirty-three when he began to play tennis as a means of exercise while he was an intern at Prairie View Hospital.

In the 1930s, he developed a practice in Lynchburg, Virginia, where he established a clinic because black physicians were denied privileges at Lynchburg's only hospital. Moreover, he allowed young physicians who had recently completed medical school or who had yet to get their license to practice under his guidance. He had played tennis only casually while at Shaw and Lincoln, but became addicted to the game while serving his internship at Prairie View, so that later, when he acquired a larger home, he constructed a clay court in his backyard. He and other black professionals played from city to city (Durham, Raleigh, Smithfield, Wilmington, and Lynchburg), each having a court in his yard. Johnson even built a court next to his father's auditorium in Plymouth, where he sponsored a tournament. At his home in Lynchburg, he held the ATA Annual Labor Day Round Robin Tournament, inviting the top ATA players, close friends, and a few celebrities such as writer-photographer Gordon Parks Jr. Tennis professionals Bobby Riggs and Frank Guernsy played an exhibition match there one year.

Johnson began to house as many as fourteen to eighteen youths at his own expense to give them the benefit of training during the summer. He wanted to see some of these young men and women develop into international champions. As a result, he was optimistic about Luis Glass of New York City and Bonnie Logan of Durham. Glass and Lenward Simpson of Wilmington, North Carolina, earned scholarships at Deerfield Academy in New England and Hill School in Pennsylvania, respectively. Other prospects included Robert Ginns of Cleveland. A few whites began to send their children to Doc's program, including Tina Watanabe of California and "Rock" Devine, the son of a Lynchburg physician.

One of his students described Johnson's training program:

> We got up around 6:30. We practiced till breakfast, then rested half an hour. Then it was practice, practice, practice all day until about 4:30, when Doc came home from the office, with maybe an hour off for lunch. We also did a lot of exercises and running. The push-ups were the hardest. We weren't exactly on a diet but there were a lot of things we couldn't eat. Everybody made progress. There wasn't much else we could do, practicing like that every day. At night part of our social activity was watching tennis movies. Doc also had a lot of books to read—about tennis, of course![67]

The working budget came from whatever sources Doc Johnson could find, but the main source was his own pocket. His son, Robert Walter Johnson Jr., remarked, "He had originally started getting collegians primarily to help them with their game. Then he finally realized that he had to reach way back to get some of the younger players." Johnson realized that the best black college players had little chance of advancement because their early training was "haphazard and primarily self-imposed."[68] When returning home on one occasion in 1951, he drove through Charlottesville, Virginia, and noted a sign that read "USLTA National Interscholastic Championships." When he discovered that no black player was to participate, he sought permission from tournament director Edmund "Teddy" Penzold to bring two finalists from an all-black qualifying event to Charlottesville the following year.

He began training students and taking them to USLTA tournaments. He eventually was able to get two of his students from Dunbar High, Victor Miller and Roosevelt Megginson, in a National Interscholastic tournament in Charlottesville. Both players lost 6-0, 6-0 in the first round. Johnson stated, "I'll never forget that. I was stunned. It was like getting religion. I had these two Dunbar High School boys I thought were unbeatable, but they got beaten love and love. I never saw tennis played by young people the way those young white boys played it."[69]

Afterward, he talked to Penzold, who was also chair of the USLTA Interscholastic Committee, about including more ATA players in scheduled tournaments. Penzold suggested that Johnson organize an ATA qualifying tournament to expand the pool of players, and the winner and runner-up in boys' and girls' events would be eligible for the USLTA competition. Johnson took Penzold's advice, founding the Black National Interscholastic Tennis Championships in 1952. Twenty-three players participated in the first tournament, held at Virginia Union in Richmond. The finalists, William Winn and Elton King, were automatically entered into the USLTA National Interscholastic tournament in Charlottesville.

Althea Gibson was eighteen when she first met Johnson in 1945 after a defeat in the ATA National Championships, losing to Roumania Peters. She recalled, "It was life's darkest moment. I was sitting in the grandstand alone when a man came up to me and asked how would I like to play at Forest Hills. I couldn't believe my ears and thought it was a joke until I looked at the expression on his face. Then I knew he meant what he was saying. I told him that of course I would like to play at Forest Hills but it was impossible."[70] Johnson arranged for Gibson to live with his friend Hubert Eaton in Wilmington, where she attended high school, but she trained with Johnson during the summer in Lynchburg. Gibson won nine ATA singles titles following that first summer and three years later entered the women's draw at Forest Hills.

In the 1950s, Ashe was another of Johnson's proteges, visiting Johnson's summer camps at his home from age nine until he was sixteen. Serving as a mentor in an ATA-sponsored youth development program, Johnson continued to work with an impressive list of junior players. Even when he was sixty-six, he handled a general medical practice in Lynchburg, played tennis daily, and devoted "every other spare moment to the encouragement, development, teaching, housing and feeding of ATA youngsters who possess tennis talent and ambition and want to go on to bigger things in the USLTA tournaments."[71]

Johnson worked to integrate black juniors in the major white tournaments so that they could have a greater opportunity to become champions. In his later years, however, juniors failed to understand his techniques. With the braggadocio of 1960s rhetoric, some youths could not attune themselves to a method of gentility that had worked well for Johnson's former students. Johnson did what he had to do to get his students into the major white tournaments, but observers saw that he never acted with fear. He integrated several institutes in Lynchburg as well and at age sixty even marched with black students to picket Lynchburg's F. W. Woolworth store.

Because of Johnson's work with so many juniors, more than one hundred by 1965, Dr. Matilda Davis nominated him for the Marlboro Award, which he won. That award, however, did not temper his thirst to seek and develop more talented youth. In 1971, Johnson suffered a heart attack at his church and died shortly afterward, leaving a young Juan Farrow, his top student, at a crossroads.

Another figure from the early years was Nehemiah Atkinson of New Orleans, who was the first black tennis player to be inducted into the Southern Tennis Association Hall of Fame. At age eighty, Atkinson had played tennis for more than seven decades. He declared that there were no black tennis players when he was growing up in New Orleans, noting, "I played tennis in the school yard with a wooden paddle the same size as a regular racquet that one of my brothers made for me when I was a kid. We didn't have access to a tennis court in those days." One of ten children, he grew up near the NORD Stern Tennis Center, the former home of the New Orleans Lawn Tennis Club, where blacks were not allowed to play.[72]

Atkinson served in the army during World War II, where he worked on the construction of the Alaskan Highway, one of the home-front's major projects. His father was a minister who recognized no racial boundaries. Atkinson said, "My father being a minister, I've eaten in many a white home. Many a white man traveled with my father." In fact, Bishop C. C. Atkinson's church, the Triumph Church, Kingdom of God in Christ, had an integrated congregation. "When the police would come to tell us we couldn't worship together, my father always had an answer for them. Integration was nothing new to me." With this attitude, he personally integrated many USTA events and supported a merging of the ATA and the USTA.[73]

Atkinson was the director at the New Orleans Recreation Department at the NORD Stern Tennis Center for twenty-two years, beginning in 1973. Lloyd Dillon, a recipient of the partial tennis scholarship at Grambling, which Atkinson had arranged with football coach Eddie Robinson, replaced him. Fifty years after being denied the opportunity to use the New Orleans Lawn Tennis Club facilities, Atkinson became a member of that club.

In 1977, Ethel Kennedy presented Atkinson the Ripple of Hope Award during the Robert F. Kennedy Pro-Celebrity Tennis Tournament at Forest Hills for his contributions to underprivileged children. He said, "It has been a great pleasure to have the opportunity to play against some of the best players of my generation such as Gardner Mulloy, Bobby Riggs, Bitsy Grant and Gardner Henley." In 1985, he was given the Annual Noland Touchstone Award during the Southern Seniors Championships at River Hills Club.[74]

At age sixty-six, Atkinson continued teaching three days a week and getting additional requests for instruction. At seventy-two, he was named honorary chair of the fifty-fourth annual USF&G Sugar Bowl Tennis Classic played at New Orleans City Park's Wisner Tennis Center in 1991. The award was presented to a candidate who had served the New Orleans tennis community in an "outstanding, exemplary

Branch Curington of Atlanta.

manner by working with the youth of the community in fostering sportsmanship and good will on and off the court."[75]

Another fascinating story is that of Branch Curington from Atlanta, who battled two forms of segregation in pre–civil rights Atlanta. Poor black tennis players had to fight a double prejudice, race and class, and poor black women players faced triple oppression because they rarely received equal support in the world of sports.

After seeing some whites play tennis, Curington developed an interest. He taught himself the tennis basics by watching the white players and learned what he could. After getting an old racket that a white player had thrown aside and some balls, he hit on a schoolhouse wall, practicing until after dark. When he became a teenager, he needed to work to help support the family, so in order to maintain a closeness to tennis he found employment at Piedmont Driving Club repairing the courts. This prestigious club forbade blacks to join or play at the facility, although they could work to maintain the surfaces. Nevertheless, this job afforded Curington the opportunity to observe matches at the club.

Exclusive attitudes were not limited to whites. Atlanta had a strong black middle class. One writer explained, "Blacks with 'fair skin,' education and/or a profession segregated themselves from those born on the 'wrong side of the tracks.' " When Branch Curington grew up in Atlanta's Pittsburgh Community, he visited Washington Park to watch the "black elites" play tennis. These courts were also off limits to him as a player.[76] Although Curington never played in their tournaments, he believed that he could have beaten most of them. He argued,

> Tennis was always considered a rich man's game. All the tennis was channeled through private country clubs. The black folks who started playing tennis were mostly teachers, maybe a few jokers working at the post office, a few doctors. The so-called elite blacks tried to play tennis because it was a social thing to do. Those who played tennis didn't care anything about working or helping anybody with tennis unless you were in that social environment.[77]

At age seventeen, Curington joined the army to fight in World War II. After the war, he returned to Atlanta and got another position at the Piedmont Driving Club as head court attendant. Welby Van Horn, the fifth-ranked player in the United States, was hired as the head pro and befriended Curington, recognizing his exceptional tennis skills. Van Horn advised him to learn as much as he could about tennis "and leave here and go to California" because there was no place for a black player or club pro in Atlanta.[78] Eventually, however, the club promoted Curington to assistant tennis pro to teach club members.

Tennis instruction at Washington Park in Atlanta in the 1960s. Courtesy of Branch Curington Library.

When Van Horn resigned, Joe Weldon was hired, and Curington took a job away from tennis for the first time in his life. In 1955, he started his own restaurant. After ten years, he returned to tennis. While Ivan Allen was mayor of Atlanta, the city built a tennis center at Washington Park and decided to hire a black coach in 1964. Out of the other thirty-two applicants, Curington scored the highest on the test administered by Atlanta's Parks and Recreation Department and became the first director of the same facility that had denied him an opportunity to play when he was a child. During the dedication ceremonies, he vowed "never to turn a child away from the courts for social, or economic reasons beyond the youngster's control."[79] According to a biographer, "Through the instruction of Curington, literally thousands learned the techniques of offensive tennis. In spite of the betrayals and obstacles thrown at him even by those he had fed and taught, Curington was able to develop exceptional tennis talent on a very limited budget."[80]

Curington has received recognition for his work, including a nomination to the Tennis Hall of Fame and the annual award given by the Martin Luther King Jr. Center for Social Change. In addition, he has been recognized by the USTA, the U.S. Tennis Teaching Association, the ATA, the Southern Tennis Association, the Atlanta Lawn Tennis Association, and the Gate City Tennis Association.

• • •

The black players and coaches of the 1940s and 1950s transformed professional tennis by opening doors for players of later generations. They challenged the racism in both the game and society in order to participate in an exclusive sport. Racism remained within the structure of the sport, however, and classism continued to permeate it even among blacks.

2

Althea Gibson

"The Jackie Robinson of Tennis"?

ALTHEA GIBSON, born August 25, 1927, in Silver, South Carolina, moved to New York at the age of three. Her parents, Daniel and Annie Gibson; brother, Dan; and three sisters, Millie, Annie, and Lillian, moved north to Harlem after having bad harvests on a cotton farm they sharecropped. Gibson loved to play sports, including football, baseball, stickball, basketball, and paddle tennis. "She was always the outdoor type. That's why she can beat that tennis ball like nobody's business," her father later told a reporter.[1] In fact, it was while she played paddle tennis outside her apartment building in New York City that Buddy Walker, a band leader who had a summer job as a play street leader in 1940, gave her two secondhand tennis rackets that cost five dollars each and watched her hit tennis balls at a nearby park. Later, Walker took Gibson to the Harlem River Tennis Courts and asked a friend to play with her. One of the people watching her was Juan Serrell, a schoolteacher; Serrell told them that he wanted to arrange for Gibson to play at the Cosmopolitan Tennis Club, where he was a member. After she played Fred Johnson, a "one-armed" instructor, a small crowd took up a collection to buy her a junior membership at the club.[2] It was at the club that she saw Alice Marble play. Gibson wrote of that experience, "One of the days I remember best at the Cosmopolitan Club was the day Alice Marble played an exhibition match there. I can still remember saying to myself, boy, would I like to be able to play tennis like that! She was the only woman tennis player I'd ever seen that I felt exactly that way about."[3]

Gibson learned the game so quickly that she made it to the finals of the ATA-sanctioned New York State Junior Girls Championship in 1942 when she was fifteen and advanced to the finals of the ATA Nationals. She won the ATA girls' nationals in 1944 and 1945. The following year she reached the finals of the women's singles at the ATA Nationals, but lost to Roumania Peters. When two physicians, Dr. Hubert Eaton and Dr. Robert Johnson, saw her play, they were convinced that she could be a champion and arranged for her to live with the Eatons in Wilmington, North Carolina. Gibson describes the belongings she packed for that trip: "I went back to my mother and father's apartment to pack for the trip south. I used two suitcases; all my tennis clothes went into one and all the rest of my things into the other. Both of them were made of cardboard and they surely would have fallen apart if I hadn't tightened a spare belt around each one of them."[4]

Although blacks were not allowed to play on public courts in Wilmington, some whites played at the Eatons. Also, Gibson remembered, the Eatons had a "handsome *en tout cas* court, . . . a gathering place for all the Negro tennis players in the district."[5]

In Wilmington, Gibson found that though she had only enough credits for the seventh grade, she was placed in tenth owing to her success on aptitude tests. She attended racially segregated Williston Industrial High School and joined the basketball team, choir, and band, playing saxophone. Because of her deep voice, she quit the choir, but sang and played sax (given to her by boxer Sugar Ray Robinson) with a jazz combo.

Gibson made tennis history for her role in breaking color barriers in tennis by playing in USLTA tournaments, first entering the Eastern Indoor Championships in 1949. Also that year she received an invitation to play Orange and Forest Hills. However, she was not the first black to play at the U.S. National Indoor Championships: Reggie Weir had been accepted in this tournament earlier.[6] Of her early experiences, she wrote, "In both the U.S.L.T.A. tournaments I played in that winter—my first experiences as the only Negro in an otherwise all-white draw—I was made to feel right at home by the other girls. It wasn't just that they were polite; they were genuinely friendly, and believe me, like any Negro, I'm an expert at telling the differences."[7]

When Gibson was twenty-one, she attended Florida A&M University on a full scholarship. After returning to the Eastern Indoor Championships in New York for the second time, she won the title and made it to the finals of the U.S. National Indoor Championships. The Florida A&M family welcomed her with banners and the marching band.

Despite the celebration, Gibson was not invited to the Eastern Outdoor tournaments, held at private eastern tennis clubs in Seabright, Newport, East Hampton, and South Hampton. Those players who performed well in the summer circuit were usually invited to Forest Hills for the USLTA National Championships. One author argued that it was one thing for major league baseball to admit Jackie Robinson in 1947 because baseball was for the masses, but another for Gibson to be admitted to Forest Hills because tennis was the sport of ladies and gentlemen.[8] However, racism existed in all classes, and the doors to baseball and other sports were opened by black athletes, community institutions, and white allies.

Jackie Robinson's success in major league baseball prefigured the integration of other professional sports. In 1950, three black men "broke the color line" in professional basketball. Earl Lloyd was the first to play in the National Basketball League (drafted by the Washington Capitols), Charles Cooper was the first player drafted (by the Boston Celtics), and Nat "Sweetwater" Clifton was the first to sign a contract.[9] In addition, the American Bowling Congress dropped its "whites-only" policy, and by 1951 fourteen black men played in major league baseball.[10] Meanwhile, Althea Gibson made a remarkable move in tennis. In order for her to play in the U.S. Nationals, she had to distinguish herself in several preliminary tournaments. However, "if [she] could be kept out of those events, the USLTA could claim that it had no basis upon which to judge her against white players, and thereby finesse its way out of giving her a spot in the Forest Hills Draw."[11] Gibson found an ally, although unsolicited, in Alice Marble.

Alice Marble wrote a letter to *American Lawn Tennis* magazine challenging the USLTA to change its policy. Some whites were not pleased with Marble's comments:

> If tennis is a sport for ladies and gentlemen, it's also time we acted a little more like gentle people and less like sanctimonious hypocrites. If there is anything left in the name of sportsmanship, it's more than time to display what it means to us. If Althea Gibson represents a challenge to the present crop of women players, it's only fair that they should meet that challenge. . . .
>
> She is not being judged by the yardstick of ability but by . . . her pigmentation. . . .
>
> . . . The entrance of Negroes into national tennis is as inevitable as it has proven to be in baseball, in football, or in boxing.[12]

Even *Time* magazine carried a story: "Negroes have played in the National Indoor tennis championships, but they have never been invited to set foot on the outdoor courts of Forest Hills, the sanctum of U.S. tennis."[13]

In March 1950, Gibson became the first black to reach the finals of a USLTA championship. A short piece in *Time* noted the monumental occasion: "In the women's tournament, lanky, 22-year-old Althea Gibson became the first Negro ever to reach the finals in a national championship sponsored by the U.S. Lawn Tennis Association. Although she lost the next day, her performance made it possible that she would also become the first Negro ever to play in the nationals at Forest Hills this summer."[14]

Although she was denied entry into one New Jersey tournament, she played in another, the Orange Lawn Tennis Club tournament, where she lost in the second round, and in the National Clay Courts in Chicago, losing in the quarterfinals. In August of that same year, the USLTA announced that Gibson was invited to play in the fifty-two-women draw at Forest Hills.

When some reporters complained about how tournament officials discriminated against Gibson by placing her on the court with the smallest seating capacity, farthest from the clubhouse, while Ginger Rogers played a doubles match in front of the clubhouse, Gibson made little of it. One author argues that Gibson used humor to "bypass political conflict," and "humor may have been her way of overcoming feelings of hatred or bitterness." [15]

The USLTA offered to arrange for Gibson to be coached by a tennis teacher in preparation to play at Wimbledon in 1951. Boxer Joe Louis paid for her plane ticket. By 1952, Sydney Llewellyn had become her coach, and Gibson had adopted a continental forehand grip. However, it was only in 1955 that she began really to make her move in professional tennis, remaining a powerful force until 1958.

In the 1955 Wimbledon, Gibson upset second-seeded Darlene Hard 6-2, 11-9 in the semifinal round. Although Gibson displayed a "dazzling display of shots," she lost to Louise Brough in the final. [16] That year Gibson was ranked number 9 in the USLTA. According to Jeanette Chappell Kalt, chairperson of Women's Ranking Committee,

> To be considered for ranking in the Women's Singles a player must play in "one of the four USLTA Championships and four other sanctioned tournaments in the United States, or in the alternative, eight sanctioned tournaments in the United States.
>
> "The rankings shall be based solely upon the records of the players for the season under consideration, and not upon the personal opinion of the Ranking Committee. Middle and late season performances in the United States leading up to the USLTA Championships shall be given greater consideration than early season performances." [17]

By the summer of 1956, Gibson had won six consecutive singles titles, and in her six months playing outside the United States she had lost only one match (to Angela Mortimer). After winning the Italian Championships in July, [18] she captured the French Open title. During the latter championship, her game was described in a photo caption as follows: "Here Althea Gibson is caught in a bad position, facing the net, yet her racket-handling ability is evident. The great body balance saves her in situations where she cannot employ proper footwork.

She handles herself on the court like a Mickey Mantle or Sugar Ray Robinson." [19]

In 1956, she traveled with "glamour girl" Karol Fageros, Ham Richardson, and Bob Perry on a State Department tennis tour of Asia and Europe, where she reportedly gained confidence.[20] Not everyone was convinced of Gibson's dominance. According to *World Tennis* writer Julie Heldman, it took the retirement of the "Big Guns" of tennis—Louise Brough, Margaret duPont, Maureen Connolly, and Doris Hart—to give Gibson a shot at the top.[21]

Despite the doubt cast on Gibson's success, the winning tradition continued. She won the grass event at Manchester, beating Shirley Fry and Brough en route to the title. In addition, she won the singles event at Surrey, beating Ann Shilcock, a former Wightman Cup player. However, she came up short in the Wimbledon singles, losing to eventual winner Fry 4-6, 6-3, 6-4 in the quarterfinals, but capturing the doubles title with Angela Buxton.

Back in the United States, Gibson won the Pennsylvania State tournament, employing her "long Continental forehand which she whips around, following a high wind-up."[22] The runner-up at this tournament the previous year, she now defeated Margaret duPont 6-1, 6-4. One her matches was considered one of two great matches of the tournament. "[S]eventeen-year-old Mary Ann Mitchell threw down the gauntlet to Althea Gibson and was beaten only after some of the most glorious women's stroke-work seen at Merion in a long time. Gibson was denied one match point at 4-5 and another at 8-9 before winning 6-2, 11-9 from the apple-cheeked youngster who might have been a Helen Wills out there, so cool and smart were her deep retorts, from the half-volley particularly."[23]

In the National Clay Court Championships, however, Gibson easily defeated the teenage sensation 6-3, 6-1. In the final, she lost to Fry, although she had a 5-2 lead in the first set. Writer Mary Hardwick argued that it was "one of the saddest matches I have ever witnessed. . . . I hope Althea will learn a lot from it." She added that the body needed rest and relaxation, and after six months Gibson was "mentally and physically exhausted."[24]

Taking time to sign autographs for young fans before her match, she won the Colorado State title. Her final match against Dottie Knode drew a capacity crowd, and Gardner Mulloy wrote in a *World Tennis* article that the "colored" champion hardly worked up a sweat in the 6-4, 6-4 win.[25]

Gibson won more tournaments than any other player in 1956. Competing in twenty-seven major tournaments, she lost only five matches to two players, Shirley Fry and Angela Mortimer. Gibson played mixed doubles with Gardner Mulloy, and they were finalists at Wimbledon and semifinalists at Forest Hills that year. Making history again, she graced the cover of the October 1957 issue of *World Tennis*. After she won the U.S. National Championships, Vice President Richard Nixon presented the trophy to her.

According to some observers at the time, Gibson had the strongest serve in women's tennis, although "she is prone to footfault due to the motion of her right leg which is sometimes planted inside the baseline before the hit."[26] Gibson explained in an interview that her coach had her practice the serve repeatedly, hitting the same spot on the court until she could do it with her eyes closed.

The following caption appeared beneath a picture of her making a low volley: "Althea Gibson, the Wimbledon and U.S. title list, is unquestionably the top woman amateur in the world. Her tremendous reach on the volley and her big serve give her an edge over all her competitors. She is perhaps the best athlete women's tennis has ever known, her relaxed loose-jointed movements being in a class of their own."[27] Another writer summarized, "Althea Gibson was ranked No. 1. Her record is too outstanding to need comment."[28]

Gibson and Lew Hoad of Australia were considered the power hitters of amateur tennis. In July 1957, it was written that Gibson was "the first Negro to crash big-time tennis, [and] has only hovered on the edge of greatness. Last week, day after day crowds of 20,000 packed the stadium at Wimbledon, England . . . to wonder if Althea was really anything more than a strong-armed also-ran."[29] Even Queen Elizabeth II weathered the one-hundred-degree heat to watch the final. After her victory, Gibson admitted that she was prepared to win Wimbledon that year. "I have to make a confession. I'd been so hopeful that I might win the tournament that, the first week I was in London, I'd gone down with Angela to her store and picked out a beautiful evening gown to wear to the Wimbledon Ball. Even worse than that, I'd worked for days on a speech to give at the Ball in case I won."[30] Not only had she worked on her speech, but she had decided not to defend her French Open title so as to play only grass-court matches, leading to Wimbledon.

Many years later a *Sports Illustrated* writer described Gibson in the Wimbledon world:

> The 29-year-old Gibson knew the customs of the All England Club. She knew about the strawberries, the white-only tennis outfits, the proper protocol upon meeting the queen. For the fortnight of the tournament she was staying in the West End flat of a friend, Angela Buxton, a Jewess, as they said in London in those days. The Jewess and the colored girl, they were a curiosity, but most Britons were too polite to fuss over them much more than that.[31]

Buxton was injured that year, but designed Gibson's tennis outfits, "all white, of course, which suited Gibson just fine, since white showed off her smooth, dark skin and her torch-singer good looks." According to Joan Bruce, who covered the tournament, "Hers, it should be said, was not a personality which particularly appealed to Wimbledon crowds, who like their heroes to be chivalrous to a fault and noticeably human. Actually, Althea Gibson was human enough. She suffered from center-court nerves and the self-imposed responsibility of representing the whole Negro population of the United States of America."[32]

The Wimbledon crowd "handled her with silent respect until the semi-final, and then prepared to be partisan." She faced a sixteen-year-old, "statuesque, 5-foot-11 schoolgirl with amber-colored hair called Christine Truman." Truman "couldn't do anything right, and Gibson never let her think she could." The final against Darlene Hard was "equally one-sided." Gibson was the "first representative of the Negro race ever to win a Wimbledon title, but the center court raised only an apathetic cheer when the Queen presented her with the big gold salver and Darlene hugged her with sisterly enthusiasm."[33] Gibson became the first to receive the award from Queen Elizabeth II, who rarely attended tennis matches. Gibson also took the doubles title, playing with Hard, and advanced to the mixed-doubles final.

Participants in the tournament became members of a prestigious club. Very little was written about the integration of the All England Club, which "had come about naturally and cordially." After all, Gibson danced with a white man, Lew Hoad, the men's singles champion, at the ball, as was the ritual. In addition, she sang "I Can't Give You Anything but Love" at the affair, causing "such a sensation as her play during the tournament."[34] "Few witnessed the event, and nobody wrote about it," commented writer Michael Bamberger forty years later. He added, "She was, as far as anybody knows, the first black woman to be a member. Nobody cared. Or if people did, they pretended not to. It is naive to think that you could write a story about two club members—tough tennis champions, one black, the other white—sharing a dance and that such a story could influence the thinking of the likes of Orval E. Faubus. But I would love to have tried."[35]

When Gibson returned to the United States, a ticker-tape parade was held in New York City, with the army, air force, and Coast Guard color guards as well as bands from the Fire Department and the U.S. Third Naval District. She rode in the car with Bertram Baker of the ATA; Hulan Jack, the Manhattan Borough president; and Richard Patterson, the Department of Commerce commissioner. The backdrop of her win was that two months later nine black students attempted to enter Central High in Little Rock, Arkansas.

Gibson was the best woman athlete in the world, attested to by her being voted the Associated Press Outstanding Female Athlete of 1957; she captured most of the votes of the 214 sports writers and broadcasters in the poll, becoming the first black female to receive this honor. Finally, Gibson could play her role as a superstar athlete and an ambassador of the game. For instance, she demonstrated her strokes at Midwood High School in Brooklyn, New York. While she was playing on the 1958 Caribbean Sunshine Circuit, a photographer caught her shaking hands with a ballboy.[36] Gibson and other players called lines on the Caribbean Circuit, but she had poor results on that tour. After losing her third match to Janet Hopps, she stated, "The tournaments don't mean anything. They were just a test. It's Wimbledon that counts, and I definitely think I'll win again this year."[37]

The strongest aspect of her game was the serve. Billy Talbert featured Gibson's serve in the June 1958 issue of *World Tennis,* describing it in these terms:

> Althea Gibson is a fine model for the service action since her toss, hit and control of weight are excellent. She has a bigger backswing than most, but there is more allowable variation here than in any other part of the serve. Her worst fault, not shown here, is a tendency to footfault since she allows her left foot to slide forward onto the line just at the start of the action. . . .
>
> Althea has excellent weight control. She uses her back and knees more actively than most women, and this gives the serve an added kick. The force of her entire body is behind the shot, which is the most important single factor in achieving power.[38]

In the summer of 1958, Gibson continued her winning form. At age thirty, she fulfilled her prophecy of winning another Wimbledon, beating unseeded Angela Mortimer, a surprise finalist, 8-6, 6-2, dropping only one set in the tournament run. After she returned to New York, Mayor Robert Wagner proclaimed Althea Gibson Day, and a reception was held in her honor at Gracie Mansion, where she presented him one of her record albums.

She later won at the Merion Cricket Club. At a summer end tournament, it was thought that in the quarterfinal match against Christine Truman, Gibson "appeared to be a much sounder player than in 1957. Her ground strokes were steadier and more fluent."[39] In the fall, Gibson won the Eastern Grass Court Championships, also taking the doubles with partner Sally Moore. Gibson was ranked number 1 in the world in 1958, winning eight of twelve tournaments, including Wimbledon and the U.S. National Championships. She also captured her second consecutive world championship. She gave much of the credit for her success to her coach, Sidney Llewellyn.

Gibson was the guest of honor at the ATA party held at Birdland in New York City, escorted by her fiancé, William Darben. Also present was Sammy Davis Jr. when she sang "I'll Be Seeing You." She attempted a singing career and released an album of inspirational songs on Dot Records in May 1958. She argued, "I had the flu at the time, and I made a hasty recording. After the record came out, I could see Dot was just using my name without any concern for my talent."[40] Her singing career became official when Ed Sullivan invited her to sing on his show.[41]

She also tried acting and in 1959 played a plantation slave in John Ford's *The Horse Soldiers*. Another money-making venture was her $100,000 contract to play matches before Harlem Globetrotters games, making her the highest-paid woman in the history of tennis. Gibson preferred open tennis, the system where players could earn money while still competing in big tournaments.

After retiring from professional tennis, Gibson joined the women's professional golf tour in 1962 at age thirty-five. However, she earned little money as a golf professional, her best year being 1967, when she made $8,000. In 1969, she earned only $1,500 in thirteen tournaments. She explained, "I am losing money on the tour in the long run, but I am not ready to give up, not hardly. I am learning more and more every day."[42]

Confidence was a major ingredient of Gibson's personality. Long after she had retired from tennis, she demonstrated that. In a tournament final in Florida between Chris Evert and Kerry Reid, Reid had to withdraw because of a broken thumb. Promoters were worried that a final would not be played. Gibson reportedly stated, "I'll play her [Evert]. I can beat her with my big serve." Approximately forty years old, she was not afraid to play the top player of the next generation.[43]

Other achievements included becoming the athletic commissioner of the state of New Jersey and a community relations liaison for the city of Orange. In 1971, she was voted into the National Lawn Tennis Association Hall of Fame.

Gibson's legacy has not been forgotten. When Zina Garrison made the finals at Wimbledon in 1990, becoming the first black woman to play a Grand Slam final since Gibson, Gibson was present. She had been interviewed by NBC the previous day when Garrison upset Steffi Graf in the semifinals. Observers made connections immediately, and Gibson and Garrison were questioned about any ties between them. The sad part of the media's interview with Gibson was that she repeatedly stressed the lack of money in order to fly to the London suburb to witness tennis history in the making. Despite her success and fame, she indicated that the sport had failed to offer enough money to be financially secure after retirement and that the prize money was even less for women professionals. In addition, she was rarely approached to endorse products. In fact, only two companies were interested, and "they didn't want to pay much." [44]

Gibson's financial situation remained dire. At the age of sixty-nine in 1996, she was ill, surviving two strokes and weighing about 115 pounds, according to friends. [45] It was also reported that she suffered debilitating arthritis, clinical depression, and mild memory loss. Three years later, however, Zina Garrison insisted that Gibson looked good for a seventy-two-year-old woman. [46] Two neighbors had been assisting Gibson in East Orange, New Jersey.

One of her former doubles partners, Angela Buxton, publicized Gibson's troubles in an interview with *Inside Tennis,* stating, "I might lose our friendship over this." After Gibson's first stroke, her bills had snowballed, and she never qualified for a pension. Her husband died in 1995, and, according to Buxton, his death "seemed to lower Gibson's already poor spirits." Her situation worsened as she could not afford proper medication and was unable to pay for heating for a while. Once Buxton publicized Gibson's predicament, players began to send contributions. When Buxton visited Gibson and helped her open some of the envelopes that had piled up in her post office box, one contained two $100 bills from Mariaan de Swardt, a white South African player, who also sent a note: "I focused on your game when I learned how to play, and I wanted to thank you." Gibson rarely made public appearances, presumably owing to her illness, almost living as a recluse since suffering a stroke in 1994 (she also suffered two cerebral aneurysms). In addition, it has been suggested that another reason for her reclusiveness was Angela Buxton's announcement that Gibson was financially insolvent. Frances Clayton-Gray, head of the Althea Gibson Foundation, explains that reporters began writing stories "suggesting that she was living in a slum." "She had nothing," according to Pamela Hayling-Hoffman, who helped raise approximately $100,000 to pay Gibson's debts. During the 1996 Women's Tennis Association (WTA) season finale, Chase Manhattan Bank donated $250 for each ace hit in four matches played on the final two days, raising $8,500.[47]

In 1997, a new tournament was inaugurated in honor of Althea Gibson, the Althea Gibson Cup, an international event for women seventy and older.[48] A school in East Orange, New Jersey, where she lived for more than thirty years, bears her name, the Althea Gibson Early Childhood Education Academy, dedicated in May 1999. According to Betty Debnaun, principal of the academy, "It's only fitting to name the school after a woman as great as Althea Gibson. She excelled in everything she did. She's a living legend."[49]

As writer Ken Kamlet argues, Gibson's legacy has been limited. "When discussing black tennis players, most people bring up Arthur Ashe first and Gibson second, if they bring her up at all. They will usually tout Ashe's three Grand Slam singles titles rather than Gibson's five." Family friend Pamela Hayling-Hoffman agrees, "I just wonder how many players are aware of her legacy. Althea broke the color barrier and made it easier for people like Ashe to get into the game. By just being an exemplary athlete who also happened to be black, she made the sport of tennis wonderful for everybody."[50]

Although USTA officials repeatedly invited Gibson to the U.S. Open, she politely declined. She instructed American Express to use an old photo of her in a print ad campaign. Friend Frances Gray believed that Gibson refused interviews in her later years because she wanted people to remember her as she was. Even so, she remained an avid tennis and golf fan. Although she liked Tiger Woods and Pete Sampras, she felt a special kinship with the Williams sisters. After Venus won

Wimbledon in 2000, Gibson raised a glass of ginger ale in a silent toast.[51]

Gibson died at age seventy-six on September 28, 2003, from respiratory failure. Several in the sports world praised her contribution. Zina Garrison stated, "Althea used to say she wanted me to be the one who broke her barrier, to take the burden off of her. When [Williams] won, I called [Gibson] and she was so happy that it was finally lifted."[52] Whereas some people like to hold on to records of note, Gibson preferred that the focus move to another player, erasing the blot on history that only one black woman in the previous forty-three years had won a Grand Slam title. Billie Jean King acknowledged, "Althea did a lot for people in tennis, but she did even more for people in general."[53] When King was thirteen years old, she saw Gibson play for the first time and immediately considered Gibson one of her "true Heroines." Martina Navratilova added, "Her life was very difficult, but she broke down a lot of barriers and doors and made it easier for a lot of us."[54] Such words were a telling tribute that Gibson's importance transcended "race." Gray believed that despite the accolades for Gibson's achievements in sports and the arts, it was, as *Chicago Tribune* writer Melissa Isaacson put it, "among her greatest sources of satisfaction, that the foundation she co-founded with Gray succeeded not only in exposing inner-city children to sports such as tennis and golf, but focused on their education as well."[55] Prior to her death, Gibson collaborated with Gray on her biography, *Born to Win: The Authorized Biography of Althea Gibson*.[56] A sign at the Florida A&M tennis courts reads "The House That Althea Built."

In a tribute to Gibson, it was written that her legacy may have as much to do with the way she played as it does with race. According to Billie Jean King, "She was imposing to begin with, and she had a swagger that added to that aura."[57] Later, another net rusher, Navratilova, had that same swagger, as does Serena Williams now.

Gibson was more than a black woman playing tennis. She was one of the greats.

3

Arthur Ashe

Citizen of the World

ARTHUR ASHE JR. is the most well-known name in the history of black tennis and one of the better-known figures in general tennis history. Ashe had impacts on professional and amateur tennis, oftentimes transcending the tennis world into broader political, social, and economic arenas nationally and internationally.

Ashe was born July 10, 1943, in Richmond, Virginia, and his early years were important to his personal and professional development. His mother, Mattie Cunningham Ashe, died after an operation when he was almost seven years old. She told her husband, Arthur Ashe Sr., "If anything should happen to me, Arthur, the boys are yours. I didn't born the children for your mother, and I didn't born them for mine. I born the children for you, Arthur." After his father told him the news, Ashe said, "Well Daddy, as long as we're together, everything will be all right." His father argued that nothing Arthur had done since then made him so proud.[1]

Arthur Ashe Sr. moved to Richmond from Lincolntown, North Carolina, to work for $2.50 a week. By the 1960s, he had a job in the city park and owned a landscaping business. In addition, he built a home in Louisa County, virtually by himself. The young Ashe noted these accomplishments in a segregated environment, where racism was open and thriving.

Growing up in the segregated South, Ashe experienced racism not only in the social avenues of Southern society, but in tennis domains. When he was twelve years old, he and Ronald Charity once tried to convince Sam Woods, the white man who practically ran tennis in Richmond, to allow Ashe to play in a city tournament; Woods denied the request.

Charity, a part-time playground instructor, was the first to notice Ashe. Charity remembers, "It was difficult to tell whether Arthur was dragging the racket or the racket was dragging Arthur, but he was soon so obviously good that I arranged to have him go to Dr. [Robert] Johnson's for a summer." [2]

During the initial days at Johnson's school of tennis, Ashe refused to do anything that clashed with what Charity had taught him. After Johnson called Ashe's father, the latter took the three-hour bus trip to tell Arthur that he might as well return home if he was not going to listen to Johnson. Arthur decided to stay. He admitted, "I have never once in all my life talked back to my father." [3]

According to Beverly Coleman, an acupuncturist who studied under Johnson, Arthur "was always a mild mannered kid that suppressed his emotions. He was always kidded by the older boys. They would always slap him on his head, and call him names. I took care of him, and tried to protect him. Arthur had it hard at camp among his peers, and also in the junior tournaments. . . . Even in tournaments, he was under continuous stress at an early age." [4]

In 1959, Ashe played in the Eastern Junior and Boys Championships at Forest Hills, where he was seeded number 1, but lost in the finals to Hugh Lynch III from Bethesda, Maryland. Ironically, two southern players competed against each other in New York, but were unable to play in the South because Ashe was not accepted for tournaments in the Middle Atlantic Lawn Tennis Association (MALTA). Ashe was unranked by MALTA, whereas Lynch was number 2. Ashe said later in his career, "Thank God for the American Tennis Association," while sitting in the executive offices of American Airlines, where he had accepted an offer to be the company's touring professional. [5]

In his first appearance in the U.S. National Championships at Forest Hills in 1959, Ashe played Rod Laver in the first round; he was so nervous that he vomited beside the court just before the match.[6]

Like many black pioneers, Ashe had to adjust to being the only black or the first black to accomplish several feats in tennis. For example, in 1961 he played on the Junior Davis Cup team, the only black member. When he was a sophomore at the University of California at Los Angeles (UCLA), he became the first black player to be named to the U.S. Davis Cup team in 1963. Ashe explained,

> Since no black American had ever been on the team, I was now a part of history. Despite segregation, I loved the United States. That year, I played only one Davis Cup match, a "dead rubber" match (one played after the best-of-five series has been decided), in which I defeated Orlando Bracamonte of Venezuela. And at the moment of my victory, it thrilled me beyond measure to hear the umpire announce not my name but that of my country: "Game: United States," "Set: United States," "Game, Set, and Match: United States."[7]

After Ashe was named to the squad, his mentor, Dr. Robert Johnson Sr., declared, "Ashe is two years ahead of the timetable I set for him. . . . I figured that he would be just hitting his trade around 1965."[8] A fixture on the Davis Cup team, Ashe was named to the squad in seven of the next eight years, where he posted a 5-1 record in three winning challenge rounds, 20-2 in singles, and 1-1 in doubles in thirteen zone matches, an impressive 26-4 record overall.[9] He earned twenty-seven Davis Cup singles victories and played on ten squads between 1963 and 1978.

He also played on the 1964 UCLA squad. Dennis Ralston and Billy Bond of USC beat Ashe and Charlie Pasarell 6-2, 6-3, 6-4 in the doubles final. Ashe revenged that loss with a win over Ralston in the Eastern Grass Court Championships. Moreover, in 1964 he won the Johnston Award, the highest honor that an American player could receive.[10]

In 1965, Ashe was ranked the number 3 player in the United

States. Meanwhile, he continued to win for UCLA, claiming the singles and doubles (with Ian Crookenden of New Zealand) titles in the National Intercollegiate. Also that year Ashe entered the world's top ten for the first time, being ranked at number 6. However, the highlight of the year was when he was chosen for the Davis Cup team to face Mexico.

The Davis Cup tie (see glossary) was held in Dallas, where sponsors—the Junior League, the Jaycees, and Niemann-Marcus—made it a major affair with parades, dances, lunches, and brunches. Although a "supporting player, not really a principal," Ashe became "a star" of the tie by defeating Rafael Osuna, Mexico's top player. The day before the matches began, the Mexican captain, Pancho Contreras, "smiled broadly when the draw pitted his ace against the relatively inexperienced Ashe." [11]

Another surprising feat occurred in the quarterfinals of the men's singles in the U.S. National Championships, where he faced Australian Roy Emerson, the defending champion, top-ranked amateur, and a heavy favorite to win the tournament. Ashe won the match 13-11, 6-4, 10-12, 6-2 and received a standing ovation. "As the large, cheering crowd rose to its feet, Ashe raised his arms in the air and stared at the ground, as if stunned by his achievement. Then he dropped his racket, broke into a quick, friendly grin and shook hands with Emerson." [12]

In his Australian debut in 1966, Ashe, at age twenty-two, defeated three Davis Cuppers for Australia to win the Queensland Championships. Fred Stolle was the number 2 amateur when he faced Ashe "in a match of cannonballs." Ashe scored twenty-one aces against Stolle's ten. Stolle said after the match, "I just couldn't pick his serves—he changed them so often—and his returns were too good to be true." Then Ashe defeated John Newcombe in straight sets; Newcombe commented, "Even when you could pick what service was coming, it was so fast you had little time to do anything about it." In the final, Ashe took down Roy Emerson in five sets to become the first player from the United States to win the Queensland men's singles title. [13]

Newcombe was able to turn the tables at the New South Wales tournament that followed, where Ashe lost amidst wind gusts of up to fifty miles per hour in Sydney. It was reported, "John Newcombe yesterday put an abrupt end to the talk of invincibility which has been building up around American Arthur Ashe."[14]

Ashe rebounded to take the South Australian title by defeating Roy Emerson in five sets, but lost to Emerson in another tournament in March. The saga of Ashe in Australia continued when he won the Western Australia Championships and received the trophy from the governor, Major-General Sir Douglas Kendrew. Ashe chronicled his own matches in the championships, writing in third person: "The Ashe-Okker match was scheduled for 1 P.M. and started promptly at 4:25 P.M. due to the extended Richey-Newcombe encounter. Most readers know how it feels to wait around for a match; cooling one's heels for 3½ hours and then playing in the shadows with a handful of people around is slightly depressing."[15]

In 1966, Ashe had a full schedule in the spring, which included the American Zone Davis Cup, final exams, a State Department trip to Uganda, and an upcoming marriage.[16] Also that spring he defeated Jim Osborne in the finals to capture a title in Phoenix. In 1967, World Championship Tennis (WCT) presented Ashe with a bid to turn professional, sending "a bushel basket of socks" with the contract. Although he returned the contract unsigned, he kept the socks.[17]

The turbulent year 1968 was also a turning point for Ashe's tennis career when he won the U.S. National Championships title twice. This tournament was one of the first majors he played after the USLTA decided to retain the distinctions "amateur" and "professional."[18] The first time he defeated Bob Lutz, who was unseeded. A writer described the match: "Arthur Ashe's victory always seemed to have been fore ordained. Some people live dangerously; Bob Lutz claimed from one peak of excitement to another, but Ashe was always at the calm center of events, unruffled, confident, serving superbly, the one cool man on the hot ground. If you looked at the whole field, you picked him as a thoroughbred at once."[19]

Ashe was twenty-five when he won the title in temperatures that reached almost one hundred degrees. According to one report,

"Sometimes it seems that Arthur creates difficulties for himself, usually by playing lazy volleys, as part of a scientific experiment, just to see whether he can serve his way out of trouble. There were times when Lutz pulled off astonishing shots and it seemed a major advance when he won the third set, but the Ashe poise was indestructible. His answer to danger was serenity."[20]

In 1968, Ashe met with George MacCall, a professional promoter, who offered him $400,000 to play for five years. In the end, Ashe and Davis Cup teammates Pasarell, Stan Smith, Lutz, and captain Donald Dell decided to put tennis first, and Ashe remained an amateur.[21]

Later that year the USLTA opened its doors to professionals, but two amateurs emerged as singles finalists in the U.S. Open. Ashe was seeded fifth behind four Australian professionals, but had been unbeaten in his previous twenty matches. In that tournament, thirteen professionals fell to amateurs, and the four men seeded above Ashe lost in earlier rounds. Nevertheless, Ashe defeated four top players, including Emerson and Drysdale. The final between Ashe and Okker was played on Monday because of the rain on Sunday. As a result, they played before a crowd of seven thousand. Ashe won the marathon match 14-12, 5-7, 6-3, 3-6, 6-3.

Ashe's victory in the U.S. Open in 1968 is best remembered because he took $280 for expenses. Ashe told friends "not to feel sorry for him because he won the U.S. National Open and received a handshake and a Cup, while losing finalist Tom Okker was the recipient of $14,000." After reading about the "unfair" distribution of the prize money, a woman in New Jersey sent him one hundred shares of General Motors stock, worth $8,900.[22] One writer described the situation in these terms: "The irony of that situation, accentuated by the fact that one of those amateurs got paid for losing while the other got a big cup and a pat on the back for winning, was only matched by the drama and excitement of a great tournament."[23] At that time a U.S. Army lieutenant stationed at West Point, specializing in data processing, Ashe had refused the money owing to his amateur status. The rules changed the next year. Ashe then won the Pennsylvania Grass Courts, defeating Marty Riessen in the final, and earned a number 2 ranking by the end of the year. In 1970, he was the leader in prize money among the independent professionals, having earned $45,000 by September.

One of the brightest spots of Ashe's illustrious career came in 1975, when he defeated Jimmy Connors in the Wimbledon final. The match had its buildup long before that July day in 1975. By 1973, a "feud" was brewing between Ashe and Connors because Ashe failed to shy from his opinion of Connors. For example, he accused Bill Riordan, Connors's manager, of picking spots for Connors. "He [Connors] is like an up-and-coming boxer who only gets thrown a carefully selected diet of palookas and washed-outs. Everything has been decided only with consideration to Connors' career." Ashe added that Connors was not his own man because his manager maneuvered him; "[i]n effect Connors has traded his soul."[24] Connors refused to join the Association of Tennis Professionals (ATP), although he profited from the organization, causing Ashe to reveal, "He never helped in our ongoing struggles with the national and international governing bodies." Moreover, Ashe could not understand Connors's refusal to play Davis Cup tennis and in 1975 stated that Connors was "seemingly unpatriotic." Just a week prior to Wimbledon, Connors and Riordan announced a $5 million libel lawsuit against Ashe, the ATP president.[25] The suit was dropped after Ashe defeated Connors at Wimbledon that year.

The bookmakers had Ashe as an eleven to two underdog. Because Connors had won three of the previous meetings, it was expected that he would emerge victorious again. However, Ashe had won in the WCT finals in Dallas. Ashe's game had been described as having been based on power, "overwhelming when he was playing well, but brittle and suspect when pressured by an opponent who could return consistently."[26]

Describing his feelings that day, Ashe admitted, "When I walked on court, I thought I was going to win. I felt it was my destiny."[27] However, most tennis fans and followers were shocked at the resulting 6-1, 6-1, 5-7, 6-4 victory. Not only had Ashe won, but he had defeated the favorite convincingly.

In a postmatch article, one journalist reported, "On Saturday it seemed doubtful whether Ashe would even take a set from Connors. We suspected Connors was no longer playing matches—merely giving exhibitions. . . . The climax produced the most piquant surprise of the tournament, and one of the most interesting men's finals for years."[28]

According to this same reporter, "One of the biggest upsets in modern tennis history began to unfold before a thrilled but incredulous crowd."[29] Ashe dismantled Connors's power game by chipping the ball to Connors's forehand, abandoning the power game of slashing winners and denying Connors what he liked most, pace. Although Connors went up 3-0 in the fourth set, Ashe remained relaxed. During the changeovers, he kept his eyes closed, head slightly raised as if meditating. In the fifth game of that set, he regained the break by hitting another great lob and a down-the-line forehand to cause a volley error from Connors.[30] After match point, the thirty-two-year-old Ashe calmly raised a fist, a black power symbol, but an action that seemed "momentous" for some whites who thought of Ashe as being quiet and shy.

When exiting the court, he spoke to Lew Hoad, who had kept a telephone line open from Spain to offer his congratulations. Even reports of Connors's alleged injury failed to daunt the enthusiasm of the victory. Connors's manager Bill Riordan reported that "Connors damaged muscles on his right shin during his first round match against John Lloyd and was in pain after subsequent matches."[31]

When asked whether a victory over Bjorn Borg had helped him in winning Wimbledon in 1975, Ashe replied, "As far as results are concerned I guess that's right, but I'd been playing well. I'd been in the finals of Forest Hills. I was twice in the finals of the Australian, semis of Wimbledon twice, the finals of WCT once. I knew I was just a couple of inches away, literally, from winning. It wasn't a matter of me not knowing I could do it. It was a matter of a little luck here and there."[32]

In an early round match against Tony Roche, Ashe "was sharp and quick, swinging easily into fluent first serves and volleying with depth and power." Although Ashe dropped the first set, he took the next two sets, dropping the fourth, but taking the fifth. After beating Brian

Gottfried in the third round, he felt that he could do no wrong throughout the rest of the tournament. "And when I walked on the court against Connors, I had this eerie feeling, like I said, for the first time, that I can't lose today."[33] He also admitted that he had decided to cut down on unforced errors on the forehand by not hitting as hard. In addition, he employed one of his best shots, the topspin backhand crosscourt. Finally, he felt that his second serve had improved, providing him with additional confidence. The win brought a full page ad for Ashe in *World Tennis,* a photo of him holding the Wimbledon trophy, with the caption "You know what Arthur's been doing lately."

Realizing the impact of the tennis ball, Ashe thought that Roscoe Tanner erred in trying to outhit Connors in the semifinals, as he had done two weeks earlier at Nottingham. However, Connors was unaccustomed to the grass at Nottingham. Also, Slazenger balls were used at Wimbledon, not the heavier Dunlop used at Nottingham. To take away the angles, Ashe generally hit the ball at Connors. Furthermore, he did not allowed Connors to hang on the baseline. He borrowed a shot from Rod Laver, a low backhand lob that barely clears the backhand reach, a shot more difficult for a two-handed player with a shorter reach. When Ashe warmed up with Rya Ruffels, he practiced the lob. One writer summarized the affair: "It was a destiny richly deserved, a triumph that spread happiness and satisfaction throughout the world of tennis because it turned a good man into a great champion. It has been a victory in which intellect had guided near perfect execution."[34]

At that time, Ashe penned his own explanation for his win: "Understand at the outset that it was not foremost a matter of beating Jimmy Connors. The primary thing is that I won Wimbledon. I beat Jimmy Connors and I beat Tony Roche, Bjorn Borg, Graham Stilwell, Brian Gottfried, Jan Kamiwazumi and Bob Hewitt."[35]

It also helped that Ashe was totally relaxed in the finals, never nervous. In his description of the match, he added, "I am known for wearing a mask on the court, a poker face, but those who know me well have told me they could discern something beyond the usual unemotional coolness." When Connors won the third set and went up a break in the third, it presented no problems for Ashe: "it was almost comforting because it violated my sense of the normal that I could beat him easily in three sets." [36]

In the 1975 year-end Grand Prix Masters, Ashe and Ilie Nastase had a very controversial first-round match. After the players split the first two sets, the match heated during the third. Ashe mounted a 4-1 lead, and Nastase found himself serving 15-40 when Ashe held up his left hand to indicate he was not ready and caught the ball that Nastase served. Nastase, who had already received a warning for hitting a ball at a linesman, complained that Ashe was never ready, even though Ashe was possibly "the one player opponents never [had] to wait for." [37] Nastase received another warning after deliberately bouncing the ball four times. Ashe walked off the court. A spokesperson announced to the press, "The referee has not been able to make a decision. Ashe has claimed default." Later, the referee, Horst Klosterkemper, stated, "There is no winner of this match. In my opinion both didn't play according to the rules . . . nobody wins and nobody loses . . . the match will not be replayed. . . . I had it in my mind to disqualify Nastase, but before I could, Ashe walked off the court." [38]

Ashe argued that he left the court because the rules had been broken, adding that he knew the rules because he had helped write them. The president of the International Lawn Tennis Federation (ILTF), Derek Hardwick, later announced that Ashe's misdemeanor was overlooked and Ashe was awarded the match, a decision Nastase accepted.

Compiling a 108-23 match record, winning nine tournaments, and earning $338,337 in prize money in 1975, Ashe was ranked number 1 after winning Wimbledon and the WCT finals and reaching the semis of the Grand Prix Masters. Ashe commented, "That was my one big disappointment of '75. I wanted to win WCT and the Masters the same year." [39] The following year he won twenty-nine of the first thirty matches he played and five of the first six tournaments.

In 1977, Ashe had chunks of calcium removed from his left heel. He hoped to play tennis again, but others thought his career was finished. Despite the setback, at age thirty-five he made the semifinals of the Australian Open in 1979 and had a match point for the final. He later advanced to the final of the Grand Prix Masters, where he lost to John McEnroe after holding two match points. Because he had dropped to 157th on the computer ranking after his surgery, he qualified for the Masters only when Guillermo Vilas decided not to play.

When it appeared Ashe was returning to form, a heart attack halted his amazing career in 1979. After recovery from a quadruple bypass surgery, he wrote extensively about the ordeal. In an article, he recounted how the events on August 1, 1979, changed his life. "I have long scars on my lower legs to mark the spots where veins were removed and used in my quadruple bypass operation. I have had to think about death, and this has made life more precious." There was hope that he could play tennis again if the surgery was successful, although "they [the doctors] didn't know anybody who had done it." However, this hope was "dashed" on March 9, 1980, while he was jogging in California, when after one hundred yards he felt a twinge of angina. He learned that he would have to live with the possibility of chest pain from physical exertion.[40] In 1980, he announced his official retirement from competitive tennis. An editor of a tennis magazine wrote of the retirement:

> A touch of class has gone out of the pro game with Arthur Ashe's decision to retire from competitive tennis. . . .
>
> Not only is the pro game losing one of its most courageous and elegant champions . . . but its most eloquent spokesman. . . . Ashe has always been a voice of responsibility off court and the personification of sportsmanship on it.[41]

After retirement, Ashe returned to tennis as the captain of the Davis Cup team. In his autobiography, Ashe wrote, "This is a job I've wanted since I was young. . . . My captaincy also proved to be much more challenging than I had anticipated. Those five years turned out to be, on the whole, a disorganized, sometimes exhilarating, sometimes frustrating and even humiliating epic of victories and defeats, excitement and tedium, camaraderie and isolation."[42]

Fortunately, John McEnroe Jr., the top player in the United States, was willing to play on the team. Ashe explained, "John has always been available, and I found that admirable well before I was asked to become captain."[43] In 1982, in the final against France, his team opposed the French team, led by Yannick Noah, whom Ashe had seen years earlier as a young boy in Cameroon.

In 1985, Ashe was named to the International Tennis Hall of Fame. The committee inducted him as soon as he was eligible, five years after retirement. Soon after, Tom Gorman replaced Ashe as captain of the Davis Cup team. Ashe had a remarkable tenure as captain, thirteen wins and three losses, and was only the second captain in thirty years to lead the U.S. team to consecutive victories in 1981 and 1982. Despite this record, he thought it should have been better because he "had led some of the most talented teams ever fielded by the United States." He confessed, "We should have done better, and some of the blame must rest on my shoulders."[44]

Throughout his career, Ashe played doubles with some remarkable talent. He played mixed doubles with Althea Gibson, then a teaching pro, in a tournament in New York in 1973. He said of her, "I'd love to be able to see Althea and Margaret Court meet, both on their best days. I'm not so sure Althea wouldn't give Margaret her toughest match."[45] He played mixed doubles with Billie Jean King at Hilton Head in 1973, losing in the final to Margaret Court and John Newcombe. He realized that King had an excellent chance of beating Bobby Riggs in their upcoming battle of the sexes. Later, Ashe won $80 betting on King. Playing with his protégé Yannick Noah, he took the court in a doubles match on Center Court at Wimbledon in 1978, a historical moment in tennis history.

• • •

Arthur Ashe was not only the first black male to win a Grand Slam, but was the first American to win the U.S. National Championships since 1955. He even made the cover of *Life* magazine, "the certification of celebrity at that time."[46] Later, his picture appeared on the cover of the *Chicago Tribune*'s *Sunday Magazine* in 1969. When he played in New York in 1970, he was the guest of honor at a reception where it was announced he would become tennis director at the Doral Hotel and

Country Club in Miami, becoming the first black head pro at a southern club.

"Race" became the center of his identity. For instance, one article in 1966 referred to him as "an American Negro," the first identity tag in a piece, noting that he was "the first male of his race to invade the highest levels of the sport of lawn tennis."[47] By 1964, Ashe had begun to receive press coverage primarily because blacks were a "novelty" in tennis. One reporter wrote, "In the white-ducked, white-skinned world of amateur tennis, 21-year-old Arthur Ashe Jr. is an athletic oddity." Some viewed him as a major breakthrough in the world of previously segregated country clubs. "[T]he Negro student from UCLA is invited to tournaments at clubs that normally admit others of his race only as waiters and locker-room attendants." Integrating tournaments was not the same as integrating club memberships. In addition, integrating tournaments was not the important aspect for Ashe, but winning them. He saw himself as a tennis player "who was also a Negro," rather than "a Negro tennis player." Ironically, he argued, "I'm no crusader. I'm simply me and not a social phenomenon."[48] Two years later, however, in response to the idea that he was "a Negro in a game that is one of the last sporting strongholds of the white man," he stated, "I guess I'm just a sociological phenomenon."[49]

Ashe was an activist against racism despite his life in the almost lily white world of tennis. Black athletes have always endured scrutiny by white sport writers. In a 1992 tribute to Ashe, writer Peter Bodo tried to analyze Ashe psychologically within a social context with underlying assertions. He wrote, "After all, Ashe had been a collegiate tennis star and an Army man—a good soldier at a time when many of us thought that was an oxymoron. He wore short hair and spoke the King's English, a language many of us couldn't or didn't want to understand."[50]

This statement is perplexing. Do such attributes make Ashe unique among blacks or unique among all Americans? Obviously, Bodo ignored Ashe's afro, and the concept of "short" and "long" was relative. Ashe wore an afro in 1975, and how whites chose to perceive it was less important than what it meant for blacks to wear it. In addition, Ashe was not as removed from the black power struggle or culture as Bodo implied. In fact, some of the most vocal black activists after World War II were veterans. In addition, Ashe did not speak the "King's English"; he spoke American English and was articulate, just as were many blacks.

The key of Ashe's character was that he was soft-spoken, a quality endeared by whites when held by blacks. In contrast, being black and loud, like Muhammad Ali, were negative attributes to many whites. Playing tennis, being articulate (in a manner acceptable to whites), and being soft-spoken made Ashe a prime candidate to be viewed in a way that Ali or other outspoken black athletes or visible personalities could not be viewed, although they may have been just as articulate.

In the early 1990s, Barry Lorge maintained that Ashe never was estranged from his roots or mentors: doctors, teachers, preachers, disciples of Dr. Martin Luther King. Nevertheless, Lorge attempted to separate Ashe from the civil rights era by reporting, "It was a tumultuous time of riots and boycotts. Muhammad Ali had been stripped of the heavyweight boxing championship for refusing to fight in Vietnam. Tommie Smith and John Carlos raised gloved fists on the Olympic victory stand in Mexico City. Ashe became a symbol of calm, reason and restraint in the era of 'burn, baby, burn!' "[51]

Lorge's assessment is a grave misconception of the struggle for blacks. "Burn, baby, burn!" was not the agenda of the nonviolent, direct action movement. First, Ashe was not a leader in that respect. According to him, he left that role for those more skillful and in a better position to play it. Ashe's voice was not one in opposition to other black leaders, but a supplementary one. Black people have never thought the same about any issue. Even if Ashe disagreed with H. Rap Brown and Stokely Carmichael's approach, as Lorge argues, was his opinion widely publicized at the time? Did he set a stage for public debate with those urging more immediate change? Interestingly, Ashe praised the work of people like Carmichael.

Even though Ashe might have preferred a gradual approach, he too was frustrated that progress was too slow for blacks in tennis. "I think he was hoping to see more USTA advancement in getting inner-city kids involved. He and I both thought we'd have more inner-city kids involved in junior tennis by now," argued Stan Smith.[52]

Writer Peter Bodo also missed the mark in mentioning a discussion with Ashe wherein the latter revealed that he wanted to open a tennis camp aimed exclusively at black players. Bodo saw this plan as "reverse segregation" and hinted that Ashe failed to skew the new agenda of multiculturalism.[53] Bodo could not or did not want to see what Ashe saw: that the USTA had failed at tapping talent in the black community. "Reverse segregation," as Bodo called it, was in reality a direct result of segregation imposed on the black community and the almost near exclusion of blacks in the USTA's strategies to develop top players.

The year 1968 was a volatile year and major turning point for the Civil Rights Movement with the assassination of Rev. Dr. Martin Luther King Jr., who had recently expanded the movement with the Poor People's Campaign. Black peace activists and others who opposed the Vietnam War raised their voices against colonialist and neocolonialist projects against other nonwhite people. In addition, too many black American lives were being lost in the military campaign. Anne Marie Braffheid, Miss Curaçao, was the first runner-up in the Miss Universe contest, marking the first time a black woman ever came so close to winning the title. Other black women competed in the first Miss Black America Pageant, protesting the racism and discrimination in the Miss America Pageant. James Brown's "Say It Loud (I'm Black and I'm Proud)" became the national anthem for the black cultural revolution, and artists began to answer the call to produce black consciousness-raising material. After it was decided that U.S. black athletes would compete in the 1968 Olympics, Tommie Smith and John Carlos held their own protest against racism at the Olympic Games in Mexico City. On the winners' podium, the two young athletes raised fists encased in black gloves and bowed their heads during the playing of the national anthem of the United States. In those games, black Americans set seven world records in track and field and won three medals in boxing. In certain sports, blacks excelled: 26 percent of professional football players,

30 percent of major league baseball, and 44 percent of professional basketball players were black.[54] Advancement for blacks in the larger society came much more slowly and at a much higher price.

During an interview in England, Ashe stated that he would devote
himself to the Civil Rights Movement after completing his tour in the
army. Ashe's brand of civil rights activism included such activities as
playing a benefit to raise money for the Black Economic Union and
Food First, a relief program in Holly Springs, Mississippi.[55] He stated,

> People like Stokely Carmichael, who are committed to the fight 24
> hours a day every day understand that it is different for guys like me,
> or say, Sammy Davis Jr. They realize we lead different lives. The im-
> portant thing is that we are really with them, working with them. Not
> just as a gesture. . . . We're not going to get what we are after quickly
> but we can't behave as if we are resigned to letting it come slowly.
> Men like Stokely are absolutely right to demand and insist that it
> must happened now. What Stokely is doing is wonderful. I've met
> him and talked with him quite a lot and I'm full of admiration for the
> guy. When people have been on the bottom as long as the blacks have
> been on the bottom in the U.S., they get conditioned. For genera-
> tions, our people were indoctrinated to believe that white was beauti-
> ful and black was ugly. So you had all the nonsense about trying to
> straighten the hair and so on. There is a dignity gap to be bridged and
> guys like Stokely are doing it. Of course, they deal in exaggerations at
> times. Stokely shouts that black is beautiful and so it is, but that
> doesn't mean that white isn't beautiful. . . . What we are doing is not
> like trying to open a door. It's more like trying to batter down a wall.
> . . . They say that Stokely is extreme but I'm telling you there are
> guys around that make Stokely look like Mary Poppins.[56]

Off the court, Ashe readily gave his opinion on many issues, which
set him apart from most athletes. For instance, he suggested wearing
colors other than white long before the so-called rock-and-roll tennis
players of the 1990s. He argued, "White is traditional, not fundamental. I see nothing wrong with players wearing color shirts."[57] Moreover, in the 1970s he argued for changing the schedules of the major

tournaments, stating, "I'd love to be a benevolent dictator of international tennis, with absolute powers, for five minutes. First, I would rearrange the schedule and spread out the major championships of the world. It's absolutely asinine for the French Open, the biggest clay court tournament in Europe, to be separated from Wimbledon, which is on grass and *the* premier event in the world, by one week." [58]

His foresight regarding the game was amazing. In 1975, he stated, "we shall see the emergence of some more 17-year-old prodigies like Borg." [59] By the 1990s, as predicted, there were many teen sensations in tennis. As for the USLTA, he asserted, "The biggest drawback in having a responsible, powerful and successful USLTA is the lack of paid employees. USLTA officials work for free, on their own time. A man gives up some of his free hours for tennis, and then says, 'Well, I've done this on my own time and I can sleep easy knowing that I've given up both time and money for a cause.' This is no way to run an organization." [60]

When asked about those who insisted that there was no budget for hiring administrative assistants in the USLTA, he answered, "No budget for it? Are you kidding? What else are they doing with their money? In the first place, it's ridiculous that a Junior has to pay to play tennis." During this interview, an announcement was made over the public-address system that enrollment dues in the USLTA had been increased. Reporter Neil Amdur noted, "Ashe's facial expression, which had been serious, now becomes heavy, almost as though what he had been saying all along has just been verified. He throws his hands up in despair." Ashe returned to his criticisms of the USLTA and how it handled juniors, arguing, "They can get the money elsewhere. I know they can. And when they do get the money, they don't spend it wisely." Although tennis was changing, Ashe felt that it was still antiquated, "like a 1940 relic trying to compete in the Indianapolis 500." [61]

A major development marked tennis history in 1970. Lamar Hunt had already been instrumental in the formation of the WCT and had signed Rod Laver, Pancho Gonzalez, John Newcombe, Roy Emerson, Fred Stolle, Tony Roche, and eighteen others. During the U.S. Open Championships of 1970, Hunt, Mike Davies, and Al Hill Jr. announced a million-dollar circuit of twenty-one tournaments, which affected the ILTF, the various national lawn tennis associations, and the agents for Independent Pros and Pepsi-Cola, who sponsored the Grand Prix. Ashe, Bob Lutz, and Charlie (Charlito) Pasarell signed a five-year contract with WCT, leaving the independents. A week later, the USLTA lost seven additional players, all women.

Ashe maintained a strong fan base. Describing this ability to attract fans, one reporter said, "He does not always win but he attracts a following that cheers for him, bleeds for him and adores him. Such a one is Arthur Ashe."[62]

Ashe played an instrumental role in the governing body of tennis. In 1972, he became one of the leaders in the formation of the ATP. In the following year, the ATP was faced with how to handle the case of Nikki Pilic, who was threatened with suspension by the Yugoslav Tennis Association Federation because he refused to play on the Davis Cup team for Yugoslavia in 1973 after committing himself to it. Ashe argued, "Nikki says this is not so, and our players union, the Association of Tennis Professionals, has taken up his case. I am especially involved because I am an officer of the ATP—and one of its founders, for that matter."[63]

During this ordeal, Ashe's maternal grandmother died, and although he was in London at the time, there was no doubt that he would fly home for the funeral. "Big Mama was one of my heroines. . . . She kept the family together, all the while working full-time in the kitchen at a white public school. She was a strong, dear, fine woman."[64]

Ashe, as president of the ATP in 1974—75, commented on the switch to the open era (see glossary):

No one was well prepared for the transition from the closed amateur (or "shamateur" as some called it) to the open era—not the International Lawn Tennis Federation (ILTF), as it was then called, nor the Big Four (the governing bodies of the American, French, Australian, and British championships). Fearful that they would lose control of the game and the players, the ILTF (later shortened to ITF) and the

Big Four pursued a reactionary strategy, impeding us at almost every turn. In my judgement, they resisted change in defense of privilege and a stuffy conception of the traditional.[65]

To say that Ashe was a renaissance person would explain his varied interests. He wrote a biweekly sports column for the *Washington Post,* created a minority hiring program for Aetna Life and Casualty, acted as the national campaign chairperson for the American Heart Association, and started a New York–based import-export firm with a friend. As a writer, he spent $250,000 and worked more than six years to complete *A Hard Road to Glory,* a three-volume history of the black athlete, published in 1988. He explained, "The more I delved into it, the more emotionally attached I got to the information—especially with people I felt had undertaken heroic actions."[66] Ashe also served as longtime editor for *Tennis Magazine,* writing instructional guides with Alexander McNab for developing players of all levels.

Ashe's other writing credits include a diary he kept from Wimbledon 1973 to Wimbledon 1974, titled *Arthur Ashe: Portrait in Motion;* a memoir, *Days of Grace;* and a couple of instructional books. He also wrote a fitness column for the *American Express Gold Card Personal Fitness Newsletter.*

He could also claim achievements beyond professional tennis. For example, for two years he taught at Florida Memorial College in Miami, where he was also a member of the Board of Trustees. He taught an honors course, "Education and the Black Athlete," which examined the comparative roles of black athletes in predominantly black colleges and in predominantly white colleges.[67]

College sports and academics were important issues for Ashe. Despite the few blacks on teams at predominately white universities in the 1960s, Ashe's role at UCLA fostered the viewing of these programs as possibilities. A history major, he belonged to the California Club, a student leadership organization concerned with "the future development of all UC campuses." According to Sue-Fawn Chung, who attended UCLA at the same time and was an active member of the organization, she and Ashe were sometimes "token minorities": "We both excelled in the things that we did so we were able to be recognized by the larger community for this contribution."[68]

In 1977, Ashe wrote, "I have become convinced that we blacks spend too much time on the playing fields and too little time in the libraries." In this article, he warned black parents that the chances of their child's becoming a professional athlete was slim. His formula was that the child spend two hours in the library for each hour spent on the athletic field.[69] In 1983, he was the recipient of the (Bob J. H.) Kiphuth Fellowship from Yale University. During a press conference, he gave his opinion on a controversial NCAA rule debate, Proposition 48, arguing, "The intent of the proposal is commendable. Many athletes are in college to play ball and not get an education, but the remedy is too broad a brush. You need to do it with finely chiseled tools, not with a sledgehammer. Basically, what you are saying is you will keep someone out of college on the basis of what they did one Saturday morning on an S. A. T. test."[70]

Ashe became the first athlete to be named *Sports Illustrated* Sportsman of the Year after retirement. He had served as ambassador for the National Junior Tennis League (NJTL), "going around the country getting mayors excited about it," according to Dwight Moseley of the USTA Minority Participation Committee. Eve Kraft, who served twenty-one years with the USTA, commented, "He would tell the kids tennis could help them, not necessarily to win Wimbledon, but to get a tennis scholarship to college, to become a doctor or lawyer." When fifteen-year-old Marvin K. Williams met Ashe at an Eastern Tennis Association dinner right before Ashe's death, he admitted, "It was like a once-in-a-lifetime experience."[71]

A relentless activist, Ashe continued to fight for the elevation of the downtrodden in the world. He was arrested in Washington, D.C., while participating in a demonstration against apartheid in South Africa. Richard Lapchick, a sports sociologist, recalled when he was fearful of the message Ashe could present to demonstrators by being opposed to the idea of a boycott of South Africa. However, Ashe told the demonstrators that he supported the boycott, and he "had been wrong in going to South Africa for several years." He thought he was doing the right thing at the time, but "changed his mind when he tried to buy tickets for some African children on a recent trip, and was told to go in the 'coloreds-only' ticket booth."[72]

Ashe's most difficult battle was against AIDS. This battle was further complicated by people's desire to know the personal lives of highly visible personalities. As a result, a *USA Today* inquiry forced him to make a public statement about his health status. In fact, his friend and tennis columnist Doug Smith interviewed Ashe, wanting to confirm whether Ashe had AIDS. Ashe admitted that he was worried that the AIDS announcement could affect his income. "Would my commercial affiliations beg off, as some eventually did with Magic Johnson? Would some parents at a tennis clinic tell their children to shy away from me?"[73] A disease such as AIDS causes even the greatest of heroes to think about their relationship with their fan base.

Another concern was international travel because some nations, including the United States, forbade AIDS patients to enter the country unless they were attending an AIDS-related event. This was a concern for countries that required visas from U.S. citizens. Although England did not require a visa, Ashe was apprehensive about what the press had done to other tennis players; up to this point he had enjoyed a favorable image in England.

He had earlier reported his medical condition to his sponsors. The companies reaffirmed their allegiance, and there were even new offers. Andy Gross, the new owner of Le Coq Sportif USA, informed Ashe that Gross's mother was a volunteer with the Gay Men's Health Crisis in New York City and that he himself was very familiar with the HIV crisis. Aetna Life and Casualty Company, Head Sports USA, Doral Resort and Country Club, ABC Sports, Home Box Office (HBO), and *Tennis* magazine remained supportive. By 1992, Ashe had represented both Head and Doral for twenty-two years.

Ashe referred to the forced announcement as an "outing," similar to the way some gays "out" homosexuals who prefer to remain "in the closet." The managing sports editor for *USA Today*, Gene Policinski, disagreed with Ashe's argument that he was no longer a public figure and had a right to privacy. Policinski replied, "You *are* a public figure, and anytime a public figure is ill, it's news. If he has a heart attack, as you did in 1979, it's news. We have no special zone of treatment for AIDS. It's a disease, like heart disease. It is news."[74]

Ashe steadfastly insisted that he had a right to privacy, and the ordeal created a stimulating debate about the media and an individual's right to privacy. *USA Today* received hundreds of letters, most agreeing that Ashe had a right to his privacy. Once again Ashe had managed to bring a major issue into a national forum. He wrote, "One good result, at our expense but worthwhile on the whole, was the spirited discussion of the rights of the press and the right to privacy that echoed in the media itself. . . . Through all of this, one issue has caught me by surprise: the media's invasion of privacy. I was totally unprepared for the ensuing emotional debate that resulted after *USA Today* went public because of the 'right to know.' " In addition, he felt that the situation was ironic because *USA Today* had done more than any other major daily to publicize the positive side of minority life in America. He considered it unfair that he was forced to admit his AIDS condition to "forestall some impending exposé by that newspaper." He argued that adjusting to the new realities had become a habit for him and his wife, Jeanne. "What may have rent apart other marriages only has strengthened ours."[75] Although the "reaction on the streets" was "more favorable" than Ashe expected, this outcome failed to "lessen [his] anger over what happened."[76]

Donna Doherty, editor of *Tennis* magazine, wrote,

His correctness spoke volumes on and off the court as a civil rights activist who learned early that tennis and politics are strange bedfellows that often cannot be separated. He was arrested for civil disobedience. He helped get South Africa banned from Davis Cup competition for its abhorrent apartheid policy.

He raised the fist to both the underdog and the black man when he became the first of his race to win Wimbledon in 1975. . . .

He has borne the mantle of both his race and his politics with the grace, dignity, courage and intelligence that those of us who know him have come to expect and saw no less of in his stunning announcement in April that he has AIDS.[77]

Doherty asked, "Did the press, specifically *USA Today,* do the right thing? Was it an invasion of Arthur's privacy to force him to choose between lying to a trusted reporter or going public with an announcement he had chosen to keep secret for 3½ years?" She argued that most of the newspaper publishers who were holding their annual meeting in Washington, D.C., at the time felt the paper had acted correctly. The electronic media felt differently. The panel on the *David Brinkely Show* unanimously and unequivocally felt the story was a travesty. Doherty believed that although a person is a public figure, news that the media give to the public is based on a need to know.

> I maintain there are definite limits. If a woman who is a public figure loses her breast to cancer and chooses to keep it her own business, is it the public's right to know?
>
> AIDS is a disease that is required to be reported to the Center for Disease Control. Does that make it public? No. Syphilis and gonorrhea are reportable diseases. If Ashe were suffering from either of those conditions, would we have a right to know? I think not.

Doherty suggested that old canons or ethics of journalism may need to be revised just as some laws have been revised. Moreover, she argued, "Sometimes we forget that there are human beings behind these news stories."

Peter Bodo placed the ordeal in more dramatic terms: "Ashe has never been a more powerful or relevant public figure than he is today. But he reached that position only after *USA Today* put a gun to his head, walked him out on the gangplank of his privacy, and forced him to jump off." [78]

Ashe thought that 1991 would be his last chance to be an analyst for HBO during the Wimbledon fortnight. However, he returned in 1992 to do another broadcast. Nevertheless, he continued to worry about British tabloid press. He explained, "I'm concerned over what it might do to my family, who really love England. My two-and-a-half weeks with HBO is the most work I do for anyone. I really enjoy it, but it won't be the same this time." [79]

On February 6, 1993, Ashe died of AIDS complications. The tributes appeared in several publications.[80] Barry Lorge wrote, "Close your eyes and you still can see Arthur Ashe with his eyes open. Alive, alert, analytical—focused on a tennis ball and later on a larger globe." He also quoted Ashe as saying, "Forty years from now, I can tell my grandchildren, 'In 1975, I was the best tennis player in the whole world.' . . . Not too many ever get there, in anything." Ashe explained that "three stars shone brighter than all the others" in his sky, or his life in tennis. One was Ronald Charity, who nurtured his love for the game; a second was Pancho Gonzalez, who was an outsider in the tennis world because he was a Mexican American; and last was the Davis Cup ties.[81]

Ashe became an icon in tennis, and the honors have been testaments to this legacy. In 1996, a twelve-foot statue of him, sculpted by Paul De Pasquale, was unveiled in Richmond, Virginia, at Roseneath and Monument Avenues.[82] In 1998, the Battery Park tennis courts in Richmond were renamed the Arthur Ashe Tennis Centre in his memory.[83] When the Institute for International Sport created the Scholar-Athlete Hall of Fame, Arthur Ashe was one of the first inductees who were chosen based on distinguished achievements in sport, academics, and contribution to society. There is an Arthur Ashe Youth Tennis Center in Philadelphia, a regional USTA training facility. An annual benefit has been held to raise money for the center. Approximately sixty-five hundred kids from ages eight to eighteen participate in programs at or around the center each year under Philadelphia Youth Tennis, which merged with the NJTL in 1999.[84]

At the time of his death, Ashe was helping former USTA president David Markin carry out expansion of the National Tennis Center. The new stadium was named the Arthur Ashe Stadium. When it opened in 1997, black players' matches were scheduled on the stadium court. That Monday was also Althea Gibson's seventieth birthday. U.S. Open director Jay Snyder said, "There was an effort made to schedule both men and women from the U.S.—especially those on Davis Cup and Fed Cup teams—on stadium Court."[85] Making sure only U.S. players competed that day minimized Ashe's contributions to international tennis, however. Each year Arthur Ashe Day is celebrated the Sunday before the start of the tournament to raise money for the Arthur Ashe AIDS Foundation.

The Aetna Voice of Conscience Award was created in memory of Ashe, who served on the Aetna Board of Directors from 1982 to 1993 and who chaired the Aetna Foundation, the company's philanthropic arm. The award was established to recognize people whose life's work embodies Ashe's ideals. Winners have included such people as Oseola McCarty of Hattiesburg, Mississippi, who donated $150,000, most of the savings from seventy-five years of washing other people's clothes, to the University of Southern Mississippi to provide scholarships for black students; Dr. Roland Gutierrez, who is the head of the HOPE clinic in North Philadelphia, a center providing health care to the homeless, working poor, and elderly; and Kobi Little, the founder and chair of the Center for Leadership and Action, an organization dedicated to training new black leaders and fostering community development.

Ashe was posthumously inducted into the Sport in Society Hall of Fame, which honors people in sport who make significant contributions to society. In 1998, Le Coq Sportif commissioned artist Jeffrey Rubin to create a commemorative painting of Ashe based on a photo taken by Melchior DiGiacomo for donation to the Arthur Ashe Endowment for the Defeat of Aids annual fund-raising auction. Le Coq also created an identical replica of the sneaker worn by Ashe and for each pair sold gave a donation to the Arthur Ashe Foundation. During the 2000 U.S. Open, the Arthur Ashe Commemorative Garden was dedicated, and artist Eric Fischl's fourteen-foot sculpture became the center of the tribute. The U.S. Post Office issued the Arthur Ashe stamp in July 2005.

In a 1999 *Tennis Match* article, reporter Kevin O'Keefe shared several of his memories of Ashe. When Ashe's daughter, Camera, had received a white doll as a gift, and she was playing with it at a televised tennis event, Ashe felt that if the media showed her playing with the doll, "some blacks would wrongly accuse the Ashe family of ignoring its African-American heritage. The doll was immediately put away." While O'Keefe was covering Mandela's visit to the United States in 1990, he did an interview with WABC-TV and commented, "even though we were peddling products such as Mandela T-shirts and mugs, the cash was going to a good cause. 'We're here to market Nelson Mandela and not Bart Simpson,' I remarked." Ashe saw the interview and suggested that O'Keefe be more careful with sound bites, "claiming," O'Keefe said, "that the ANC [African National Congress] was not happy with my association between its heroic leader and the bratty cartoon character. It was only later that I found out Arthur was kidding." [86]

After covering tennis during the last five tournaments of the initial WCT tour in 1971, tennis columnist Barry Lorge wrote that he "came to appreciate one of Arthur Ashe's most endearing traits: the absolute, unabashed delight he takes in little pleasures." These simple pleasures included a love for prosciuto, hard-boiled eggs, paella, Pripps beer, paperbacks, tapes, the Sunday *New York Times,* and challenging crossword puzzles. To represent Ashe's temperament, Lorge added, "While several colleagues fidgeted through an unexpected overnight train excursion from Zurich to Bologna, . . . Ashe curled up and seemed to enjoy what the others considered a gross inconvenience. He gazed out the window, his attention riveted until dusk on the undulating Swiss countryside. He read. He treated everyone to some white wine. He worked on his crosswords. He listened to his everpresent cassette tape player." Lorge included Ashe's analysis of his own personality: "It doesn't show on the surface, but I get enthusiastic about a lot of things, mostly little things. There are times when I can be charming, outgoing, pleasant to be with, and there are times when I can be, as they say, aloof and stand-offish. Sometimes things just get to me and turn me sour." [87]

His concern for people extended to replying to "the some 150 letters" that he received each week when he was at the peak of his career. It was reported that "[h]e sits down periodically and makes his self-appointed rounds, delivering all the pieces into one of four stacks: autograph requests, correspondence to which he can dictate a response and send it back to this secretary, correspondence he thinks he should answer personally, and everything that doesn't fit into the other three categories." [88]

Lorge pointed to another difference between Ashe and many other tennis professionals. Whereas players such as Vitas Gerulaitis drove a Rolls Royce at age twenty-two and Martina Navratilova purchased a Mercedes at age twenty, Ashe did not own a car. Billie Jean King, who owned an inexpensive car, argued, "To a lot of young players, the big money in tennis is second-nature, and they spend it in amounts that shock me. They don't even think about it. Arthur and I went through the days when you played for cheese sandwiches, and I don't think we'll ever be free spenders." Ashe commented, "My apartment is comfortably furnished, but I don't really have much there. More books than anything else. I'm not much of a collector, actually. Every once in a while I buy a piece of art, but that's about all. I love gadgets."

Ashe has been an inspiration to many. Michael Jordan claims him as a personal hero. "When I was a rookie, he advised me on how to deal with the corporate [endorsement] challenges I would face." [89] Geoffrey Green, a British journalist, wrote, "Against the odds, Ashe grew to find his place in a wholly white-oriented sport, unlike Muhammad Ali, the fighter, and Pelé, the footballer. Now he helps to point the future of an expanding game where success can lead to the dollar millionaire." [90] Mike Lupica wrote in 1979, "If you look at the whole picture, Ashe has been the most significant male tennis player of the open era." [91]

It is fitting to end this discussion with comments from Yannick Noah, who promoted Ashe's memoir *Days of Grace* in France. Noah explained the reasoning behind the promotion: "Arthur Ashe has mattered much to my career, in my life. He had much influence on my way of being, of playing. . . . Speaking of Arthur is speaking of my life." Noah attempted to describe what distinguished Ashe from other champions: "Arthur had the capacity of transposing the power that he possessed as a black tennis player, in order that it goes beyond the tennis world. He did much for the American social world, for blacks in particular. He was one of the first black athletes to go to South Africa and in speaking in a coherent manner. Some days before dying, he still marched in front of the White House in Washington for the integration of Haitians." [92]

4

A New Horizon

THE DECADE OF THE 1980S witnessed the greatest numbers of blacks competing on the professional tour. However, there were talented players prior to 1980. For instance, Marlene Everson won the Detroit News Novice Tournament in 1956. In 1957, Western Wightman Cup winners included black team members Darnella Everson and Gwen McEvans. In 1960, Jim Harris played tennis for Brother Alban, who had turned a gym into a tennis court at Bishop Laughlin Memorial High School in Brooklyn.[1] This team won the Catholic High Schools tournament in 1961. Sylvia Hooks and Bonnie Logan made the finals of the Middle Atlantic Women's Doubles in 1964. Logan also won the Girls' 16s in the Maryland Junior Championships in Baltimore in 1963 and impressively maintained a seven-year hold on the ATA national singles title from 1964 to 1970. In addition, Logan was one of the first black players to compete in a tournament in racially segregated South Africa. Logan's older brother, George, taught her to play, and because no other girls in her community played tennis, she competed against boys. Like Althea Gibson, she thought that she could do whatever any boy could do and played basketball, football, and baseball. After winning a trophy at age ten, she decided to focus on tennis. In 1963, she won the *Sports Illustrated* Award of Merit.

Other juniors had some success. Doug Sykes defeated Rodney Kop in the 1961 National Junior Public Parks Championships in Golden Gate Park in San Francisco.[2] In addition, Luis Glass won the Eastern

Pennsylvania Junior Clay Courts tournament in 1965. Teaming with Hugh Curry, Glass advanced to the doubles final of the National Interscholastics in 1964. The following year he took the men's ATA title.

Many blacks who began to play after 1975 have credited Ashe as the main reason for their attraction to tennis. According to Branch Curington, however, the "new" tennis boom started prior to Ashe's Wimbledon victory that year. He argues that tennis "spread like wild fire" in 1971. "People started walking through airports with tennis rackets who couldn't even play tennis. It was a social and popular thing." [3]

After Ashe, the most heralded black junior player was Juan Farrow, who won the 1968 Eastern Pennsylvania 12-and-Unders when he was ten years old. He also captured the USTA National Boys' 12s and 14s championships and with Chip Hooper won the Boys' 14s doubles championship. [4] In addition, he became the national amateur champion at age sixteen.

Dr. Robert Walter Johnson coached Farrow, and he believed that Farrow was the most talented boy he had coached since Ashe. Farrow's parents, who had no interest in tennis, lived next door to Johnson. Farrow got his first "racket," an old broom handle, when he was four years old. Johnson had him hit a ball five hundred times consecutively against a wall with the broomstick. In 1992, Farrow explained, "He said if I was consistently able to hit it with a broomstick, I would have no trouble hitting with the center of the racket." After five months, he got his racket. Doc Johnson died when Farrow was twelve years old, and Farrow believed that if Johnson had lived, "things might have been different." [5] After Johnson's death, Farrow left his family and moved to St. Louis to work with Richard Hudlin, who desired to work with a talented black youth. While under Hudlin's tutelage, he won three Missouri State singles titles from 1974 to 1976.

Farrow attended Southern Illinois University and captured the NCAA Division II title three times and was named an all-American every year. Money was the major obstacle for Farrow after college. He had to work in order to earn traveling funds and could not afford a coach. He signed with a Dallas agency, Improsel, and played on the

satellite tour (see the glossary), attaining a ranking of 260. When Improsel dropped him, he was left with $9,000 in bills they had promised
to cover.[6]

Farrow failed to land major financial support, and Ashe believed
that Farrow's personality "didn't work in his favor—he's a bit reti-
cent." Farrow agreed,

> If I had talked to people more and tried to get myself out there, I
> probably could have had many sponsors. But here were people they
> would look at me and say, "Good luck, Juan, you'll do fine," and then
> they'd drive off in their Mercedes. I don't care if I never make it, I'd
> never ask them for a dime. My response to this frustration of not
> making it to the upper echelon of tennis, "Sometimes I wish would
> make my game go terrible so I could stop this crazy stuff."[7]

After leaving the pro tour, Farrow coached at Match Point Racket
Club in Griffith, Indiana, in the early 1990s and taught tennis once a
week at Calumet High School in Illinois.

Another promising player to emerge after Ashe was Atlanta's Horace Reid, who had major success in the Juniors Boys' 14s and Boys'
16s and won the 1972 ATA National Championship title. According
to his first teacher, Branch Curington, Reid started learning tennis at
age seven. "Everyday, I'd see him peeping through the fence. One day
I told him to come in. When he got in I asked him if he wanted to work
and learn how to play tennis."[8] Another version of the story was that
Reid began playing in 1963 at Washington Park, when Curington
caught him trying to take a stray tennis ball and bribed him with ice
cream to help collect the tennis balls.

The doors to white-controlled tournaments were being opened to
blacks when Reid learned to play. As a result, he was the first black to
play in the Georgia State Tournament when he was twelve years old
and was the first black from Atlanta to win a Georgia high school singles championship. At age sixteen, he had his first "real lesson," but
credited Curington and other players at Washington Park for his tennis
development. He recently reported, "There was not even a concept of

an academy then. I would basically open and close the place for Branch and go play all day. I was kind of natural at it."[9]

Prior to his junior year at Washington High, he was offered a full scholarship to the Harry Hopman Tennis Academy in New York. Ashe saw him, began to support him financially, and helped him get accepted at UCLA, where he played for two years. Reid thereafter played on the professional circuit for six years, reaching the top three hundred in rank. The major highlight of his short career was advancing two rounds in doubles at the 1978 U.S. Open.[10] In recognition of his accomplishments, Reid became the first black inducted into the Georgia Tennis Hall of Fame in 1997.

Albert Brooks Jr. and Keith Allen were among the youths who played at Washington Park Center, where Curington coached. Allen described Washington Park as "a tennis mecca for blacks at that time." Children in Allen's neighborhood played tennis although it was a poor area of the city. More than thirty years after Curington's experiences prior to World War II, classism still existed among black tennis players in Atlanta. Allen maintains, "There were always conversations at the Center from these high profile 'negroes' and there was never a kind word spoken about the boys from the 'hood so to speak. I had the general feeling that they almost thought they were white, and a much higher grade or a choice cut well above the poor kids from the other side of the tracks."[11]

According to Allen, Horace Reid was the best in the program, so it was expected that he would be promoted while others received less attention. However, the black elites "controlled" the selection of youths who received support.

Rick Davis emerged in Miami, Florida, during the tennis boom of the mid-1970s. Davis learned tennis in a tennis facility staffed by blacks, but racially diverse in terms of participants. Initially, Davis had no interest in tennis, preferring to play basketball. However, the only water fountain with cold water was in the tennis facility, located next to the basketball courts. Bobby Curtis, of the Florida Tennis Association, headed a NJTL program there that included Jean Desdunes and Kim Sands. One day Curtis told Davis that the water fountain was for tennis players only. Because Curtis was white, Davis at first "thought he was racist," but Curtis then informed him that if he played tennis, he could drink the water.

Davis's first experience was disastrous. "One day Bobby said, 'I need another player for NJTL match,' and he put me on the court. I wasn't ready; I got beat 0 and 0 in about thirty minutes. I didn't like losing that way." This experience motivated him to learn the game. He eventually left basketball for tennis because he believed that he was too short to play basketball. He was then in the ninth grade at five feet, two inches. Nevertheless, he had a strong desire to be a professional at something. He dreamed of winning Wimbledon, but people kept telling him that he started too late. "I knew I had a lot of catching up to do. I was self-motivated. My parents didn't push me to play. There was a strong desire on my part to play. Basketball was very limited; I only played in Dade County. I played tennis all over the state, sometimes outside of the state." [12]

Davis feels that he was fortunate to be a part of great tennis network. Because the Orange Bowl was one of the biggest junior tournaments, he met many other black juniors such as Zina Garrison, Lori McNeil, Kelvin Belcher, Edgar Adams, Cheryl Jones, and Jerome Jones.

Another player with great potential was Benny Sims, who began to play tennis when he was a sixteen-year-old quarterback and who also played baseball and ran track at Charlton Pollard High School in Beaumont, Texas. He asked a young girl, Brenda Richards, to play tennis with him because it looked like fun. "She did the playing, but I was hooked," he explained. He played tennis in Pipkin Park, where one had to sweep away the shattered glass before playing. [13] He chose tennis over the other sports because "tennis was the most demanding mental and physical test." [14] In spite of his late start, he earned a tennis scholarship to Texas Southern University to play for Herb Joseph Provost.

Sims won the Beefeater Trophy of Excellence at the 1975 ATA National Championships by defeating Richard Williams of Los Angeles in the finals in San Diego 6-4, 4-6, 6-0, 7-6. His performance in the finals was "at times reminiscent of Ashe when he unleashed startling topspin

Rick Davis, Atlanta, 2000. Photograph by Jinaki Wilson.

winners or appalling errors, with almost equal alacrity." A senior at Texas Southern University in 1975, Sims had a magnificent year. In addition to becoming the ATA national champion and the National Association of Intercollegiate Athletes (NAIA) national doubles champion, he was an NCAA all-American, an NAIA all-American, and All-SWAC (Southwest Athletic Conference) and all-NAIA for the fourth year. Despite playing tennis for only six years at that time, he was talented, but had no sponsorship money until his senior year. Provost secured the support of six Houston business people to finance Sims for three years on the professional tour.[15]

Sims attempted the professional tour, but left it to teach tennis. In 1977, he moved to Boston and taught tennis in a youth development program for inner-city youths at the Sportsmen's Tennis Club in Dorchester. In 1982, he became the first black and only the ninth teaching professional at Longwood Cricket Club, established in 1877 in the Boston suburb of Chestnut Hill. The following year he was appointed to the staff of the National Tennis Teachers Conference.

By 1980, new black players were on the horizon, including Lori McNeil, Zina Garrison, Yannick Noah, Chip Hooper, Jean Desdunes, Kelvin Belcher, Lloyd Bourne, Rodney Harmon, Bruce Foxworth, Ronald Agenor, Leslie Allen, Rick Jones, Cheryl Jones, Kyle Copeland, Renee Blount, Kim Sands, Dianne Morrison, Camille Benjamin, Nduka Odizor, Marcel Freeman, Eric Riley, Andrea Buchanan, Troy Collins, Adrian Clarke, Doug Burke, and others—a few of them having some success on the professional tour.

In 1981, Leslie Allen headed the list of five black female players, all from the United States, ranked on the professional tour.[16] She was ranked number 19, followed by Sands (60), Blount (82), Buchanan (106), and Morrison (119). Although Blount won a 1979 tour event on the Avon Futures circuit, making her the first black woman to win an event since Gibson, Allen, ranked 45 in the world at the time, was the first to win a major title, the Avon Championship in Detroit in February 1982, defeating Hana Mandlikova, ranked number 5, 6-4, 6-4. With this win she qualified for the season ending Avon Championships in New York. Allen had made a major move this year, jumping from number 152 to 41 in the world.

Born in Cleveland, Ohio, Allen was introduced to tennis by her mother, Sarah Allen. She played tennis in the Middle Atlantic region, competing in the summer. In 1982, Allen admitted, "I didn't like it because it was hot and you had to run and I wasn't any good. I played one summer when I was eleven and didn't play tennis again until I was fourteen. Those are prime years."[17]

When she began playing tennis in high school, it was more difficult for girls, who had few if any opportunities to play sports before Title IX. She explained, "A girl could be a majorette, sing in the choir or march in the band. I didn't know anything about singing or playing an instrument. I was too tall to be a cheerleader and I didn't know how to twirl a baton. I decided to try sports, but they didn't have any girls' team."[18] As a result, her tennis was limited to playing doubles on Saturday because she did not own a car. Although Allen was the only girl who practiced with the boys' tennis team, she was the best player. Other schools made an issue of her playing, and her school "didn't like rocking the boat" because it had good teams in other sports and wanted to maintain sources of funding.[19]

Allen attended Carnegie Mellon University in Pittsburgh, the Fashion Institute of Technology in New York, and Texas Southern University in Houston. At Texas Southern, she became frustrated when a promised women's tennis team failed to materialize. As a result, she transferred to USC in Los Angeles, where she graduated magna cum laude in 1977, one of the few top tennis professionals who have earned a college degree. At USC, she played number 5 singles on the team and won the national women's intercollegiate title in 1977. Although she failed to make the four-woman traveling squad, she played as well as her all-American teammates.

After graduating in 1977, she turned pro with no national USTA ranking. However, she won the ATA National Championships that year, which earned her a wild card (see glossary) to the qualifying rounds at the U.S. Open. Although she lost in the first round of that tournament, an official of Tennis Australia invited her to play on the Australian satellite circuit. The next year the qualifying rounds for the U.S. Open were played at Flushing Meadows, and she lost again in the first round. The following year her ranking was high enough to get into the main draw. Allen remembered Althea Gibson "jumping to her feet, cheering and raising her arms with clenched fists" when Allen won the first set in a third-round match against Dianne Fromholtz. Arthur Ashe argued, "She literally didn't take it seriously until she graduated from college. Leslie made it on sheer athletic ability."[20]

One of Allen's most notable matches received attention because Chris Evert, her opponent, was dubbed the "Comeback Queen" in 1982 when she defeated Allen 6-3, 3-6, 7-6 (7-3) in the quarterfinals of the Avon Championships of Oakland. Evert was down 0-4 in the final set before making her move to win the match.[21] Despite the attention given to Evert, Allen demonstrated her talent. She had Evert on the ropes again in Dallas before being beaten.

By 1981, Allen was number 17 in the world rankings and vice president of the WTA Board of Directors. She feels particularly proud of her success because she held no junior ranking, but made it to the top twenty in the world and the top ten in the United States.[22] However, by the end of the 1980s, she had retired, founded a tennis academy in Florida, renovated historical houses, owned a restaurant on Amelia Island, and gotten married. In 1990, she returned to professional tennis as a manager for the women's tour sponsor, Kraft General Foods, working on the corporate and media sides. She joined the USTA staff as tournament director for the U.S. Women's Hardcourts, a WTA tour event, in 1994 and was an assistant to the U.S. Open tournament director and member of the U.S. Open Committee. She has also managed the Arthur Ashe Endowment for the Defeat of AIDS booth at the U.S. Open.

Kim Sands and Andrea Buchanan started playing in their teens; Sands started at age fifteen, Buchanan at sixteen. Sands's major professional highlights were the semifinals at Providence, Fort Wayne, and Dallas in 1978 and the quarters at Montreal and Atlanta in 1979. Buchanan died at age twenty-six, victim of a double homicide in a Los Angeles fish market, where she worked part-time. She had played on the pro tour for three years.

It was different for Renee Blount and Dianne Morrison. In a 1982 interview, Blount said that her parents played "Sunday Tennis,"[23] but she too began late, starting at age ten. However, she "could not afford the expense of a full-time coach, tennis equipment, or the cost of traveling to major tournaments to play against the best."[24] Blount had great success in junior tennis, winning single titles in all of the higher age divisions in the Missouri Valley sectionals. As a professional, she won the Futures (see glossary) of Columbus, Ohio, in 1979. After retiring, Blount built a tennis facility near Richmond on two hundred acres of land.

Morrison's parents stressed taking formal lessons, believing it was important to learn the right way. She began playing at age eight at Los Angeles Rancho Cienega Park, where Bruz Freeman was the pro, and later became the only black pro who had major junior experience, having competed on Junior Wightman and Junior Federation Cup teams.

The winner of the 1975 ATA National Championships title at age seventeen, Morrison earned an academic scholarship to Stanford. In 1974, she attained a number 17 ranking in the USTA for players sixteen and younger. The following summer she played the junior circuit as a member of the Southern California intersectional team.[25]

Although the five ranked black women made inroads in professional tennis, it was the next class of black female players—Garrison, McNeil, and Benjamin—who advanced to a higher level. Garrison and McNeil are discussed in chapter 5. Camille Benjamin had a great run at the 1984 French Open that caused people to notice her. Seventeen years old and ranked number 47 in the world, she upset number 13 seed Lisa Bonder to reach the semifinals, joining the top three ranked women on tour: Martina Navratilova, Chris Evert, and Hana Mandlikova. That was her best showing at a Grand Slam in her five tries. Before that, she had reached the semifinals in a 1982 tournament in Mahwah, New Jersey.[26] She lost to Evert in the semifinals. Like Pam Shriver, Benjamin would be able to count that one tournament as her only major accomplishment in a Grand Slam. Unlike Shriver, she would quickly become a forgotten player.

Benjamin was born in Cleveland on June 22, 1966. Her father, Carl, who had played tennis at Central State College in Xenia, Ohio, was a math professor at Bakersfield College and taught her and her sister, Chevonne, to play tennis. Her grandparents had migrated to Panama from Jamaica to work on the building of the Panama Canal. Her parents had met while attending college in Ohio.

Benjamin's strokes were described as "loose and extremely wristy" and were "as unorthodox as you'll find in the pro ranks." "Oh, a lot of people tease me. Sometimes I swing on high volleys and a lot of people talk about that. But that's me; that's the way I hit it. If they don't like it, they don't have to hit it that way," she explained. In the 1990s, many baseline players began to swing on high volleys, but Benjamin did it when it was not the fad. Camille's mother, Claudette, a physiotherapist, refused to view being "unorthodox" as a negative thing. She argued, "People often say, 'unorthodox,' in a negative manner. But I think it is a positive factor. We saw our role as guides. We never encouraged Camille to be a clone." Benjamin explained that her father refused to change her strokes, especially the forehand, because it was one of her strengths. One analyst described her forehand as "a noodle-armed, bent-wrist, topspin stroke that often looks like a bit of pres-tidigitation. She hits the ball on its descent and sweeps it up with the full force of her free-swinging arm. The ball lurches low over the net with surprising speed." Benjamin argued that her game was not flawed, but she needed improvement like the majority of players.[27]

The feat of reaching the semifinals in Paris did not bring respect from all reporters, even in 1984. Benjamin complained, "At the French Open, I was really mad because some reporter ripped me apart saying I shouldn't have been in the semifinal; I should have been at home at high school graduation. If my shots had been going in, Chris wouldn't have beaten me love and love. I had an off day, and Chris played well."

Benjamin started to play when she was around six years old and had won her first tournament by the age of nine. She was ranked number 1 in the Girls' 16s in the United States at age fifteen. She joined the professional tour at age sixteen. Her successes include two finals in satellite tournaments and the quarterfinals of three championship tour events. Her upsets included those of Helena Sukova at the U.S. National Clay Court Championships and of Andrea Temesvari and Rose Fairbank at the Virginia Slims of New Jersey. The year 1984 turned out to be a great year for her: she defeated Zina Garrison, a player on the rise, and reached the semifinals of the Marco Island tournament.

Katrina Adams started playing tennis at age six when she was introduced to the sport through a summer program sponsored by the Dr. Martin Luther King Jr. Boys Club in Chicago, held in Garfield Park on the west side of Chicago, near her home. Adams had a stellar career as a high school junior. In 1983, she won the Illinois High School Association Girls' Championship and was a semifinalist in the Chicago Classic. She was honored as the Chicago District Tennis Association (CDTA) Junior Competitor of the Year in 1984, an award presented at the CDTA Benefit and Awards Dinner during the Virginia Slims of Chicago tournament. When she was sixteen, she won the eighteen-

and-under division in Seventeen's Annual Tennis Tournament in 1985. That same year she advanced to the quarterfinals of the USTA National Indoor Girls' 18s. In 1986, she and Nicole Arendt won the Girls' 18s Indoor National Championship at Indian Creek Center in Overland Park, Kansas.

A 1985 graduate of Whitney M. Young High School, where she was a top player, Adams moved on to play for Northwestern University. She won her first USTA title in 1991, winning the USTA Women's Circuit of New Braunfels. Even though she attained a WTA ranking of 67 in 1988, her doubles career was far more striking. She won several doubles titles on the challenger circuit and the WTA tour between 1986 and 1998. One of her most spectacular years in doubles was 1989, when she won seven titles. She also played team tennis for several years, noting, "World Team Tennis gave me an opportunity to be in a team atmosphere that I experienced in college. You are with other teammates, both men and women and the camaraderie that's developed lasts beyond that particular season. . . . I was able to develop a different fan base."

After twelve years on the tour, she retired. She expounds,

Traveling the world some thirty weeks out of the year, the desire was fading. You truly have to love what you're doing to stay on the tour for a long time. I had injuries that were creeping in, and mentally, I wasn't prepared to fight through them anymore. You have to stop before you began to hate what you're doing. I loved playing professional tennis. I loved the friendships that I developed and the places that I traveled to near and far.[28]

After retiring, she became a USTA national coach in 1999, replacing Bryan Shelton. "Coaching juniors for the United States Tennis Association" was her way of giving back to the sport.

• • •

There were far more black men than black women on the tour in the 1980s, and several hailed from countries other than the United States. In addition, several promising juniors were in the wings, including

Phillip Williamson and Datus Murray of Jamaica. The black player with the greatest success in this period was Yannick Noah, who is discussed in volume 2. Notwithstanding Noah's success, he was French, so the U.S. media continued to seek a black American to follow in Ashe's footsteps.

Born in Los Angeles, California, October 18, 1958, Lloyd Bourne was ranked among the top juniors in the United States in 1979, and he led his Stanford team to three NCAA Tennis Championships. After turning pro in 1980, he played team tennis for the Chicago Flyers with Billie Jean King. Bourne had a great run in 1982 by advancing to the finals of the South Australian Open in Adelaide, his first Volvo Grand Prix tournament, and two weeks later advanced to the quarterfinals at the Benson and Hedges Open in Auckland, New Zealand. He followed with an appearance at the Mediterranean Open in Cap d'Agde, France, defeating Heniz Günthardt in the first round and Pavel Slozil in the finals. In that year's Canadian Open, he defeated Wojtek Fibak before losing to Jimmy Connors in the quarterfinals.

It appeared that Chip Hooper might fulfill the role of becoming "the next Ashe." None of the black male players had had a major tournament win or great success at a Grand Slam since Ashe. This changed when Hooper upset number 8 seed Peter McNamara in the first round of the 1982 Wimbledon.

Lawrence Barnett Hooper III, professionally known as "Chip," was born October 24, 1958, in Washington, D.C., the son of a general surgeon and a high school guidance counselor. He began playing tennis at age five in Sunnyvale, California, and when he was ten, he was number 1 in the Boys' 10s singles in northern California. By 1970, he was number 3 in the USTA National Boys' 12s, being considered a "possible threat," and number 1 with partner Juan Farrow in doubles.[29]

Hooper's talents were noted in the USTA National Boys' 12s in 1970. That year he met his idol, Arthur Ashe, at a tennis clinic, which led to a well-publicized mentor-protégé relationship, something very common for Ashe and aspiring black players. However, it was not a smooth situation. "We didn't understand each other. We didn't have too good a rapport because I was always saying, 'Hey, do this for me and do that for me.' I think he only halfway listened, but now he is all ears," Hooper explained in 1982. Even though he was a ranked junior player, he was labeled a late bloomer as a professional because of "self-doubt" and a body that developed late and rapidly.[30]

In the 1990s, it became the norm in tennis for male players to be more than six feet tall. However, in the 1980s Hooper was one of the tallest players on the tour, standing six feet, six inches. Also, he was one of the few players who used other sports to improve his tennis career before that approach became popular. He played team sports, lifted weights, swam, and used ballet in an attempt to improve his mobility. Before Navratilova and Ivan Lendl's success with weight lifting, it was taboo in tennis, when players were "primarily concerned with the technique and timing of their strokes."[31] Hooper began lifting weights because his brothers, both football players and much larger than he, teased him. By the time he was twenty-three and on the pro tour, he could bench press three hundred pounds.

Hooper became a collegiate all-American at Arkansas. When he was a senior, he was ranked number 407 professionally. As he saw it, "The thing that motivated me the most [to turn pro] was looking at my contemporaries and players of my stature and knowing that they were doing well."[32] After turning pro in 1981, he was soon sidelined for eight weeks when he had eye surgery to remove pterygia. However, after winning the Texas Open in Amarillo, he made the semifinals of two Grand Prix tournaments. He needed a wild card to compete in the qualifying rounds of the U.S. Pro Indoor Championships in Philadelphia, where he defeated Peter Fleming, Roscoe Tanner, and John Sadri to reach the semifinals, where he lost to Jimmy Connors. He followed that success with a win over big server Steve Denton at the U.S. National Indoor Championships in Memphis and with quarterfinal finishes at Rotterdam and Monterey. In addition, he advanced to the semifinals in the Trevira Cup in Frankfurt, Germany. In the first half of 1982, he jumped from number 235 to number 17 in four months.

After his upset win in the first round of Wimbledon in 1982, Hooper lost in the second round to a minor player, but one of his most remarkable tournaments was the 1985 Wimbledon, where he advanced to the fourth round. He did not view his results as "very exciting," though.[33] During the fortnight of the tournament, Bud Collins of NBC interviewed several of the black players from the United States, and Hooper was confident about his chances of advancing further in the draw.

After that remarkable run at Wimbledon, Hooper failed to achieve any other major results. Retiring in 1987, he returned to college to earn a bachelor's degree from California State at Hayward and obtained a teaching certificate from the University of Guadalajara in Mexico. From 1988 to 1996, he taught bilingual education at William Oaks Elementary School in East Palo Alto, California, served as a job program administrator in San Jose, and worked as a tennis coach and substitute teacher at Central High School in Kansas City, Missouri. He has also worked independently with several top juniors. About this work, he has said, "Having been a pro and learned what I have, I bring an added reality. Being a schoolteacher also taught me a lot about dealing with parents—a pretty big factor in tennis."[34]

After Hooper, Rodney Harmon carried the Ashe torch. Born August 16, 1961, in Richmond, Virginia, Ashe's hometown, Harmon began playing tennis at age eight. Being from Richmond and growing up "three houses from the tennis courts," he was a product of the tennis boom that emerged after Ashe won the 1968 U.S. Open. He lived near Battery Park, which had a thriving junior tennis program. The highlight of his junior career was winning the Easter Bowl. In addition, he won three national doubles titles with partner Mike DePalmer.[35] He played one year at the University of Tennessee in 1980 and transferred to Southern Methodist University (SMU), where he graduated in 1983.

Standing six feet, three inches, Rodney Harmon seemed to be well on his way to stardom in 1982. Warren Bosworth, the "Dr. Feelgood" of tennis, helped Harmon during his "erratic" period on the tour. Harmon was described by reporter Ray Kennedy as being so erratic in a first-round match at the 1982 U.S. Pro Indoor Championships in Boston that "some of his shots would have gone for extra bases in Fenway Park." Harmon confessed, "One of my wristy forehands took off and hit the scoreboard. I was so embarrassed that I went to Connecticut right away and spent two days working with Warren." The latter overhauled Harmon's rackets and changed the stringing pattern. Afterward, Harmon advanced to the quarterfinals of the next four tournaments, including the U.S. Open,[36] despite suffering from food poisoning during the qualifying round of that tournament,[37] where he lost to Connors. Ashe had advised him to "soften" his game—in other words, to be more patient. After the loss, Harmon said that he should have played his normal game and slugged it out. He was still a senior at SMU when he made his move at the U.S. Open and was unsure about whether he should turn pro.

His professional career ended after five years because of a broken bone in his foot. "I had pain in my feet my whole life." Later, at age thirty-six, Harmon served as the USTA's director of multicultural development, where his "priority in a broad sense [was] to look at everything the USTA [did]—be it national teams, recreational leagues, advertising, marketing whatever—and make sure all cultures [were] being properly represented and their concerns properly addressed."[38]

Yet another black player, Martin Blackman, was part of an elite class at the Bollettieri Academy in the mid-1980s, together with Andre Agassi, Jim Courier, and David Wheaton. He won the USTA National Boys' 16s singles in Kalamazoo in 1986 and qualified for and won a round in the U.S. Pro Indoor Championships. He attended Stanford for two years and was on winning NCAA championship teams both years. As a professional, he attained a ranking as high as 150 on the ATP tour.

Blackman, who lived in Barbados, where his father worked at the Central Bank of Barbados, received a wild card into the qualifying rounds at the U.S. Open in 1987 at age sixteen after a tennis agent, Bill Shelton, took Marilyn Fernberger, tournament director, to see him practice on the back courts at the U.S. Open.

Years later, Blackman dreaded discussing his tennis career because it led to the question, "Why did you stop?" He thought that he had failed and that he lacked the maturity to grasp the qualifications to succeed on the tour. More important, he had come to hate tennis. In 1997, he elucidated the problem:

> For the first three and-a-half years of my pro career, I had a love-hate relationship with the game. I was fighting myself, dealing with the frustrations of trying to succeed by denying that it was important to succeed. I came to resent that people didn't understand how "good" I really was, even though the results weren't there, and I wasn't doing the things to get them there. Lots of times I dealt with a tough loss by telling myself, "It's only tennis. It's not important."

He revealed that he wanted to win, but was disinterested in the process and felt guilty about refusing to work on weaknesses in his game: "That was another way of copping out, because not trying is a great way to rationalize losing. I felt guilty because my parents had invested a huge amount of money and emotions in my career, but I also resented the fact that it mattered so much to them whether I won or lost." [39]

He needed a coach who believed in him, and he needed to listen to that coach. As he saw it, many of his coaches seemed "to need to break me down in order to build me up, and I didn't like that. I was very sensitive to criticism early on, especially when it came from people I really trusted." [40]

A top regional player during his collegiate years in the early 1980s, Chip Dorsey was ranked number 16 in Maryland in 1983, number 26 in the mid-Atlantic region of the USTA, and number 17 in the ATA. Dorsey played singles and doubles for the University of Maryland. Although school took up much of his time, he was able to win several tournaments, including the Netman's Tennis Tournament in 1982 and 1983 and the Baltimore Open in 1982 (at which he also reached the finals the following year). In addition, he coached the Baltimore Youth Game teams and was on the Head Advisory Committee. Instead of joining the Penn Circuit as planned, he obtained a law degree and gradually stopped playing competitive tennis. [41]

Eric Riley was an oddity in the sport. As a junior, he played in the

Chip Dorsey at the 1984 Netman's Coed in Baltimore.

Banana Bowl in Rio de Janeiro and later competed in the "number one singles" for the University of Pennsylvania, while majoring in Oriental studies and international relations. He spoke Spanish, French, and Chinese. Despite his academic and intellectual achievements, Riley wanted to be an athlete. As a result, during the late 1980s and the early 1990s he played on the satellite circuit, playing doubles with his twin brother, Mark, who later became the director of tennis at the William H. G. Fitzgerald Tennis Center in Washington, D.C. Eric had wins over Wheaton, Jim Pugh, and Alex Antonitsch, all of whom later had success on the major circuit. However, Riley rarely broke even in tennis earnings, which meant returning to Philadelphia to teach tennis to earn money to continue playing on the tour. He has helped coach other professionals such as Pam Shriver, Betsey Nagelsen, and Kathy Jordan. In 1991, he explained, "Some people think that I've been kind of a waste in that I've gone into tennis when I had other academic options. But, I don't see it as a waste. I know the connections I've made and the people I've met and the places that I've seen. These experiences have helped my values more than just being one of 15,000 lawyers practicing law in Philadelphia."[42]

At the close of this era in black tennis, the number of blacks on the professional tours declined. As a result, commentary appeared about the lack of black professional tennis players, along with suggestions as to how to attract top black athletes, mainly male, from popular team sports to tennis.

5

The Houston Triumvirate

ONE OF THE MOST REMARKABLE STORIES in the history of blacks in tennis is that of John Wilkerson, an instructor at a public park, and two of his students, Zina Garrison and Lori McNeil. Wilkerson started a free tennis clinic at MacGregor Park in Houston in 1974. Although Garrison and McNeil have been the most famous names from the clinic, others who participated in the program received college scholarships, and another, Kelvin Belcher, became a professional player.

John Wilkerson

Wilkerson himself had a rich tennis history. Born in San Antonio in 1939, he played various sports, including football and basketball. He eventually decided to try tennis at age eighteen. In a 1987 interview, he expounded,

> My brother and his friend used to play tennis on weekends and they always tried to get me to go along.
>
> I was a pretty good hitter in baseball, with good bat control, and a racquet just felt natural in my hand. All the guys that went to the park that day were footballers, very macho, and they really whacked the ball. I just kept getting the ball back, ran them all over the court, and beat every one I played.[1]

Afterward, Wilkerson tried out for and made the high school team, defeating everyone on the team. His accomplishments included winning the district and state singles and doubles titles that year. However, he demythologized those achievements, arguing, "Remember now, that high school sports in Texas were segregated then, and I was playing in the Negro Interscholastic League and the competition was not as tough." Later, he received a tennis scholarship from Prairie View A&M. He spent so much time playing tennis that he failed to concentrate on his course work and as a result became ineligible to play. He joined the armed services and served in the Airborne Eighth Brigade in Germany; he considered the experience in Germany positive: "After two and a half years in Germany, I had a better sense of direction and I also played all my tennis on clay, learning more about the strategy of the game than I dreamed possible."[2]

After his stint in the armed services, Wilkerson worked for a short time in a post office, then enrolled at Texas Southern University on a tennis scholarship and graduated in 1973. While at Texas Southern, he won the singles and doubles titles in the SWAC, the black intercollegiate title, and the ATA National Championships.

Lee Le Clear hired Wilkerson to teach at MacGregor Park when the former transferred to the then new Southwest Tennis Center. When Wilkerson began teaching at MacGregor, "There were a few black players at MacGregor, but they were from middle to upper income families, mostly professional people, and were merely interested in the sport socially."[3] As a result, he offered free daily tennis clinics to attract youths to the game, holding them from nine to eleven in the morning for children from three to fifteen years old. When he started the program, he charged a fee, but discontinued the practice after very few registered.

Although he had set hours, he offered extra helped to anyone who needed and wanted it. Wilkerson's clinics eventually attracted about two hundred children a day during the summer. After he and two assistants worked with the children for approximately six weeks, thirty of the most promising students were invited to join the year-round program, and the others could enroll in a Thursday afternoon program.

Wilkerson refused to marginalize the girls. The key element of the program was its co-ed nature, with both sexes between ten and fifteen creating fierce competition. According to Lori McNeil, "John had the patience and the personality to build up kids' egos. He knew how to keep us involved, how to give credit and attention. There were plenty of instructors around, but only one as patient as John."[4]

Wilkerson insisted that the participants in the program follow his rules. A reporter explained,

> Wilkerson didn't have a lot of rules, but the ones he did have he enforced. If you didn't have a hat, . . . you didn't play. There was no gum chewing or talking on the court. During a tournament there was no sulking, no temper tantrums, no arguing. And there was no soda pop, period.
>
> Oh yes, there was one more requirement. The kids had to be eager to learn, not only how to play tennis, but how to act amongst their peers.[5]

Garrison also described the atmosphere: "John was a strict coach, but to be a part of the clinic was like being part of a big family. He always had a sense of humor, still does, and the knack of knowing how to bring out the best in each person."[6]

In 1981, the city decided to "promote" Wilkerson to direct fifty neighborhood centers around the city. Wilkerson, however, viewed the proposal differently: "MacGregor Park was a most disheartening thing. They said they were promoting me to oversee all the kids' programs in the city. What they really did was put me behind a desk, had me working with older people and took me out of a position where I was most effective."[7] After five months, he left the new position, which enabled him to continue working with juniors until 1983, when he became a full-time traveling coach for Garrison and McNeil.

Wilkerson dreamed of a tennis program with housing facilities to prepare others from Houston to take the torch from Garrison and McNeil when they left the game. However, he had no desire to create a "factory," but a place where deserving youths could develop their skills.

Zina Garrison

In 1963, Zina Garrison's mother was diagnosed as having a tumor, but after seeking another opinion, she discovered that she was pregnant. Garrison was ten years younger than her next older sibling. Before Garrison was a year old, her brother William died after being hit in the eye by a baseball months after he had been drafted by the Milwaukee Braves. Shortly after that, her father, Ulysses, died.

Garrison began working with Wilkerson when she was ten years old. Her brother Rodney, who played baseball at the park, told Wilkerson that he had an athletic sister. Wilkerson saw her sitting by the fence watching the others do their drills. Wilkerson stated, "She was a standout from the start, very fast, very aggressive and alert. She was out there every day at 8 A.M. when I opened and was usually the last to leave in the evening. By the end of 1975 she had developed so fast I couldn't believe it."[8]

Garrison first received national attention when she lost to Andrea Jaeger in the finals of the 1978 USTA National Girls' 14s. She was ranked number 1 in Texas, the first black female ever to be ranked in the state. She was also the first black to be ranked number 1 in the Girls' 16s by the USTA and won the title in 1980. The following year she won the junior titles at Wimbledon and the U.S. Open, and then received the International Tennis Federation's (ITF) 1981 Junior of the Year Award. After graduating from high school in 1982, she played in the French Open and advanced to the quarterfinals.

After turning professional at the French Open, she had some significant wins that year, which propelled her to number 16 in the world. Although she won her first title in 1984, at Eastbourne she lost to Virginia Wade after having a lead, a match that the tennis world forced her to remember. In an interview several years later, she said she believed that people criticized her because she cried after the match. For her, "It was a very emotional match, and a lot of people will never forget it because psychologists used me as an example of getting emotionally upset under pressure. And I just couldn't handle it. Since then I've learned a lot of discipline on the court and been able to compose myself a lot more."[9]

Wilkerson argued that controlling emotions was Garrison's greatest problem and that it had less to do with choking. "Zina has these personal crises and her emotions come up when she has one of these crises. Then she takes the crisis on court with her and she's battling more than her opponent." He added, "Her sisters and brother never let her make any decisions about her future. Making mistakes helps her grow up, and they never let her make her own mistakes. There's no communication in that family, just a lot of yelling."[10]

Garrison admitted, "I really feel fortunate to have met John because he cared, not just about my tennis, but about me. We used to have a lot of talks about whatever was on my mind—social life, grades, whatever."[11] Her family, however, believed that Wilkerson was trying to control Garrison. As a result, her sisters became interested in her decisions, but advice from so many sources created quarrels within the family, which made Wilkerson decide to take care not to raise his voice to her as her family did. He related an incident when Garrison's mother was in the hospital for two and a half months in a coma. Her brother came to the court one day and waited for Garrison to arrive. When she did, he was very upset and "socked her with his fist." Rodney argued that his abuse was the result of a painful and stressful situation.[12]

Garrison had several arguments with her mother before her death about when she should turn pro and who should manage her. "My mom didn't know a lot about tennis, and it was easy for people to get hold of her and influence her. But at the time that I turned pro my mom and I had a lot of disagreements and I wish I could take them all back."[13]

One summer night in 1983, Garrison felt that her mother, Mary Garrison, had died. When she called her family, they told her that their mother was alive, but in intensive care. She learned, though, that her mother had died that night but was revived by cardiac resuscitation. Her mother finally passed away on September 12, 1983. Garrison denied her death: "For a long time after her death, I had problems with myself because there is a part of you there that feels like no one else

really cares." [14] She experienced mood swings, particularly when inter-
acting with other players.

After defeating number 2 seed Hana Mandlikova in the semifinals,
she upset Chris Evert at Amelia Island in the Sunkist/WTA Championships in 1985, at the time the biggest victory of her career. Evert
noted, "I think she played a great match, she deserved to win. She just
came up with some great shots and ran me around." [15] That year Garrison also advanced to the Wimbledon semifinals, where she lost to
Navratilova.

One of her best tournament performances of that year came in the
Family Circle New South Wales Open, where she won her first grass-
court title, defeating Helena Sukova, Wendy Turnbull, and then top-
seeded Pam Shriver in the final. It was remarkable that she defeated
three top serve-volleyers on a surface that favors that style of play.

That same year Garrison played the Maureen Connolly Brinker
Memorial/Virginia Slims in Dallas at Moody Coliseum on the campus
of Southern Methodist University.[16] The semifinal match against
Navratilova was one of the most inspired matches Garrison ever
played. With the Texas crowd behind her, the place was rocking with
each winner that she hit; the crowd gave numerous standing ovations
and cheers during the first set. The strategy was for Garrison to take the
net from Navratilova. In addition, Garrison used her speed to chase
Navratilova's volleys to execute perfect passing shots. This approach
brought her a 6-0 first set. However, the tables began to turn in the
second set. Although Garrison eventually lost the match, she learned
that the strategy could work against Navratilova, and she used it to beat
Navratilova years later.

Ashe said of Garrison in 1986, "She's a very good athlete, and she
has some of the fastest feet on the women's tour. She'll be up there a
long time." [17] That year, at the Ecker Open in Tampa, Florida, marked
the first time that a final was played between two black women when
McNeil defeated Garrison. By 1987, Garrison was the first black
woman to win $1 million in prize money on the pro circuit and the sec-
ond black player to do so, following Ashe's success. Moreover, she was
the first black woman to be ranked in the top 10.

Zina Garrison *(left)* with fan Sarah Ward at a WTA tournament in Dallas, 1986.

Things were complicated when Garrison faced McNeil in the "round of sixteen" in the 1990 U.S. Open. In the third set tie break, after Garrison had held a match point, McNeil hit a netcord that fell on Garrison's side, giving McNeil the match. Later, McNeil and Garrison lost in the doubles semifinals to Steffi Graf and Gabriela Sabatini. In addition to being coached by Wilkerson, Garrison had worked with Willis Thomas, a tennis instructor from Washington, D.C. Feeling that Wilkerson was spending too much time with McNeil, Garrison decided to work exclusively with Thomas. After McNeil signed a contract with International Management Group (IMG), she informed Garrison that they could no longer play doubles together. Garrison blamed "the media for blowing the breakups out of proportion," stating that there were no hard feelings between Wilkerson and herself, and that McNeil and she were still "Lori and Zina."[18] Wilkerson asserted, "I think the breakup . . . was hard for her, because there were people who were telling her she needed to split from me to grow. It was hard for both of

Lori McNeil and Zina Garrison at a community center in Atlanta.

us, because I was like a father for her. But it really was the best thing. It's been good for her—I could never have taken [her] to the level she's at now."[19]

In 1989, an unnamed former touring pro was quoted as saying, "Zina's a very demanding person. She had a love/hate relationship with John, just like you have with any father, but it became so bad that she was never happy. When John paid attention, she hated him for pushing so much. When he didn't pay attention, she hated it even more."[20]

Early in 1988 Joe Breedlove, who had worked with Martina Navratilova, began working with Garrison. In the 1988 Olympics, Garrison won a bronze medal in singles and teamed with Pam Shriver to win the doubles gold medal. When in New York, she visited Public School 125, located near the Grant Housing Project to speak to the students. Later, they sent letters to her, and she cried when reading them. "They couldn't believe an Olympic athlete would actually come see them when it was raining."[21] That year, after twenty-one previous attempts, Garrison finally defeated Navratilova at the U.S. Open quarterfinals after first blowing a 6-4, 5-0 lead.

Late in 1988, Garrison met Willard Jackson, a co-owner of a hazardous waster disposal company. A few weeks after dating, they were engaged and married in September 1989. Jackson managed her off-court business, scheduling transportation and meals, setting up practice time, and handling tour officials. He even attempted to coach her until her coach at the time, Sherwood Stewart, made it clear that he (Stewart) was the coach.[22]

Garrison made tennis history with her 1990 appearance in the Wimbledon final. No black woman had made the Wimbledon final since Althea Gibson's feat in 1958. Gibson traveled to England to watch the match. Garrison said, "I was really happy that Althea was here, but it didn't affect me in any way. She came out and watched me practice. She's a very nice lady and I was really happy to see her here."[23]

Garrison's appearance in the 1990 Wimbledon final followed criticisms of her not having advanced to a Grand Slam final in the eight years she had been on the pro tour. Although Garrison was ranked in the top 10, one writer asserted that "she continually stumbles against the game's elite in late-round matches," which justified labeling her a choker. Garrison maintained, "When I get people down, especially top players, I don't pounce on them like I should." Her hitting partner, Angel Lopez, believed that Garrison possessed the "ammunition but may simply be misfiring."[24]

Garrison played the tournament of her life, using her speed to defeat two top players. The tennis public was looking forward to a Steffi Graf–Monica Seles semifinal as a rematch of that year's French Open final. However, Garrison spoiled the possibility of that matchup, as well as a possible final between Graf and Navratilova.

In the quarterfinal match between Garrison and Seles, Seles had rallied from a 1-4 deficit in the third set and was leading 7-6, 40-30, and it appeared that Garrison was going to permit another lead to vanish. "I always felt that I'm a really good grass court player, and I just never did as well as I did in 1985," she explained. Even though Seles "romped through the first set with confidence and power" and had a match point in the third set, Garrison used her experience on grass to win the match 3-6, 6-3, 9-7. Graf admitted, "To tell the truth, I was hoping to play against her [Seles, in the semifinals] really badly, so I am a little bit disappointed about it."[25] For Garrison to defeat Seles on grass was one thing, but to beat Graf would be a greater feat.

Garrison had "trained expressly to arrive at Wimbledon" and felt most confident in winning. She served and volleyed with "far more precision and authority" than Graf. Although the media made note of Graf's sinus infection and of the tabloid reports about the "supposed disharmony between her parents," Graf attributed her loss solely to "her own inability to match Garrison's flawless playmaking." After the match, the twenty-one-year-old Graf revealed that she thought she "would be able to extricate herself from trouble once she had won the second set." Garrison, however, managed to get a break for a 3-1 lead in the third set. "After Garrison fooled [Graf] into break point with a lob and then floored her with a backhand service return winner down the sidelines to break her . . . , Graf's spirit seemed to flag."[26] According to one tennis correspondent, "Garrison . . . has put a full stop to a number of sentences in tennis history. She has ended the monopoly of the Wimbledon final by Graf and Navratilova, who have contested the last three finals, and broken Graf's run of 13 consecutive grand slam final appearances."[27]

The win over Graf was great for Garrison, who had lost in the first round of the French Open that year. Navratilova argued that she did not assume that Graf would definitely win the match, citing a prior mistake from 1986. "I've been there before when I concentrated so much on playing Chris and then Hana [Mandlikova] beat Chris in the semifinal. It really threw me for a loop because I had prepared to play baseliners. I really wasn't mentally prepared and I wasn't going to make the same mistake again. I know [people] were supposing that Steffi was going to be in the finals, but I wasn't going to take anything for granted."[28]

In the final, Garrison walked onto center court with many fans supporting her, some because of what she represented for blacks in tennis, others because she was an underdog, and others because she had become a crowd favorite owing to her upsets in the earlier rounds. Navratilova also had much at stake because she was going for a record ninth title. Navratilova won easily, 6-4, 6-1 in seventy-five minutes. When asked whether it would have been more gratifying to have defeated Graf for the championship, she answered, "It would have been more fitting, but Zina earned her place here. There's no belittling her effort or ability." [29]

Arthur Ashe sat in the Players' Tea Room almost an hour before the championship match and revealed his delight "to see Garrison make such a substantial change in her outlook and performance." He remarked, "She seems to have been able to wipe the slate clean and start all over." [30] Another former professional, Rosie Casals, was also impressed: "She was so frantic in the past, but now she has slowed down her momentum. She isn't rushing between points anymore. Zina has always been a hell of a tennis player, but getting to the final of Wimbledon has gotten her over a hurdle." [31]

One journalist reported, "Garrison's . . . Victory over No. 3–seeded Seles in the quarterfinals and . . . win over the top-seeded Graf in the semifinals won her new respect from a tennis establishment that labeled her a choker when she lost to Virginia Wade in the second round in 1984—and never let the label loose. It also earned her a clothing contract." Her coach, Stewart, was credited for the change because he had "revamped Zina's technique, giving her a keener understanding of strategy and showing her the value of a more professional approach of the sport." [32] After the match, Garrison attested, "It's even more exciting when you get a chance to see that trophy up close. I couldn't take my eyes off of it." [33]

Garrison faced Navratilova again in a losing effort in a 1994 Wimbledon semifinal. Lori McNeil had defeated number 1 seed and defending champion Steffi Graf, and Bryan Shelton had beat the number 2 seed in men's singles. Their wins inspired Garrison. She defeated Arantxa Sanchez-Vicario en route to a semifinal showdown with Navratilova. At least one observer thought Garrison's performance "restore[d] faith in [the] women's game." He wrote, "Women's tennis is supposed to be in the doldrums; the teenage baseline clones are either overpaid or burnt out, and life without Steffi Graf is unthinkable. Yesterday, at Wimbledon, however, Zina Garrison-Jackson led the revolt against popular thinking by knocking out Arantxa Sanchez-Vicario." [34]

Prior to the 1994 Wimbledon, Garrison had played Lori McNeil in the final of the grass-court tournament in Birmingham, England, defeating McNeil 6-3, 6-3. The two had faced each other several times during their careers, and McNeil had won the two previous finals they had contested. Both had excellent runs to the Wimbledon final in 1994, without losing a set. Garrison said, "I decided this morning to go for my shots and not be upset if I didn't get them. Lori was a little bit nervous, too, so that helped." [35]

In her career, Garrison defeated two famous players who were at the end of their careers. She defeated Evonne Goolagong in Goolagong's final Wimbledon, where Goolagong was awarded a sentimental sixteenth seed. In addition, in a quarterfinal round in 1989, she was the victor against Chris Evert in Evert's last U.S. Open appearance. Her defeat of Evert was considered one of her "claims to fame." Garrison argued, "I will be remembered as a villain." [36]

For some time, people were telling Garrison that she needed to lose weight despite the fact that she was the one of the fastest women on the tour. Apparently, critics, including Billie Jean King, believed that losing weight was one of the most important improvements Garrison needed to make if she were to be a better player. However, when she made that magnificent run at Wimbledon in 1990, most were unaware that she was suffering from bulimia. Garrison's problems with this eating disorder began after the death of her mother in 1983. She explained, "I was eating all the time. Then I'd go and purge. . . . You definitely feel guilty. Your self-esteem is down. You know that it's wrong. It's really depressing. You're hiding, so you never feel very comfortable with yourself. The relationships that you have with others are unstable. You always feel they are going to run away and that they're not going to be there. I felt insecure all the time." [37]

The insecurity was also in her game. "I felt insecure on the court, so I didn't have any confidence. I felt weak. I didn't have the strength that I needed to compete." She lost a match in Kansas City, Missouri, where she was weak although she had just eaten. After seeing commercials for clinics and a movie about an actress who suffered from bulimia, she asked her trainer on the professional tour for help, and the trainer found a counselor in Houston. The desire to be thin contributed to such drastic action. She explained, "There is pressure to be thin in this society and people will do whatever it takes. People don't realize that women who are ultra-thin have a naturally high metabolism rate. I believe you should eat as healthy as you can. You have to be comfortable with yourself." She believed that "suffering from bulimia is worse than being addicted to drugs or alcohol because you *have* to eat. You constantly have to make choices about what you eat." [38]

Garrison was unable to acquire major product contracts although she was ranked fourth in the world in 1989. According to friend and doubles partner Katrina Adams, "She looked different; she wasn't the blond, blue-eyed athlete that a lot of the endorsements were looking for." Jackie Joyner-Kersee has suggested that this rejection might have played a role in Garrison's bulimia because Garrison wanted to look a certain way. Meanwhile, her marriage was crumbling. Sara Fornachiari, her former agent, argued, "Willard was everything that I think Zina was not; he was a handsome, dashing, articulate guy." According to childhood friend Larry Thomas, "She found out he was cheating on her. That really sent her for a loop." Garrison admitted, "All of a sudden I became in his eyes, ugly, fat, things that he knew would throw me off." The negative comments about her were not things "you'd say to a person, who is a recovering bulimic." Early in 1995 Garrison announced her pending retirement at the end of the year. Her husband, however, wanted her to keep playing, presumably for the money. Soon after her retirement in 1996, he left her, and she fell back into depression and started "the whole bulimia thing all over again." In 1999, she ingested a dangerous mix of Sudafed and Tylenol, but thought better of it and called a friend. Garrison was able to jump this hurdle, and, as her sister commented, "She realizes now that she is very, very pretty." [39]

After retiring, Garrison played on the Virginia Slims Legends Tour, the only black player on tour in 1996, joining such greats as King, Navratilova, Evert, Casals, Turnbull, Goolagong, Wade, Shriver, Casals, and Tracy Austin.[40] She replaced King as the Federation Cup captain and served also as the women's team coach in the 2004 Summer Olympics in Athens.

Lori McNeil

The final member the Houston triumvirate was Lori Michelle McNeil, daughter of Charlie McNeil, a cornerback for the San Diego Chargers. McNeil was born December 18, 1963, in San Diego. Her father's being an athlete might have placed more expectations on her, yet she, like Garrison, was not the most gifted or the most athletically endowed in Wilkerson's program. Nevertheless, they prevailed, primarily because they, along with Kelvin Belcher, often kept hitting a ball until someone made them leave the courts. Wilkerson described McNeil's "strikingly casual demeanor" as a "protective mechanism," predicting, "If Lori ever lets go and lets her real self get involved, you'll see one hell of a tennis player."[41]

McNeil had a very productive junior doubles career with Garrison, winning five national junior titles together, and was named to the Junior Federation Cup team in 1983. She attended Oklahoma State from 1981 to 1983 and was ranked number 8 on the U.S. intercollegiate list, while also being ranked number 4 on the USTA satellite circuit in 1983. At the 1984 U.S. Open, McNeil led Hana Mandlikova in the second set of a fourth-round match before losing.

She cracked the U.S. top ten in 1986 by winning three tournaments and reaching the quarterfinals at Wimbledon. She won tournaments at Tampa and Tulsa, defeating Garrison in Tampa 2-6, 7-5, 6-2. They were friends and doubles partner and had the same coach, so it was difficult for them to play against each other, particularly after they had practiced together two hours before a match.

McNeil's first big headline came in 1987, when she, as an eleventh seed, upset Chris Evert in the U.S. Open in the quarterfinals 3-6, 6-2, 6-4, marking the first time that Evert had failed to reach the semifinals of the U.S. Open and ensuring that for the first time in thirteen years she did not win a Grand Slam title.

Evert seemed to be in control of the match after winning the first set. In addition, she led 2-1 in the third set after three straight service breaks before McNeil began to charge the net every opportunity she got. In two earlier meetings that year, McNeil had stayed on the baseline. After the first set, McNeil changed her game, explaining, "It took me a little time to get rhythm with what I wanted to do, whether I wanted to come in after every return of serve or stay back and mix it up. It is tough being indecisive with a player like Chris." [42]

Determined to keep the pressure on Chris, McNeil began to advance to the net even on Evert's first serve. "She played a very smart match, but my bread-and-butter shots, my passing shots, weren't working. I think they left me two weeks ago," Evert stated after the match. [43] "Nobody, not even Martina [Navratilova], takes my first serve and comes in like Lori did. She rushed me, she made me feel like I couldn't get anything going." [44]

The news of the win "sent shock waves through the National Tennis Center, reaching the women's locker room and shaking up Navratilova just a little." Navratilova, who was preparing to play Sabatini, explained, "It didn't help me a whole lot. It was like, 'Oh, my God.' Hana lost. Chris lost. Now I have to score one for the old guard." [45]

McNeil became the first black woman to reach the semifinals of the U.S. Open since Gibson in 1958. Wilkerson commented, "In modern-day tennis, this is a big accomplishment." [46] After she and Garrison lost to Graf and Sabatini in the doubles, a crowd of reporters wanted to interview McNeil. Wilkerson argued, "She's not used to this. I want her to keep her mind on tennis, but sometimes it's not easy." [47] McNeil demonstrated why the Women's International Tennis Association had voted her the most improved player the previous twelve months.

The semifinal match against Graf was the first time McNeil played on the Stadium Court. Some had complained that the match between McNeil and Garrison was scheduled on an outside court, but turned out to be a three-set match, including two tiebreakers. Although Mc-

Neil said little about it, Garrison criticized that decision. "I don't think it was good. Lori and I are two very exciting players. We should have at least gotten a Grandstand Court."[48]

Before losing to Graf, McNeil provided excitement for the New York crowd, taking the first set 6-4. Graf said after the match, "I knew she couldn't keep playing like she did in the first set. I knew the mistakes would come, and they did in the second set."[49] After McNeil lost the second set 6-2 and was down 3-1 in the third, it seemed the match would end quickly. However, she broke Graf and held serve to tie the set at 3-3. During Graf's next service game, McNeil missed a volley that could have given her a break of Graf's serve and a 4-3 lead. Instead, Graf held serve. In the following game, McNeil held serve easily, and Graf struggled to hold serve, playing two deuce points, but finally broke McNeil to win the match.

McNeil revealed her plan, stating, "I tried to hit to her backhand; I didn't want her to take control of the match. I was taking my time out there. I tried not to let her dictate the tempo. I wanted her to win the points, wanted her to pass me. I wanted to make her win." She also explained why she missed what was a seemingly routine volley. "I took my eye off the ball. As I was hitting it[,] I was watching her."[50] One writer assessed McNeil's performance: "People talk a lot about why relatively few blacks make it in big-tennis, and McNeil gave those fans and officials something to feel good about. Her poise and appealing, athletic game were irresistible."[51]

In 1992, Lori McNeil proved that grass was her best surface, perfect for her serve-and-volley game, by winning Eastbourne. Also in 1992, she defeated Graf at the Virginia Slims Championships. The next time McNeil made tennis headlines occurred at the 1994 Wimbledon against Steffi Graf. McNeil played some of her best tennis in 1994, defeating Garrison and Brenda Schultz at the Birmingham DFS Classic and Lindsay Davenport at the Virginia Slims in Chicago. However, none of these wins compared to her win over Graf at Wimbledon or to the run she made afterward. At age thirty, she defeated the defending champ and number 1 seed in straight sets, 7-5, 7-6 (7-5), marking the first time in Wimbledon's 108-year history that the defending women's champion lost in the first round. According to one writer, "An ill wind blasted through Wimbledon's first Tuesday like a buffoon at tea time, rattling nerves, fingering crumpets, flipping the table with a glorious smash. There went No. 1–ranked Steffi Graf, a victim of what British tennis legend Fred Perry called, 'wet, greasy and slippery' gusts, as well as the cool intensity of unseeded Lori McNeil." [52]

McNeil posed a genuine threat to Graf. "A champion at Edgbaston—for the second time, a fortnight ago—and Eastbourne, [McNeil] is one of the most accomplished grass-court players in the field," wrote one tennis correspondent. The win threw open the women's championship, and the "odds on McNeil, a 30-year-old ranked 33rd in the world, becoming Graf's successor were swiftly amended. She was a 100-1 outsider;" she became a seven-to-one outsider. [53]

After the match, McNeil stated that although she still recalled the forehand volley that she missed when she lost to Graf in the 1987 U.S. Open, she did not think about it during the match. Her career began "petering away" after that match, however. According to the WTA tour media notes, the victory over Graf was not the "shocker of the tournament"; that honor went to McNeil's win over Yone Kamio the next day in three sets. "McNeil can beat anyone in the world, especially on grass, yet she's always had trouble stringing wins together." [54]

Stringing wins together this time, McNeil advanced to the semifinals. Prior to her semifinal match, one correspondent noted, "A place in Wimbledon Championships' modern history awaits Lori McNeil. . . . [S]he is on the threshold of a personal breakthrough as well." [55] But she lost to Conchita Martinez, the eventual champion, in three sets, 10-8 in the third, playing through pain. Tendinitis below her right knee had flared before the French Open, and after she finished the match against Martinez, she could barely walk, but limped through a loss in the mixed-doubles final the next day. Despite the injury, McNeil remained "wonderfully composed throughout, concentrating on getting her first service deep and coming in to volley as often as possible." [56] Too often, however, her approach shots were too short, and Martinez easily passed her. Nevertheless, McNeil had her chances, and each player responded to the other's resurgence. After two hours and thirty-four minutes, Martinez managed to win the match.

For almost a year, McNeil had worked with Marvin Webster, who had coached the Wichita Advantage, a World Team Tennis team on which McNeil had played. In addition, she worked with sports psychologist Jim Loehr for more than two weeks in the spring. He asserted, "Lori may seem indifferent on the outside, but she feels things very deeply. She's had some real tough things in her personal life that have compounded the problem of her search for peace and calmness on the courts."[57] Wilkerson had given McNeil a copy of Loehr's book *Mental Toughness Training for Sports* ten years earlier.

"I feel that I'm maturing as a person off the court, and I think that has helped me on the court. Right now, I think I'm doing all that I can, and I'm pleased with that," she said of her newfound success in 1994.[58] Prior to that win, her mother, Dorothy McNeil, felt that McNeil had never been focused. When her father watched her play, he knew that "Her mind is in Hawaii, and the job is right here."[59]

Earlier that same year, McNeil's father committed suicide at age fifty-seven. Knee surgery had forced him to retire from professional football, and after surgery "he bounced from a job in real estate to another in offshore oil to driving a cab." He had not worked for two years prior to 1994 and had "lapsed into depression. He sought professional help, but it didn't take." McNeil was in Sydney, Australia, for a tournament when Wilkerson and Garrison informed her of the suicide. Garrison said, "I couldn't look at her. I kept saying, 'You need to call home.' And she said, 'I'll call them later.' I said, 'No. Now.' "[60] After the funeral, she missed the Australian Open, ending her record streak of thirty-five straight appearances at Grand Slam events. She declined dedicating that Wimbledon win against Graf to her father. "I'm always out there trying to win first for myself. I know that my dad is watching. I know that he's proud. It would be nice, but . . . I won't put that [pressure] in there."[61]

Despite that remarkable run at Wimbledon, McNeil's final years on the professional tour were marked by disrespect. Commentators continued to cite Jana Novotna as the only serve-volleyer on the women's

professional tour, although McNeil and Helena Sukova were still playing. After earning more than $3 million in prize money and attaining a
career-high ranking of number 9, she retired from the singles competition of professional tennis at age thirty-six. Since retirement, she has
worked with the Junior Tennis Champions in Washington, D.C.[62] In
2001, she began playing professional doubles again. She and partner
Amanda Coetzer won the U.S. Pro Indoor Championships in Oklahoma City; later, she began coaching Coetzer.

6

The "Post-Soul Era"

DURING THE 1990S, several black teens in the United States were considered the next crop of black tennis professionals. A few were highly ranked juniors. However, most disappeared from notice in the tennis world by the dawn of the new millennium.[1] Meanwhile, Phillip Williamson, Steve Campbell, Jeri Ingram, Martin Blackman, and Sude Ladipo joined a number of black veterans on the tour. The most promising new players of the decade—part of the "Post-Soul era" (see glossary)—were Chanda Rubin, MaliVai Washington, Bryan Shelton, and the Williams sisters.

Chanda Rubin

Born February 18, 1976, in Lafayette, Louisiana, Chanda Rubin began playing at age five; tired of hitting the ball against the fence, she ventured onto the court and engaged in a brief baseline rally with her mother. "I knew she had something special right then," her mother said. "When I told Ed later that day, he didn't believe me. I made him come out to the court to see for himself."[2]

Rubin and her brother, Edward Jr., who also wanted to be a tennis professional, grew up in a tennis family. Their parents met while students at Louisiana State University. Their father, Edward Rubin Sr., was from a poor family of eleven children, but became the first black elected district judge in Lafayette parish. He began playing tennis when he was thirty-one, but managed to develop a game that earned a state ranking. Their mother, Bernadette Rubin, a high school track and basketball athlete, also took an interest in tennis. She explained, "When our house was built, I asked my husband to build a tennis court because I wanted to learn to play." When asked about her Jewish last name, Chanda Rubin explained, "I am not Jewish in the sense where I have not really received training on the subject."[3]

Rubin had a remarkable career in the juniors and was ranked number 1 in the Girls' 12s when she was eleven, and at age twelve she captured the top spot in the Girls' 14s. Her biggest win was the Wimbledon junior title at age fifteen.

Although she had no idols, she watched some players more than others, including Steffi Graf, Ivan Lendl, Zina Garrison, and Lori McNeil. Garrison, who lived two hours away in Houston, became the first professional with whom Rubin hit. When Rubin was fourteen, she informed her mother that she wanted to play professional tennis. "I knew that I was going to turn pro before going to college because it would have been just too long for me to wait."[4] At age sixteen, Rubin turned pro in 1992 while still a junior in high school, participating in the USTA Touring Pro Program. The women's head coach, Lynne Rolley, helped arrange a playing schedule that allowed Rubin to finish high school in 1993 at Episcopal School of Arcadiana.

Armed with a lethal forehand, Rubin demonstrated promise. However, when she was nineteen, the tennis media focused on another weapon, her fortitude, beginning with a remarkable win in 1995 over Jana Novotna at the French Open. Novotna had already earned a reputation for choking in the 1993 Wimbledon final against Steffi Graf, where she lost the match after leading 4-1 in the third set and being one point from a 5-1 lead. After the match, she cried on the shoulders of the duchess of Kent.

Novotna did little to improve that image or to stop the criticisms when she faced Rubin in the third round of the 1995 French Open. Rubin, who was ranked number 53, won the first set in a tie break and had a break in the second set; however, Novotna won five of the next six games to take the second set. Novotna raced to a 5-0, 40-0 lead in the third set, seemingly in total command of the match, but she began

Chanda Rubin. Photograph by Jinaki Wilson.

to falter. Rubin saved five match points when Novotna served for the match, another in the next game on her own serve, and three more match points at 4-5. Rubin eventually won six straight games to serve for the match at 6-5, but then lost her serve. Finally, she won the match 8-6. After the match, Rubin said, "If you told me I would have won, at 5-0, I wouldn't have believed it."[5] She added, "I think just about everybody watched that final, and it was pretty painful to see. I started thinking about that a little bit during the course of the match. It definitely popped up in my mind when she started missing a few easy balls."[6] A year later she admitted, "That was probably the biggest win yet for me. It isn't the comeback, although that's what people remember and always ask about, as much as it was the fact that I beat a top player at a Grand Slam event. It gave me confidence and motivation."[7]

In the 1995 Wimbledon Championships, Rubin defeated Patricia Hy-Boulais 7-6 (7-4), 6-7 (5-7), 17-15 in three hours and forty-five minutes and established Wimbledon records for longest final set (two hours and four minutes) and highest number of games in a set (thirty-two) and games in a match (fifty-eight). Rubin managed to enhance her reputation for great matches at the 1996 Australian Open. After defeating Gabriela Sabatini, she and Arantxa Sanchez-Vicario hit more than three thousand shots and played for 325 points. Rubin, seeded number 13, finally defeated the number 3 seed 6-4, 2-6, 16-14 in three hours and thirty-three minutes, the longest women's match ever at the Australian Open.[8] The match set records for most games (forty-eight) in a match and most games in a final set (thirty). She eventually lost to Monica Seles, the eventual champion, in the semifinals. She closed the remarkable run with her first Grand Slam title by winning the women's doubles with Sanchez-Vicario. Rubin later agreed that the marathon matches gave her greater confidence. Her coach, Marcel Freeman, agreed: "Certainly she's worked really hard at getting better."[9]

In several matches, it seemed that Rubin had the match on her racquet, but allowed the opponent to make a comeback. When she faced Sabatini in the 1996 Lipton (Key Biscayne), she had three match points in the second set, but did not win the match until an hour later in the third set.[10] Although she had remarkable wins, there were problems. Freeman, a former tour player, thought that Rubin could be "up a set and a break, and then try to protect that lead, only to lose." This problem stemmed from the self-imposed pressure to do well. A former coach, Ashley Roney, declared, "What you're seeing is typical Chanda in that she's always been somewhat introverted and inclined to progress cautiously, looking for a little more confidence to jump to that next plateau." In the same article, writer Peter Bodo argued that Rubin's stable upbringing hurt her as a pro:

[T]he stability that provided her with great examples to follow, solid values and good work habits also may have contained elements of privilege and protection which may have prevented Rubin from getting in touch with the uninhibited competitor that dwells within champions. This shortcoming may be the thing that distinguishes her from the player with whom Rubin has the most in common, Chris Evert. Bern Rubin always encouraged her daughter to emulate Evert, and Chanda generally did so. Like Evert, Rubin chose to attend and finish high school. Like Evert, Rubin is poised, understated and outwardly cool. At a comparable age, Evert also tended to be introspective and sometimes moody. And while Evert was loath to admit it, she was always keenly, intensely aware of where she stood with her rivals.

Zina Garrison, in contrast, commented, "She's not intimidated by anything at all, and nothing seems new to her. She's also very competitive, and I like that. . . . She knew a lot coming in, where Lori and I had to learn it all, on the job." [11]

In recognition of her achievements, Chanda Rubin Day was celebrated in Lafayette on September 12, 1995, which included a reception with the mayor, an official proclamation, and a key to the city.[12] Rubin feels that she enjoys the lifestyle of a professional player although it is not as glamorous as some might believe.

Rubin moved from number 69 in 1993 to 23 in 1994, then to 15 in 1995, and then to a career high of number 6 in April 1996. She posted great results between 1995 and 1996 in singles and doubles. Just when she was having spectacular results on the tour, however, she suffered an injury, which was initially diagnosed as tendinitis, but later was determined to be a stress fracture. It required surgery, which kept her from competing for two months.

Although she had a rocky start after returning to the tour, she managed to win the Hopman Cup team title with Justin Gimelstob, the first for the United States.[13] In 1995, Rubin was one of two blacks on the team representing the United States in the Pan Am Games, and she won a silver medal in doubles and a bronze in singles, becoming the second black woman on a U.S. tennis team to win a medal (Althea Gibson had won a gold medal in the Pan Am Games). Rubin has also played Federation Cup for her country. She defeated Sanchez-Vicario in 1995 when the United States faced Spain. In 1999, in a match against Croatia, she beat Iva Majoli in a two-hour, forty-five-minute match. She then teamed with Monica Seles to win the doubles match. Owing to her accomplishments in Federation Cup play that year, she received the Most Improved Player Award. In addition, she was USA Weekend's Most Caring Athlete, and the WTA nominated her for the Player Who Makes a Difference Award.

Three injuries interrupted Rubin's progress. When she was number 6 in the world, her wrist injury impeded her development. In August 1996, she had surgery on the wrist. In 1997, she had severe problems with her forehand grip, which continued through the 1998 Australian Open. Bud Collins wrote of her poor play in Michigan, and he called coach Benny Sims, who met with her in Lafayette and became her coach. Before she could manage to recover her form, however, she had surgery on her left knee in 2001 and again on the same knee in 2002. She admitted this second round of surgery was very difficult for her to take because she had worked so hard after the first operation.[14]

After hiring Benny Sims, Rubin began to show flashes of the brilliance she had demonstrated in 1996. One of her biggest wins was over Martina Hingis, the defending champion of the Evert Cup in 1999, earning her a spot in the semifinals. In November 2000, she captured the Bell Challenge Singles title, defeating Jennifer Capriati.

MaliVai Washington

While Rubin advanced on the women's tour, MaliVai Washington emerged on the men's tour. Born June 20, 1969, in Glen Cove, New York, the second of five children of William and Christine Washington, MaliVai Washington wanted to be a firefighter when he was a child. His father, who played recreational tennis, began to teach him and his older sister, Micheala, in the summer of 1975. When MaliVai was ten or eleven, his father took them to the U.S. Open, where MaliVai got his first tennis autographs from Noah, McEnroe, and Connors. It was then that he thought about being a professional player for the first time.[15]

MaliVai Washington on the grounds at the U.S. Open.

As a junior, he reached the third round of the 1987 U.S. Open Junior Championships and finished the 1987 year ranked number 4 in the USTA National Boys' 18s. His only USTA Nationals junior title was in the 1981 USTA Boys' 12s Clay Court Doubles Championship. Washington followed these performances with a successful tennis career at the University of Michigan.

It has been declared that since Ashe "became the first and only black male to be ranked number 1 in the world, he was the unofficial judge of black tennis talent in the United States." Ashe, who was a part of a program sponsored by the Volvo Tennis/Collegiate Series, was impressed with Washington, saying, "He's one of the nicest kids I've met on the circuit. He's got his feet firmly planted on the ground and he's been well advised by his father and his college coach." When asked if Washington could be number 1 in the world, he replied, "He's definitely top 30. He's probably the least flashy player you'll ever see, but he's got great court sense."[16] Washington credits his family as the solid base for his character. "My parents always put the emphasis on working hard, whether it's for tennis or an education or whatever." His parents are from rural Mississippi, although they have lived in the North for some time. In 1993, he reflected, "[W]hen my parents grew up, it wasn't the easiest era in American history for black people. It was instilled in them that they had to work for everything they got, and even though they've moved to a different socio-economic level, they still have a grasp of two things: how much they could attain, and how much work it took to attain. That part rubbed off on me, for sure."[17] His father functioned as his coach, but Washington also worked with Brian Gottfried while Gottfried was on the USTA coaching team. In 1993, he began working with Gavin Hooper.

After two years at the University of Michigan, he turned pro, winning the 1990 Rookie of the Year Award. That year he also achieved his first victory over a top-ten player, Lendl, at the Volvo International in New Haven. He won his first two professional titles in 1992 at Memphis and Charlotte and reached the finals of four other tournaments on both grass and clay surfaces. In 1993, he was ranked as high as number 11. Washington viewed Pete Sampras as an example of what could be achieved despite what critics said. "I look to a guy like Pete Sampras. A few years ago, it was said that he was too laid-back or too flaky or whatever. But he's become one of the most consistent guys on the tour. That base of consistency paid off and he's No. 1 now."[18]

The most important tournament of Washington's career was the 1996 Wimbledon, where he reached the final, becoming the first black male to do so since Ashe in 1975 and being the only black American male to reach the top twenty since Ashe in 1979. He had to rally against friend Todd Martin in the semifinals to advance to the final, recovering from 1-5 down in the fifth set to defeat Martin. The win was credited to play in the fifth set, described as "one of the most astonishing chokes [by Martin] ever seen on Centre Court," and to Washington's "relentlessness and daring that put the pressure on Martin": "in the end it was Washington who drilled the winning backhand volley." [19] That was the first time Washington advanced beyond the quarterfinals of a Grand Slam event.

The memories of Ashe's 1975 Wimbledon victory loomed over Washington's appearance in the final. Carrying the banner of the next Ashe was a complicated position for Washington, causing him to insist, "There can only be one Arthur Ashe. To be able to accomplish some of the things that he accomplished would be great, on and off the court. But what you see is me." [20]

While Washington was posing for the photographers before the match, a woman streaked on the court. Washington described the incident: "I looked over and I see this streaker. I see this, this . . . wobbling around. She smiled at me and I think she was wearing an apron. She lifted it up, and was still smiling. I got flustered, then three sets later, I was gone." Washington lost in straight sets in a match with three rain delays. His opponent, Richard Krajicek, served fourteen aces in the match. Washington argued, "That was the difference. His serve was coming in real strong. He was averaging 120 miles an hour on his first serve. When a guy is doing that, and he can do it consistently, it's tough to break." [21]

Recognizing the significance of the occasion to his career, he reflected, "Winning that final would have helped my status, but it still did a lot for my career. I felt at the time that it would have put me one step closer to my ultimate goal, which is to be no. 1." [22] After that final, he played no matches until the following U.S. Open, where he won an astonishing first-round match against Karim Alami, playing for two and one-half hours.

Although it has been difficult to recruit top-ranked professionals for the U.S. Davis Cup team, Washington made no secret of his desire to play on the team. Nevertheless, he and other players ranked below the top ten or twenty competed only when the very top players declined invitations. Washington took the opportunity to compete in ties against the Bahamas and Brazil. When he was not selected to play against Australia in 1993, Tom Gorman, the Davis Cup team captain, explained that the decision was based solely on performance. However, Washington replied, "But I don't know, how can you tell? I'd like to believe that the decision was made with a sound mind, with the simple intention of putting together the best team." [23]

Substituting for an injured Andre Agassi, Washington played in the tie against Brazil in Riveirao Preto in 1997 Davis Cup competition, when he was ranked number 24 in the world. He took three hours and ten minutes to defeat Gustavo Kuerten (Kuerten won the French Open in 1997, 2000, 2001). The match was close, and Washington admitted, "There were times when it wasn't looking good, but you have to keep fighting and hope things will go your way." [24] He injured his knee during the match against Kuerten. He affirmed, "That match is one of my best memories, which is kind of odd since it was devastating to my career. Davis Cup is pretty important and if something is going to happen to you, it might as well happen at Davis Cup than at some smaller, unimportant tournament." [25]

After having arthroscopic surgery, Washington was out for the year. When he attempted to play in 1998, he discovered that he needed additional surgery. In the Bermuda Open in April that year, he iced his knee after each match. [26] By May, he had withdrawn from four tournaments. By June, he had not made it past the second round of any tournament. [27] In November, he had a second surgery and began practicing in March 1999; meanwhile, he worked as an on-court announcer for ESPN. He wanted to attempt a comeback in 1999, playing his first tournament at the Miller Lite Hall of Fame Tennis Championships in Newport. Later, he lost in a first-round match at the ATP Championships in Cincinnati and decided to retire in December 1999 at the age of thirty.

Washington has received several awards. In 1996, he was the recipient of the Role Model of the Year Award (voted on by underprivileged kids) from the Otis F. Smith Foundation. [28] In 1997, he was given the Sports Image Award and the Boys and Girls Club Children Are the Reason for Excellence (CARE) Award. The following year he earned the Arthur Ashe Athletic Association Leadership Award.

Bryan Shelton

Washington's best friend on the professional circuit was Bryan Shelton. Shelton, from Huntsville, Alabama, turned pro in 1989. His father, Nathaniel Shelton, was a retired army officer and technical writer, and his mother, Regina Shelton, was the vice president of the Alabama Tennis Association.

Shelton began playing at age eight, but was ranked by age ten. He won the USTA Boys' 18s Interscholastic National Championship at Duke University in 1983, where he also played in the Men's Open draw. When he was a teenager, his mother took him to junior tennis tournaments in various states in the summer. Bill Tym, former coach at University of Tennessee at Chattanooga, who bought the Huntsville Athletic Club in 1979, coached Shelton. Shelton earned the number 1 ranking in Boys' 16s of the Alabama Tennis Association in singles and doubles. In addition, he reached the semifinals of the USTA National Boys' 18s Championships in 1984. It was then that he realized that he wanted to be a professional tennis player.

At the Huntsville Club, Shelton met Kenny Thorne, and they became doubles partners and roommates on the junior circuit, at college, and on the professional tour. After graduating from private Randolph Academy in Huntsville, Alabama, in 1984, he attended Georgia Tech, majoring in engineering.

The summer after his first year in college, Shelton played the satellite circuit and won the West Penn National Amateur Clay Court Championship in Pittsburgh, defeating Thorne in the final. He qualified for two satellite tournaments in the New York area and played the Junior Davis Cup tournament. He also won the U.S. Amateur National Championships title, giving him a birth in the qualifying rounds of the U.S. Open, where he lost in the first round.[29]

Shelton was an all-American as a senior in 1988 and advanced to the quarterfinals of the NCAA tournament. At that tournament, he was introduced to Bobby Blair, a former collegiate player at Arkansas, who assembled a traveling team of rookie pros after playing on the tour himself. Shelton and Thorne joined Blair USA Team, based at Hilton Head Island, South Carolina. This arrangement included coaching, practice facilities, transportation, and lodging in return for a percentage of the winnings. Shelton played only eight weeks on the satellite tour that summer before returning to Georgia Tech to complete his studies.

Breaking from the group in June 1989, Shelton, Thorne, and Shelby Cannon, another Blair teammate, played the grass-court circuit in England. Shelton lost in the qualifying at Queens Club and at Bristol. However, back in London, he won three qualifying matches to make the main draw of his first Grand Slam. He then played Boris Becker in the first round of the main draw. Afterward, he rejoined the Blair Team for tournaments in the United States.[30]

Shelton won his first title in Newport, Rhode Island, in 1991, making him the first black American to win a men's title in the United States since Ashe won at Los Angeles in 1978. He successfully defended his title a year later. With his big serve, grass seemed to be the surface for Shelton to make his major breakthrough.[31]

One of Shelton's major wins came at the expense of Michael Stich, a former Wimbledon champion (1991) and number 2 seed, in the first round of the 1994 Wimbledon. Shelton, ranked 120, had to qualify to get into the main draw. His defeat of Stich followed McNeil's ousting of Graff. The next year Shelton's expertise on grass enabled him to dispose of number 12 seed Krajicek. About the defeat, he stated, "It doesn't quite top last year's win over Michael Stich, Stich being a former champion. But I beat a very good player, so I'm happy about that." About his Wimbledon experiences, he said, "Each time you go on the court, you feel like you're going to play the best match of your life. This place lifts you up. . . . I've won two events and have played some big matches here. I feel I can do some damage here. I try to find the right formula for myself and then let my natural game take over."[32]

After retiring from professional tennis in 1997, Shelton briefly coached MaliVai Washington and spent a year and a half as a national coach with the USTA. Just prior to the 1999–2000 season, he became the women's tennis coach at Georgia Tech. He led the team to their first NCAA tournament berth in 2000, defeating top-ranked Stanford.

Steve Campbell

After Washington and Shelton retired, Steve Campbell was hailed as the "best African-American tennis player"; he was ranked number 78 at the time. He moved from 117 to 78 during the Asian Challenger circuit, "tennis's equivalent of baseball's minor leagues." In Kyoto, Japan, he reached the singles final. To play in the qualifying round of the Lipton Championships, he left Japan on a night flight and arrived in San Francisco the same Sunday evening, boarded a flight for Miami, arriving late Sunday night. Then, he played Chris Wilkinson in the first round and fell behind 6-3, 4-0. But he came back to win that match and qualified for the main draw, where he defeated Todd Martin and Wayne Ferreira before losing to Alex Corretja in the quarterfinals. Sports writer Peter Bodo characterized Campbell as a "grinder," but "the most interesting aspect of his saga may be that he is an African-American grinder which is a particularly daunting role to play."[33]

Campbell felt this success was in part owing to hard work and faith in his game. How did he do it? What advice did he have? How did he feel? He expounded, "It's funny, but people ask those things as if there were some magic formula, some series of steps or actions that get you to your goal. There is no magic formula. You have to work really, really hard and get or make enough breaks to move ahead another step." Bodo asserted, "Campbell never was good enough to become part of the elite international tennis culture that operates outside of the quotidian social framework." Campbell agreed. "I have no resentment against anyone, because I was never a top prospect. I never put up the kind of results that would demand attention. That's one of the things I try to convey to black kids when I talk to them. You don't have to travel some golden path laid down by the USTA, or anyone else, to succeed. That's for a select few. The rest of us have to develop discipline, dedication and goals."

Campbell was a product of the Metropolitan Racquet Club (MRC) in Detroit run by Tim Ballard and Dr. Emeral Crosby, who charged kids $15 for membership, which included clinics. Later, Campbell played for Rice University, where he earned degrees in political science and business management. At the number 1 position, he received the John Van Nostrand Memorial Award for outstanding play in the Southwest Conference. In his senior year, he won the Rolex Southwest Regional Intercollegiate Tennis Championships and reached the final of the Rolex National Indoor Intercollegiate Championships in 1992.

After graduating in 1992, he played on the satellite tour and was plagued by nagging injuries and insufficient capital. At the time, he commented, "Sometimes it is hard. But I really enjoy my life, too. I guess it comes down to the same old thing, about having to pay our dues to get anywhere in life. I'm fine with that."

Boris Kodje

Injury put an end to Boris Kodje's professional dreams. Playing tennis since the age of three, the German had the same coach as Steffi Graf, Boris Becker, and Anke Huber. He became one of the top three players in Germany by age sixteen, but was motivated to attend college because of two herniated discs in his back; he believed that the back problems were "too risky to pursue tennis exclusively." He attended Virginia Commonwealth (1991–95), where he played tennis and studied acting. Since then he has become an accomplished actor, including a starring role on the HBO series *Soul Food,* but he still loves tennis with all his heart and hits with Serena Williams.[34]

Venus and Serena Williams

Despite the moderate success of other players, the most amazing story in tennis at the close of the twentieth century was that of sisters Venus and Serena Williams, who quickly captured the imagination of millions with their quick rise in professional tennis. Not since the emergence of Gibson had so much attention been placed on black tennis players. Furthermore, the Williams sisters' heralded "unorthodox" manner of reaching professional ranks has caused even those who criticized their father, Richard Williams, to reassess his method and to consider that various methods might be used to develop a champion. Other previous tennis pros had also traveled a nontraditional road to success. Gibson's

Venus Williams and Serena Williams.

road was very different from the norm, mainly owing to race segregation and poverty. Later, Garrison, McNeil, and Belcher developed into professionals without the high-profile tennis camps, lush country clubs, and well-known coaches.

From Compton, California, Venus was born June 17, 1980, and Serena was born September 26, 1981. While pregnant, their mother, Oracene, played a match every morning at five-thirty before going to work.[35] When the girls misbehaved, their father attempted to frighten them by taking them to jailhouses. That approach failed, but they were "spooked" by a bag lady in downtown Los Angeles who talked to herself while pushing a shopping cart. Serena thought, "We'd better go to school. We don't want to end up like that." They were poor, so the girls distributed phone books to earn some money, and their mother made most of their clothes. They remember being on welfare. The balls with which they practiced were so bad that Rick Macci, a former instructor, thought they were the kind "you give to a dog as a last resort." In order to prepare them for different situations on the court, their father had people hold up noisy boom boxes during their matches. He even trained them how to play against cheaters.[36]

Their father admitted that he specifically trained them to be professional tennis players. Many criticized him because he pulled them out of junior competition, which most argue is essential to success on the professional level. Because other teenagers, such as Martina Hingis, had successfully competed in juniors and moved up the rankings quickly on the professional tour, they were considered proof that the junior circuit was *the* road to the professional ranks. However, it took only a short time for Williams's daughters to begin to challenge and surpass those who used the junior circuit as a stepping stone. As a result, the critics had to retract their statements. One columnist noted, "His [Richard Williams's] unorthodox, anti–tennis establishment methods and tactics have unsettled many but vindicated him. His vibrant daughters have battled back from injuries, and accusations of not taking the game seriously enough, of being too well-rounded (as if that's a fault). I know this: When Venus or Serena takes the court, they make me want to watch tennis again." [37]

Since the Williams sisters' emergence on the tour, many have analyzed their games. For example, in 1998 Nick Bollettieri assessed them in these terms:

> Both girls have a similar game in one aspect that clearly stands out. They will not push the ball and not continue the point. They have the ability to physically and tactically beat their opponents.
>
> I witnessed Venus playing one of the best boys from the United States. She made this boy look like—and more importantly, feel—he didn't even belong on the court with her. This boy's head was hanging down so far that it almost touched his knees. I am sure she also has this effect on most of the WTA tour players.
>
> Serena also has the athletic ability to make incredible shots from impossible positions on the court. This in turn will make her opponents go for better shots, eventually leading to unforced errors. [38]

When the sisters met in the 2001 U.S. Open women's final, Richard Williams felt vindicated in the way he and his wife "had handled their daughters—not playing bushels of tournaments, taking time off for fun." He explained, "Why rush it and tear it up and burn it out?

Why have them out there at 3 years old, 4 years old, every day. When Venus was 4, and I learned how much she loved the game, we took off for a year and wouldn't let her play, no matter what she said. . . . When I went to different places to train, they wanted Venus to practice all day, drop out of school and all that. We said no." One observer noted, "Williams and his wife, Oracene, have played it right. Not perfect, but right. They have been the lightning rods, the firewalls, the offensive line effectively keeping out the stampeding defensive rush. They've given their daughters time to breathe." [39]

In spite of the sisters' success, columnist Bruce Schoenfeld questioned the feasibility of replicating Richard Williams's method. He suggested in 1998 that because Venus had been on the tour only two years and had already reached one Grand Slam final, the "trickle-down effect" would start immediately because in tennis trends tend to be set after one success story. Moreover, he maintained that this was not the same for football players, who follow a "straight, if narrow" path with the "best of them starting in junior high or high school, mature into college standouts, then end up in the NFL [National Football League]." Nevertheless, a few players have dared to break the mold. For instance, several players have left college early for the NFL, rather than remain in school for four years, as had been the "tradition." In the National Basketball Association (NBA), the success of a few players who went directly from high school to the professional ranks has caused others to consider this alternative. In short, the "traditional" rules change in sports, creating new "traditions." [40]

Bill Ozaki, the director of programs and development for the USTA's southern section in Norcross, Georgia, argued that the Williams sisters' success might be like "running from the law of averages. It worked for them, but I guess I can't see it working for most." Ernie Jackson, whose daughter Jamea was a top junior at the time, wondered, however, if the desire to win USTA matches might not hamper the "learning curve": "He [Williams] took away the pressure to win so his daughters could learn. Kids get scared of losing. When you remove the pressure to win, they learn a lot easier." Ernie Peterson, director of a junior development program in Atlanta, guided the development of his own daughter, Jewel, and argued that Williams charted his daughter's careers very carefully. "They're the most obedient kids I've ever met in my life, and they've got a real desire to win. Does that mean what he's doing is for everyone? No, but it certainly worked for them. I don't think there's any question about that."[41]

Constantly targeted by the critics and cynics, Richard Williams explained, "From day one others attempted to tell me a 'better' way to raise Venus, and later Serena, to be tennis champions." In addition, he admitted that the "negativity" did get to him. "When people criticize you, I don't care how much you say it doesn't bother you, it does. It bothers you when people criticize you, especially when you're doing the best that you can do."[42]

Even when Venus began to win on the tour, he realized that she was not a complete player. "I wanted to make sure her groundstrokes were decent enough to rally with whoever was No. 1 or No. 2 in the world, she could rally well enough to knock them off the baseline before we move to Phase 2." Phase two was to follow her big serve to the net. The rallying was important because he had heard that black players, including Ashe and Gibson, could not rally. Regarding Serena, he remarked, "Serena has better shot selection than anyone in professional tennis right now [1998]. What makes Serena frightening, though, is that if you want to hit the ball softly, she'll hit it softly. If you hit it hard, there's no one in professional tennis who can hit the ball as hard as Serena on both sides with her accuracy."[43]

Another controversy stemmed from Rick Macci's assertion that he was "betrayed" by not receiving any credit for coaching the girls from 1991 to 1995 or for having a great impact on their development. In an interview, Macci admitted that Richard Williams gave him credit on the phone (the day before Venus's appearance in the U.S. Open final in 1997), adding, "but he never says that to the media. To the media, it's like the mom [Oracene] and the dad are the coaches. There's no question Richard's done a lot for them. I want to credit him for that." Macci was disappointed that his "steadfast loyalty toward the parents and the girls . . . has not been reciprocated." He claimed that he experienced a similar situation with Jennifer Capriati.[44]

Soon after Venus's run at the U.S. Open in 1997, the USTA and NJTL took the opportunity to promote themselves on the heels of the sisters' successes. In a USTA publication, Mark Winters claimed, "What isn't known is their interest in tennis was fostered by the Amateur Athletic Foundation's USTA/National Junior Tennis League in Southern California. Not only did the sisters benefit from the introductory instruction, they participated in special events that are part of the NJTL program." Winters also reported that Richard Williams taught in a NJTL program at East Compton Park. James Pyles, brother of Judy Jones, the recreation supervisor of the Los Angeles Court Parks and Recreation Department, helped Williams put Venus and Serena through workouts at the "East Compton Country Club." Pyles maintained that he "worked mostly with Serena and about a quarter of the time with Venus." According to Jim Hillman, the director of Junior Tennis at the Southern California Tennis Association since 1977, "Venus started in NJTL and went on to play sectional championships. She was undefeated in the division, and an attorney came to the (sectional) final with her. After that, a story appeared in the *New York Times* and the press coverage took off." [45]

According to Andrea Leand, former tour player turned journalist, "When they first came on the tour . . . the William sisters possessed unparalleled potential with superior speed, strength and athleticism. Their ascension to the top seemed just a matter of time. To some, this brashness transcended gender and cast female athletes in a positive but more assertive, aggressive light." [46]

After Venus and Serena dared to proclaim that they would be numbers 1 and 2 on the WTA tour, it took little time for critics to emphasize that the sisters had failed to win Grand Slam titles in four years. In Venus's first U.S. Open in 1997, she advanced to the final, but lost to Hingis. Then number 1, Hingis defeated Venus for the 1998 Italian Open title, but argued that Venus was really number 2 in the world despite her computer ranking of number 7. "She's my rival now for No. 1." [47]

Venus won her first title in the 1998 IGA Tennis Classic in Oklahoma City, defeating Joannette Kruger. Afterward, she and her sister won the doubles. When Venus won the Italian Open, Bud Collins recalled that this championship was also the first major title for Gibson in 1956.[48] After capturing the 1998 Compaq Grand Slam Cup, she won two Grand Slams in mixed doubles with Justin Gimelstob in 1999 at the Australian and the French Opens.

After being sidelined for six months because of wrist tendinitis, Venus returned to the tour in the spring of 2000 and by summer's end had captured Wimbledon and the U.S. Open. Peter Fink, tennis columnist, wrote, "Appearing in only her second major final and her first on the daunting Centre Court, she played through her nervous patches and produced some astonishing tennis at times. What she lacked in shot-making dependability she made up for with her magnificent court coverage."[49] Her absence had caused several rumors from burnout and retirement to sibling rivalry, and the media took advantage of such stories.[50]

In the midst of the longest winning streak of her young career, Venus defeated sister Serena in the semifinals of the 2000 Wimbledon 6-2, 7-6 (7-3) and upset defending champion Lindsay Davenport in the final 6-3, 7-6 (7-3). Venus continued her domination of the tour by defeating Davenport again in the U.S. Open.

In 2001, Venus defended her Wimbledon and U.S. Open titles. She became the first woman to repeat a win at Wimbledon since Steffi Graf in 1995–96. She defeated Justine Henin of Belgium in the final. It was argued that Venus's serve took on "Pete Sampras and Goran Ivanisevic proportions." Lindsay Davenport stated, "Women's tennis has never seen that kind of serve." Her fastest during the final was 118 miles per hour, but she had clocked 125 miles per hour earlier in the tournament, which placed her in the top twenty-five among men for the tournament and ahead of players such as Agassi (124 miles per hour).[51]

The 2001 U.S. Open marked the first time since 1884 (when Maud Watson defeated younger sister Lillian at Wimbledon) that two siblings vied for a major championship title and the first time two blacks competed for a Grand Slam title. In the semifinals, Venus dismantled Capriati, while Serena defeated Hingis. Richard Williams argued, "To me, it looked like a pickup junior match from both of them, to be honest with you. Venus walked out, looked scared to death, like her heart was going to stop. Jennifer got scared as if someone had both her feet taped up; Venus acted like someone had something tied over her eyes." Hingis cried after the match, and when someone suggested that she hire someone other than her mother as a coach, Richard Williams disagreed. "Her mother is good enough. Hingis and her mom need to sit there, do what they're doing and figure out something a little bit different here and there."[52]

The final was also the scene of black royal procession much like the scenes at the All-Star Games of the Negro Leagues. The Harlem Gospel Choir and Diana Ross performed. Highly visible personalities such as Vanessa Williams, Spike Lee, Rick Fox, Sean Combs, Robert Redford, Joe Namath, Sarah Jessica Parker, Jay Z, Star Jones, and Brandy attended.

CBS decided to showcase the women's final during prime time, a "risk" for the network. As noted, "TV appeal of tennis, as opposed to team sports, is heavily dependent on its stars. TV ratings for tournaments can gyrate depending on the star power of who makes it to the final."[53] Prior to that final, the only tennis match aired in prime time was the Billie Jean King versus Bobby Riggs battle of the sexes in 1973, although other matches "unexpectedly stretched into the prime-time hours."[54]

After the sisters won their respective semifinals matches, their father stated, "All my life I've been waiting for this. And now it can happen." Serena added, "It will be great history. We just go out and work hard. Good things come to hard workers, like the ants."[55]

It was difficult to monitor how the crowd would react. According to one analyst, "the crowd wasn't really there to see who won. At this point the sisters are still so inseparable . . . that there were not a whole lot of people who could parse favoritism. . . . It [the crowd] was there to celebrate a new era in women's tennis, the one that Richard, who wore a T shirt on Saturday with his own picture on it, had been predicting for 20 years."[56]

It appeared that Venus Williams "never had to play her best tennis to defend her title." In fact, "her straight-set victory over Serena in the final proved anticlimactic. . . . [B]oth women did their best under the difficult psychological circumstances of facing a sibling." It was argued that "not even off-court concerns rattled the sisters, who handled adversity with intelligence, maturity, and good humor."[57]

When Venus Williams defended the Oklahoma City IGA Tennis Classic title in 1999, Serena Williams won the Open Gaz de France, her first WTA tour singles title, defeating Amelie Mauresmo of France 6-2, 3-6, 7-6 (7-4), making it the first time that sisters captured tournaments in the same week on the WTA tour.[58]

Serena followed that title with the Evert Cup (Indian Wells), upsetting seeded players Lindsay Davenport, Mary Pierce, and Sandrine Testud en route to the final, where she beat Steffi Graf. In her fifth tournament (Chicago) at age sixteen, she upset Mary Pierce and Monica Seles. When she captured the U.S. Open in 1999, defeating Hingis, she became the first black player to win the title since Ashe in 1968 and the first black woman since Gibson in 1958. Hingis had defeated Venus Williams in the semifinals, spoiling the possible all-Williams final. Serena reportedly said, "She [Venus] was really down. That really encouraged me to be even tougher out there. . . . I've never seen her that down before. If anything, it's going to motivate her."[59] Serena was seventeen when she won her first Grand Slam and moved up to number 4 in the world. Even more remarkable was the fact that in the women's doubles final, three of the four women were black; Venus and Serena Williams defeated Chanda Rubin and Sandrine Testud.

Serena first defeated her older sister in the final of the 1999 Grand Slam Cup 6-1, 3-6, 6-3. Venus won in the final of the 1999 Lipton, the first meeting of sisters in a tour final in the open era. Serena was the *Tennis Magazine* Female Player of the Year in 1999. In addition, she became the fastest player in WTA tour history to beat five top-ten-ranked players in sixteen matches. In the summer of 2000, Serena defeated Davenport in the estyle.com Classic in Manhattan Beach, California, defending her title.

When Serena faced Davenport in the quarterfinals of the 2001 U.S. Open, it proved to be the only match to jolt "the buzz in the women's competition"; the "three-set extravaganza against Serena provided the best quality tennis in the women's event." Although Serena squandered a 3-0 lead in the third set, she was able to win the match. She had asked her sister how to handle nerves, and Venus told her that "champions do not get nervous." Serena stated, "I told myself in the match not to be nervous and just to play."[60] After she lost to Venus in the final, it was her turn to give advice: "She [Venus] said she didn't feel like she really won. She said she always felt like she had to protect me. But I told her, 'Just enjoy, take it, it's yours. You won.' "[61] Serena remembers the first time she played her sister in a final. When she was eight and without her father's permission, she entered a tournament Venus was playing. Both of them advance to the finals, and Venus won 6-2, 6-2. Afterward, Venus traded her gold trophy for Serena's silver second-place trophy, telling Serena that she preferred silver to gold.[62]

In 2002, Serena dominated the women's tour, winning four consecutive Grand Slam titles—the Serena Slam—beginning with the French Open. She missed the Australian Open that year, but captured the title in 2003. With the four titles, she became number 1. Adding to the history was the fact that she played her sister in all four of the finals. Their father's vision of their being the two best players in the world became reality. Although Serena lost in the semifinals of the 2003 French Open, she took the Wimbledon title, then surgery forced her to skip the U.S. Open, so that she lost her number 1 ranking.

Described as the outgoing one, Serena also acts. She played a teacher on an episode of the sit-com *My Wife and Kids* and has been slated to play a reformed gang member on parole on the Showtime Network crime drama *Street Time*.

According to one writer, Serena "restores integrity to the women's game." During the Federation Cup tie, Billie Jean King wanted to know how Serena was holding up as number 1. After talking to her, King commented, "She's the player everyone wants to beat, and there are a lot of outside pressures. But with Serena, it's as if she was made to be the queen. She's just having a ball." It was also noted that Serena had managed to win over "the hearts and minds of the critics," and that as the sentiments shifted, so did the vocabulary. Her "irreverence" became her "taking the path less traveled." Her "arrogance" was recast as "confidence"; and her "brute force" became "sleek power." Serena began to find her own identity in the game. She explained, "I had to stop feeling sorry for myself. Also, I had to realize that I wasn't Venus. I used to want to be her—not be like her, *be* her—and I think that held me back."[63] The media started seeing them as separate individuals rather than as an inseparable duo.

Some sport writers began to question Venus's dedication despite the fact that she advanced to four consecutive Grand Slam finals. She started devoting some of her time to studying interior design through Rhodec International, a London-based correspondence school. Her parents had "cautioned her to maintain a balanced life, at one point halting her tennis instruction because she seemed too obsessed with the game." In contrast, Serena's dedication lacked the same scrutiny, and she was winning although she continued to pursue acting. The tennis voices wondered about Venus's reaction to Serena's dominance. Venus remarked, "My goal has always been to be No. 1 in the world. But not to take the No. 1 ranking from my sister." Serena admitted, "It's never been easy for me to play Venus. Beating her was a bit of a mental block for me. To finally win a match against Venus in a big tournament was a pretty big confidence booster." According to one writer, Venus failed to work through "whatever conflicts she feels as neatly—or as profitably—as that."[64]

The sisters won the 2000 Wimbledon doubles title, defeating Julie Halard-Decugis and Ai Sugiyama 6-3, 6-2. A reporter from *West Africa* magazine commented, "Remaining true to a declaration of tennis brilliance, the African-American Williams sisters played their way into the record books by becoming the first siblings to win the Wimbledon doubles title."[65] The sisters ended the 2000 season with an Olympic gold in doubles, and Venus won the gold medal in singles.

The sisters have also been a major force in Federation Cup. In 1999, they joined Lindsay Davenport and Monica Seles to form a very formidable team. When they joined the team for the first time, there was uncertainty. Coach Billie Jean King explained, "I wasn't sure what to expect from Venus or Serena. I had heard that they liked to stick together and did not do too much with other players, so I wasn't sure how they would mix in a team situation. But, fortunately, it couldn't have worked out better. Everyone got along and it turned out to be a dream team to coach."[66]

Sports Illustrated for Women selected Venus as Sportswoman of the Year for her exploits of 2000. She was chosen for her fantastic year, but also for "the gracious way she acted during her run, the way she carried herself not only as a winner but a champion as well."[67] Other awards included *Tennis* magazine Female Player of the Year and an ESPY for Best Female Athlete in Tennis. Venus and Hingis were among the women featured on the *Ladies' Home Journal* Most Fascinating Women list of 1997. In addition, Venus was one of the year's "Strong Women" in *Life* for 1997, and the sisters were honorees at the 2001 Essence Awards. Serena won two ESPYs in 2003, for Best Female Athlete and Best Female Tennis Player. Moreover, she was Sportswoman of the Year at the Lawreus World Sports Awards (Monte Carlo), edging out sprinter Marion Jones, marathon runner Paula Radcliffe, and skier Janica Kostelic. Venus presented the award to her sister.

The sisters developed the J. P. Morgan Chase Tennis Challenge to help raise awareness and funds for their mother's education foundation, the Oracene Williams Learning Foundation (OWL), which provides funds for special educational programs for youth and adults.[68]

The Williams sisters' popularity has permeated many institutions, and they have become role models for a cross section of youths. For instance, they and Anna Kournikova were listed among role models for teens who take pride in remaining virgins.[69] They are even mentioned in E. Lynn Harris's novel *Any Way the Wind Blows*.[70] Cora Master Barry, wife of former mayor Marion Barry, invited the sisters to the grand opening of a $5.1 million tennis and learning center in Washington, D.C. At times during the ceremony, "security guards were almost overcome by the enormous crowd," but Barry assured them that the crowd's actions were "just love." She added that many of the "youngsters only see [the sisters] on television since they can't afford to attend tournaments like the US Open."[71] Their popularity became such that

Serena dyed her hair "platinum blond to avoid recognition while shopping in public."[72]

Either one or both of the sisters have graced the covers of virtually every tennis publication of note, but they have also appeared on other magazines such as *Jet, Essence, Sports Illustrated,* and *Top Spin.* They were only the second tennis players to make the cover of *Olympian Magazine,* and Serena is one of the few women to appear on the cover of the male-focused *ESPN the Magazine.* Furthermore, they were featured in fashion layouts in *Elle* and the first athletes to appear on the cover of that magazine since model–volleyball player Gabrielle Reece was on it in May 1995.[73] In addition, British filmmaker Terry Jervis directed a behind-the-scenes documentary on Venus and Serena titled *Raising Tennis Aces: The Williams Story.*[74] Several children's book on the sisters have been published, and they published their own book, *How to Play Tennis,* and penned articles on each other in *Tennis* magazine and the publication of a newsletter.

Part of the sisters' appeal lies "in the fact that they're the newly admitted blacks in the country club—much like Tiger Woods in golf—and they're handily beating the white folks." Their presence has expanded the black tennis fan base, and blacks "are now more than twice as likely to identify themselves as avid tennis fans as whites," according to *Time* columnist Joel Stein.[75] However, their appeal has reached beyond a black fan base, and they have become legitimate crossover stars. Ian Maxtone-Graham, coexecutive producer of *The Simpsons,* admitted, "I'm always rooting for them obsessively in matches. I was watching Serena play Martina Hingis on television . . . , and I got so nervous for Serena that I just couldn't watch anymore."[76] When the sisters were taping an episode of *Hollywood Squares,* Whoopi Goldberg walked on the set and started bowing toward them; at the 2000 Wimbledon, Dionne Warwick serenaded them with "That's What Friends Are For."

In 2001, newspaper reporter Todd Holcomb maintained that more "minorities" play because of the Williams sisters. He cited that of the 261,000 Americans introduced to tennis through the USTA's USA Tennis 1-2-3 program in 1999, 25 percent were black and 44 percent were other "minorities." However, he failed to make clear the direct tie between this number and the Williams sisters, nor did he provide statistics on the level of increase from prior years.[77]

Venus Williams's success in 2000 was marred by media attempts to create a story surrounding Serena's 1999 U.S. Open title and Venus's "jealousy" over not being the first to win a Grand Slam title. For example, one writer argued, "The public remembers her sitting in the stands during the 1999 U.S. Open final, garbed in black, watching stone-faced as her little sister won the family's first Grand Slam singles tennis title. . . . It seemed obvious then that something terrible was happening to Venus Williams."[78] Another noted, "Venus Williams sat in sullen silence . . . while her sister, Serena, won the US Open, earning the Williams family's first Grand Slam singles title. Although Venus denied any jealousy or sadness . . . , her subsequent actions told a different story."[79]

In 1999, people made assumptions about Venus's feelings and attempted to get her or Serena to substantiate them. According to Venus, she was miserable watching Serena play in the U.S. Open final not because Serena achieved the "big prize first," but because she came "face-to-face with herself."[80] Venus publicly demonstrated how proud she was of her sister's success when at the 2002 French Open she took a camera to photograph her sister when the latter was on the podium with the winning plate. The fact that they love each other has been lost on some who wanted to see stellar matches when they faced each other. The speculation of the sisters "fixing" matches when they played against each other circulated broadly in the media. The sisters consistently denied the allegation. Serena explained, "People speculate because maybe they can't comprehend the love that Venus and I have for each other."[81]

The Williams sisters have also been the object of scorn, as was the case at the Evert Cup at Indian Wells in 2001, when the public believed that Venus withdrew from the semifinals, faking an ailment, only to avoid playing her sister. Some believed that their father made that decisions. As a result, the crowd jeered Richard and Venus when they took their seats. Richard heard a man say, "N——, if this was 1975, we'd skin you alive," and someone commented to Serena, "F—— you and your sister!"[82] Others screamed "Loser!" and "Cheat!" When Serena began to win points in the match, her father clapped, something he had never done. Richard Williams "turned the tables and accused the crowd of racism." He stated, "I really just think a lot of people in the tennis and business world are jealous of me. They'd rather see me sweeping the floor at the U.S. Open or picking cotton somewhere. But I'm not."[83]

The controversy sparked several articles.[84] Venus argued, "This country has a history of treating minorities badly, and that's sad because it is a country of promise." Evert Cup tournament director Charles Pasarell added, "I was cringing when all that stuff was going on. It was unfair for the crowd to do that. If Richard says someone yelled something, maybe they did, but I know that's not Indian Wells people."[85] Reporter Joel Drucker asserted, "Reading each sister's remarks hardly reveal the story. Each was scarcely emphatic in their denials of the fixing." And "Venus was also barely remorseful for the way her extremely last-minute decision had compromised so many."[86] Tennis commentators argued that she should have at least attempted to play the match or make a statement to the crowd. Of course, this counterfactual suggestion could not guarantee a better reception for Venus. For instance, Monica Seles was booed during a 6-0, 6-0 lost to Hingis at Key Biscayne although she attempted to play with an injury. Bart McGuire, Sanex WTA Tour CEO, released a "terse" statement: "The Tour is aware of assertions being circulated regarding Venus and Serena Williams' head-to-head matches. We have seen no evidence to support those assertions, and both players have denied them. They are elite competitors who are driven to win." Drucker attacked even this explanation, however: "How much more delicately would you expect a CEO to act when his tour is being held hostage by a family that thinks it's bigger than the game? . . . The bigger problem is the constant agenda of narcissism projected by this family."[87] The debate resurfaced after the 2001 U.S. Open semifinal victories. Venus retorted, "I'm just appalled anyone would hint something like that. I don't think that has ever been the case."[88]

In 2001, writer Joel Stein argued that the sisters had received "a lot of flack for saying tennis isn't the only thing in their life—for planning for their next careers." He added, "That may be the only thing that gets them through a sibling rivalry that could otherwise make Cain and Abel seem like the Waltons."[89]

A few black personalities took issue with white writers' criticizing the sisters. For instance, Judge Greg Mathis maintained that even while the media attempted to make all black youths seem like thugs and criminals, the "white public [was] trying to destroy the positive work of the Williams sisters."[90]

As noted earlier, when Serena won the 2003 Australian Open, she held all four Grand Slam titles, the first to do so since Graf, who held them in one calendar year, and Navratilova, who held all four simultaneously. Serena remarked that she might have been too young (seventeen) when she won her first major,[91] but she had dedicated herself to becoming number 1.

The sisters' domination on the tour in 2002 began to fade slowly in the course of 2003. When Serena lost to Maria Sharapova in a lopsided 2004 Wimbledon final and Venus also dropped in the rankings, the discussion of outside interests affecting their tennis reappeared. It mattered little that Serena had defeated Capriati convincingly in the Wimbledon semifinal.

By this time, Serena had formed her Arenes clothing line, making a splash in the fashion world. Some of her designs were modeled at the 2003 WTA bash, and she has sold custom-made evening wear to celebrities.[92] Both have designed their tennis outfits with their respective companies, and Venus designed the set for Tavis Smiley's talk show airing on PBS.

Alexandra Stevenson

Another promising black player making an appearance in the 1990s was Alexandra Stevenson from San Diego, California. Stevenson won her first pro title at the Dow Corning USTA Challenger in Midland, Michigan, in 1998. However, Stevenson's fame came with her advancement to the semifinals in the 1999 Wimbledon, the first qualifier to reach the semifinals in twenty-two years. In addition, when she and Venus Williams advanced to the quarterfinals, they became the second pair of blacks to advance to the quarterfinals in the same year since Mc-Neil and Garrison did so in 1994. During that fortnight, Stevenson decided to turn pro and not to attend college, preferring to take the prize money instead. Moreover, she liked the attention. "I like it when people know me. I think it's fun. I was getting very upset the first week at Wimbledon. I would walk through Wimbledon and no one would know who I was."[93] However, much of her being in the spotlight had little to do with her on-court achievements. For example, her mother, Samantha Stevenson, threatened to sue the WTA tour if her daughter was denied the prize money owing to her amateur status at the start of the tournament.[94] Also, that former NBA star Julius Irving was her father created more headlines than her fifty-seven aces at Wimbledon or her receiving the 1999 Rolex Female Rookie of the Year Award.

Prior to that stunning run, Stevenson had advanced to the quarterfinals of Birmingham, where she retired because of a pulled muscle. She was also a member on the U.S. tennis team in the XIII Pan Am Games in the summer of 1999. Cecil Mamiit, a Filipino American, was also a member, making the team one of the most diverse in history. Stevenson lost in the semifinals, winning a bronze medal. She was also the member of another diverse team, the New York Junior Tennis League team,[95] which traveled to Liverpool, England, in July 1999 at the invitation of the Cities Programme of Liverpool to compete in the City Championships of Liverpool Tournament sponsored by the British Tennis Association, where the team won first place in the two-day tournament.

The magic of Wimbledon, however, quickly faded as Stevenson thereafter won only six matches in fourteen tournaments in eight months. Some of the losses were to top players, but others were to relative unknowns. According to one analyst, the losing streak stemmed from coaching problems and tactical weaknesses.[96] Prior to the 2000 Wimbledon, her record was 10-22. Former tour player and tennis analyst Mary Carillo argued, "This kid dreams big, big dreams, and she's not afraid to tell you about them either. I'm not as convinced as she is that she can put together that couple of weeks. For her to get as far as she did last year is a real, real long shot. She talks big, but it hasn't showed in her results." Stevenson revealed that Pete Sampras talked to her about how difficult a rookie year could be. She thought that she could "start winning all the time."[97]

James Blake

While Rubin, the Williams sisters, and Stevenson served notice on the women's tour, several young talented black male players looked to advance from the satellite circuits. James Blake turned pro in 1999. Blake's father, Thomas Blake Sr., began playing tennis after Ashe's 1975 Wimbledon victory, while serving in the air force. Later, he began hitting with Betty, his wife, who was a better player at the time. Betty had moved from Oxfordshire, England, to Yonkers, New York, in the 1960s.[98]

James and his brother, Thomas Jr., began to play tennis with their parents, who were volunteers with a youth tennis program in Harlem, which held workout sessions at a shelter that was a converted armory. James was three when he began playing in the program, working with Dante Brown. Brian Barker, fresh off the pro circuit, began coaching James and his brother three years later. The Blakes commuted on Sundays to Harlem from Yonkers. When the family moved to Fairfield, Connecticut, Brian Barker, a teaching pro at the Tennis Club of Trumbull, began to work with the boys, who eventually had great junior careers. While playing at Fairfield High School, James compiled a 80-3 win record. His senior year he obtained the number 1 ranking in the USTA Boys' 18s in 1997.

When James began to attend Harvard, Thomas was already the number 1 player there and a senior. James played the number 2 position and earned a number 4 collegiate ranking. By the end of his freshman year, he had won the Boys' 18s and Under at the U.S. National Clay Court Championships and at the National Indoor Championships and had reached the finals of the National Boys' 18s at Kalamazoo, gaining a number 1 junior ranking. Thomas and he returned to Harlem whenever time permitted. "It's like their home away from home. They feel they should give back to the program because of what it has done for them," explained their mother.[99]

Thomas Jr. graduated with a degree in economics and began to compete on the satellite tour, making his ATP tour debut at the 1999 Miller Lite Hall of Fame Tennis Championships, where he defeated David Wheaton, a former top-ranked player. His successes also included advancing to the finals in a USTA circuit tournament in Kansas City and at the USTA Men's Future in Phoenix in 1998.

Neither James nor his coach, Brian Barker, nor his parents believed that he could ever become a top professional even after he turned pro. At age thirteen, he had been diagnosed with scoliosis, an abnormal curvature of the spine, and for four years wore a back brace for correction, although he removed it to play tennis. James attempted to hide the brace from most people by "wearing baggy clothes, but it was still apparent." He learned to joke about it.[100] His parents pushed academics, and when he was sixteen, he worried about getting a driver's license and if the "cute girls" would want to go out with him.[101]

James Blake won USTA Futures titles in Altamonte Springs, Haines City, and Clearwater, Florida, in 1999. Defeating MaliVai Washington was his first win as a professional in 1999. Thomas always had confidence in James's ability. When the family learned that Washington was to be James's first opponent, Thomas told James, "You can beat him. . . . Play your game." Washington, at age thirty, was the oldest player in the main draw. After Washington won the first set, Blake calmed down. "Once I stopped thinking about it and just had fun, I just fell into my serve and stepping into my shots and being aggressive and before you know it, good things are happening when you're just loose."[102] Another of James's major upsets came at the Hopman Cup in Perth, Australia, where he defeated Wayne Ferreira.

James Blake's match against Patrick Rafter in the third round of the hard-court tournament in Cincinnati in 2001, after having defeated Arnaud Clement in the previous round, was considered a breakthrough. In the match, he had two set points against Rafter, but ultimately lost. After the match, Blake reported what Rafter told him: "He asked me if I now believe I can beat someone like him or him."

When Blake answered, "I hope that I'm close," Rafter said, "You could have beaten me today. You could beat me on any given day. It's just that maybe you didn't believe you could. You had your chances and you didn't stick to your game." Those words were a "big boost of confidence" for James.[103]

While Andy Roddick, appointed the next big hope of "American" tennis, moved from number 160 to 27 in eight months, Blake moved to number 120 from 262 in two years. Blake explained: "[T]here've been times my game's gotten better and I haven't got the wins."[104]

In 2001, Blake competed for the United States in the Davis Cup tie against India, in which he won both of his single matches. He had some major successes in 2002. He had advanced to the semifinals in Newport in 2001, but had especially made others take notice when he played a tough five sets against Lleyton Hewitt at that year's U.S. Open. The following year at the Open, he again challenged Hewitt, but it was another losing effort. Those close challenges were problematic. People commented how great it was for him to get so close to winning. He responded, "But to be honest, that's why it hurts so much! Looking back now, I can feel good that I was playing well enough to have gotten that close, and being able to compete at that level is definitely fun." During the 2002 summer in the United States, he had moved up in the rankings by placing astonishing results on his tennis resume. He maintained that he needed to "solidify" his backhand, especially on returns, and felt he had done that by the summer.

Although the Williams sisters have been featured in many fashion layouts, Blake got his chance to do one in *Deuce,* an ATP magazine. He signed a contract with IMG Models, an offshoot of the company that manages his tennis career. Concerning fashion on the court, Blake argued, "I have never noticed who wears what. I guess no one has noticed me on that score, either! The South Americans usually take a lot of care over how they look, as do the Swedes. In fact, we Americans are probably the least-well-dressed people around!"[105]

Being the only top-ranked black American player currently on the men's tour, Blake has been compared with Ashe. Although he threw tantrums as a child to such an extreme that his coach advised that he take an extended break, he eventually became "decent, dignified, and quietly determined." He continues to throw a racket on occasion as a pro, showing more emotion than Ashe ever did. However, he demonstrated great calm during the 2001 U.S. Open match against Lleyton Hewitt, when Hewitt commented about the similarity between Blake and a black linesman after a call. Blake did not react even though people in the stadium "practically begged [him] to take offense." Also, like Ashe, he has remained humble. His college roommate Chris Stakich believes that success has made Blake more humble. Serena thinks that he could be in politics because "he says all the right things."[106]

When Blake's ranking fell from 28 in 2002 to 37 in 2003, he admitted to listening to "too many signals from too many well-intentioned sources and lost focus as a result." The most common advice was to play more consistently and less aggressively, but Blake began to play not to lose rather than to win. He began to believe that a more aggressive approach (many winners and errors) brought better results. At the 2004 Australian Open, he was plagued by an injury and early-round losses.[107]

Levar Harper-Griffith

Another possibility for the future in the late 1990s was Levar Harper-Griffith, from Brooklyn, New York, where he recalls that "[f]irst, the little kids would make fun of me. Then, the old people playing checkers, and the teenagers playing basketball. They'd say, 'Here comes Arthur Ashe.'"[108] Harper-Griffith won the 1999 Coffee Bowl in Costa Rica, defeating Jean-Julien Rojer of the Netherlands Antilles. Also in 1999, Harper-Griffith and Phillip King represented the United States in the Connolly Sunshine Cup, the ITF's official team championships for boys eighteen and younger. Harper-Griffith won the 1999 USTA National Boys' 18s doubles with Andy Roddick and turned pro in 2000.

Much was made of the fact that John McEnroe, the U.S. Davis Cup team captain, invited Harper-Griffith to travel to Zimbabwe as a practice partner. Harper-Griffith wrote of his experiences:

I understood a bit about social responsibility from my family and friends, and I've always respected the paths that Althea Gibson and Arthur Ashe blazed for people of color. My Zimbabwe experience helped me realize that though I'm only 18 and just beginning my career, I don't have to wait to contribute. Though I had seen social hardships and poverty on TV and read about suffering in newspapers, they were always a safe distance from my reality. Zimbabwe brought them up close.

John and the U.S. Tennis Association asked me to participate in a clinic at Chitonguiza, a township just outside of Harare. We traveled on dirt roads to reach the impoverished community. There was no running water. People cooked on the streets. I was moved to see these kids, hundreds of them, enjoying the tennis clinic, despite their hardships. Though many of them had no shoes or socks, they chased down balls and enjoyed themselves. Several of them asked me for my T-shirt and my tennis shoes. I understood how fortunate I was.[109]

7

The Additional Burden of the Professional Black Player

THE MAIN PRESSURE for a tennis player is generally self-imposed. An individual player decides whether she or he wants to be number 1 or in the top ten, and so on, and the eagerness to attain that goal can result in undue pressure. Marcel Freeman, a professional player, believes that focusing on rankings, specifically number 1, is an "overwhelming idea," and if a player begins "fixating on that it really becomes oppressive."[1]

For players on the satellite tour, the pressure to win has come in another form—that is, to win in order to obtain and/or to maintain sponsorship. In 1983, Chip Dorsey explained what he sought in a sponsor: "I want to find a sponsor who will have faith in my game. I will then be able to play on the Penn Circuit. I see other blacks play under a lot of pressure for only three months because they know they must win in order to maintain a sponsor and to stay on the circuit."[2]

The pressure of winning becomes more intense when players have limited funding on the satellite tour and know they must win quickly or return home. According to player Rick Davis, for a player to be successful, he or she needs three things: (1) money, (2) lots of talent shown very early to keep sponsorship, and (3) a parent or parents who can support him or her in the pursuit of success.[3]

In 1984, Marcel Freeman noted, "Black players face special pressures not encountered by most whites, ranging from funding sources of money to finding good facilities. A lot of black tennis players feel like they're up against the wall. The majority of them have a tremendous chip on their shoulder because they're black. They don't have the connections, they're not getting a fair shake, and it's one extra thing they have to overcome."[4]

In addition to all these factors, black professionals sometimes have had an added burden of "representing the race." Of course, players of other races, ethnicities, or nationalities face similar pressures, particularly if they are the only player or one of the few players of a certain race or from a certain country on the tour, or if no one from their race or country has won a major title in a long time. For example, Tim Henman has faced the pressures of winning Wimbledon because a British man has not held the title since the 1930s. The last Brit to win the covenant title was Virginia Wade in 1977. There are several examples of a player being virtually the lone representative of his or her country. For instance, Marcello Rios became a national hero for being the first Chilean to be number 1 in the ATP rankings. In this respect, even lesser-known players carry a similar burden.

The burden on black athletes, who were the first to break barriers, has been even greater. Jackie Robinson and Althea Gibson faced the pressure of having to behave in an "appropriate" manner so that whites could not use racist stereotypes as justification to continue to deny blacks' participation in sport. Closely connected has been the burden of producing great performances or developing a winning tradition. Gibson felt this very early in her tennis career. When she played in the ATA Nationals in 1944, she sensed that some of the ATA people from New York were disappointed with her performance. In her autobiography, she illuminates her response to their perception: "Maybe they thought they hadn't got their money's worth out of me because I had lost. I remember one of them saying something to the effect that they were through with me, that they didn't think much of my attitude, and I know I was a pretty dejected kid for a while."[5] Other disapproving comments followed. Prior to her success in major tournaments in 1956, an article in *Jet* referred to her as "the biggest disappointment in tennis."[6]

For black American players, any success means that both blacks and whites begin to ask if the black player in question is the next Gibson or Ashe. When no black players from the United States are available, any black player suffices. Pressure is immediately placed on them to represent the race on the professional tour and to become a top-ranked player. When Leslie Allen won the Avon Championship in Detroit in 1981, Gibson's legacy was quickly attached. Many years later, Allen wrote in response,

> There is nothing like the intensity or pressure of a singles match at a Grand Slam event. Ever since I won the Avon Championships in Detroit, I was always introduced as the first black woman in 23 years—since Althea Gibson—to win a big tournament. The luxury of being recognized simply as a top player was not an option. I saw how Arthur's play impacted people—that there was intense pride for the race with every victory and disappointment with each loss. It sometimes felt as if I were also playing for the entire race—the black fan in the stands, the worker at the club, the front-desk manager at the hotel. I felt additional pressure because I started late and was desperately trying to catch up and learn how to play the pro game.[7]

Allen never won another major championship, and the search for the next black player to take on the mantle continued. Then it was a matter of whether Zina Garrison or Lori McNeil or both could do it. McNeil was the focus when she made the semifinals of the U.S. Open in 1987. Garrison's chance came in the 1990 Wimbledon final against Navratilova.

When Chanda Rubin was asked whether there were particular expectations of her as a black tennis player, even if self-imposed, she evaded the question. Instead, she commented on how difficult it is for players from inner-city areas to have the opportunities to play and obtain good coaching.[8] Juan Farrow felt the pressure to excel both from himself and from others. He began smoking cigarettes at age nine in order to relax. MaliVai Washington responded differently when asked about following Ashe's footsteps: "It's a blessing that I've been given the ability to do what I do, and to know that people look up

Yannick Noah at the WCT finals, 1987.

to me for it. I feel honored. I don't want that honor to become a burden, so I have to take a first-things-first attitude, which is that I'm a tennis player with, hopefully lot of good years ahead of me to fulfill my potential."[9] On the men's side, Ashe left a legacy that has yet to be filled. Nevertheless, a few players have over the years been spotted as "the next Ashe," including Farrow, Harmon, Hooper, Shelton, and Washington.

Black players from countries besides the United States have experienced two types of pressures. For example, Yannick Noah not only was a hero for black fans internationally, but was also a hero for France; the French wanted a French player to win the French Open because that had not been done since 1946. When Noah won in 1983, the pressures were so great that he moved from Paris to New York. Columnist Marilyn August maintained, "Although nothing is more antithetical to Noah's nature than militantism of any kind, the dreadlocks cemented his image as the Black Folk Hero of the 1980s." She quoted Alain Giraudo, tennis writer for *Le Monde,* as arguing, "I'm very shocked at the way some Americans try to make Yannick into someone he's not. Perhaps they are looking for someone they can identify with, but it makes me very uncomfortable to see an issue being made out of his so-called 'black identity.' "[10]

Earlier in his career Noah took issue with Ashe, seeing him as "some sort of Great Black Hope" in tennis. He argued that when he lived in Cameroon and France, he never had the same problems with "being black" as Ashe had.[11]

By 1980, Noah was already seen as the "tennis savior" for the French and by twenty-two was a star for the French Davis Cup team, "the man who will lead France back to the glories last enjoyed during the days of the famed Four Musketeers in the 1920's and 1930's."[12] Noah and several young French players, including Thierry Tulasne and Pascal Portes, were expected to be in the top ten by 1982. Philippe Chatrier, the president of the ITF and the French Tennis Federation, ordered a costly renovation of the Stade Roland Garros in the mid-1970s. In 1981, journalist Richard Evans wrote, "Now, at first glance, it might seem as if the modernization program was ordered with the new Musketeers in mind. Or did Chatrier, like some conjuror producing rabbits out of a hat, bring the whole thing together with the wave of a magic wand? Save for one exceptional piece of luck, the truth is neither as mundane nor as fanciful. Noah was the luck."[13]

Noah became the first Frenchman to be ranked in the top ten in the open era. His early successes just created more pressure to revive honor and respect for France in international tennis. For Giraudo, it was legitimate for France to hang its hope of tennis rejuvenation on Noah (Giraudo did not criticize that pressure on a young player), but it was inappropriate for black Americans to see him as a black hero. Noah lamented, "In France everybody wants me to be very angry and serious, and I don't care to be. For me, it's not the main thing. I still practice very hard, and I try hard. But, you know, I like many things besides tennis, and I think that's why I'm happy now. For me, winning is not the main thing." [14]

The pressure of the fame that followed his 1983 French Open singles title caused Noah more troubles. The man who loved fans became so besieged by photographers that it was suggested that he pick up a large rock and throw it at photographers, who insisted on taking countless photographs of him and his wife of one month at Boca West in Florida. His compatriot, Henri Leconte, assessed Noah's state of mind: "I think after last summer Yannick lost his mind a little. Too many press, too much pressure and all the time too many people around him." [15]

In the fall of 1983, after having wandered in the streets of Paris "with tears in his eyes and suicide on his mind," Noah announced that he was moving to New York City. He also wished that tennis was more like a team sport, where friendships could be created, and have the excitement of a big game. Tennis "doesn't have as much color" as basketball, for example. "The independence is great, but tennis can be very lonely. The players are friendly, but a lot of it is a polite thing for all of us." [16]

Noah began to question who he was. "I began to act all day and I don't want to act. I'm sorry, but you can't be yourself when everybody is watching you. It's impossible." When he returned to Cameroon for his wedding in 1984, it was "a week of fresh air" because he was not compelled to play the "temperamental star." At that point, he realized that when he was in Cameroon, he was different. "I lose my typical European concerns and ways. I don't try right away to determine what people want from me. In Cameroon, I always feel like I only left home yesterday. The people are warm. They're direct." [17]

When similar pressures began to affect other French players who were teen sensations, it became quite a concern, especially after Noah's thoughts of suicide. Pierre Darmon, Noah's agent and head of the

Paris ProServ office, admitted that Noah's situation could not be ignored, and it was "a striking statement about the dark side of the exalted status in a country desperately searching for idols."[18]

The battle within Noah continued throughout his career on the ATP tour. A key period in his life was 1991, when he stopped playing on the ATP tour. In his autobiography, he wrote, "If playing no longer makes me so much better, it is that playing made me feel so badly. What had led me to no longer like the game, I who had adored it, I who had devoted all of my energy to it? It is interesting because I sensed that this time my thoughts would lead me to a true knowledge of myself. Then, to a form of happiness. A means of being liked for whom I really was and not for what I represented."[19]

Noah explained that he stopped playing prematurely because he was impatient to throw himself into "true life" to accept himself without a racket. "Feeling an impression of stability. I said to myself, 'Shit, but I like myself a lot without a racket!' It was a real relief."[20]

He formed a philosophy during these years, particularly relating to the athlete: "The inner athlete doesn't try to learn to detach himself from glory. He knows even to profit from it. . . . The inner athlete understands the secret of happiness: he places sport in the service of his life. And not his life in the service of a sport." Moreover, "Too many athletes translate their existence into an equation: Sacrifices = results = glory = happiness. The day when they are no longer in a position to obtain good results, they question themselves on the sense of sacrifices."[21]

Ronald Agenor of Haiti never achieved Noah's status, but early in his tennis career he realized the importance of representing his country. He explained, "People all over the world think of Haiti as a country with a lot of misery, which is not entirely true. I can show them that it is not like that. Even when I am playing as a professional, I will be like an ambassador for my country."[22]

It is impossible and unnecessary to determine how the hopes of tennis for blacks weigh on black professional tennis players as a group. Nevertheless, it is a burden that generates a continual topic of discus-

Ronald Agenor at the 2000 Eddleman USTA Challenger in Birmingham, Alabama.

sion and a common question in interviews that players might have to answer carefully.

When Juan Farrow discussed the elusive dream of a lucrative tennis career, he did not see expectations as a burden. He argued, "I never felt there was too much. . . . I was just looking over my articles and things, I've got millions of the them—'the next Arthur Ashe' and all. That's just a little ironic to me. . . . As a kid, I always used to say I wanted to be no. 1 in the world." Ashe argued, "There is a danger in expecting that without big numbers of minority players in the system. If there's only one player, that player is expected to go to the top."[23]

Many viewed MaliVai Washington as the next Ashe because he was number 1 at the University of Michigan. As with Noah, his support base was not limited to blacks in his home country. "I have a lot of support from the black community in the States and around the world, and it's great when you can win, because you're winning for yourself, and you're winning for your family, and you're kind of winning for those who are pulling for you. It's an honor to be the first black since Arthur to be in the final [Wimbledon 1996]."[24] He also admitted, "There was no pressure trying to live up to Arthur Ashe. What Arthur accomplished on and off the court was great, but I am my own person. I had my own goals and my own very high standards. The comparisons are inevitable and I appreciate the comparisons." Similarly, James Blake argued that he felt no "added pressure being an African American." He added, "It would be nice if a kid says they have James Blake to [look] up to. But I just want to play tennis."[25]

Hooper, Harmon, and Shelton also played under this pressure, or at least played with the expectation of being the next black tennis hope. This pressure has, on the men's side, been called the "Ashe syndrome." In 1984, Harmon explained, "Everyone who's ever been any good has been compared with Arthur. You're visible, everybody's looking at you, and the pressure is there." Ashe felt that this pressure was unfair to up-and-coming black players: "I think that this is an obvious comparison to make right now until we [blacks] have a greater presence in terms of numbers in the professional ranks. As soon as there are sizable numbers of black players on the pro tour, winning major titles, this will all stop."[26]

Houston's John Wilkerson commented, "The key is not one role model, but many role models. You look at Mal and that's the exception, not the rule. It's too much pressure on Mal to expect him to be the representative for all black tennis players. It's too much for one person." Washington often listed McEnroe and Connors, rather than Ashe, as tennis idols. Wilkerson said, "He respects Ashe, but does not necessarily want to be his second coming."[27] (Ironically, Ashe also named white players, not Althea Gibson, as a role model, but Ashe argued that gender had much to do with it.)

One might argue that no other black male player was available as a model for Ashe. The truth is that there *were* black male players, but they were not ranked on the professional tour. This discrepancy creates two important questions: Does one have to be a highly ranked professional player with Grand Slam titles to be a role model in tennis? And is it automatically assumed that a black player selects only other black players as role models and idols? In the 1980s, one black youth out of Cleveland, Brent Lovey, completely patterned his game after John McEnroe, his role model, despite the number of black players on the tour at the time.

Oftentimes, the hopes of having another black player to do well in the professional ranks have created unreal or unfair expectations and undue criticisms when the player loses, which he or she will inevitably do at one point or another. A simple loss for the individual, however, becomes a great loss for a race of people. Add to this the pressure of winning—particularly in a country such as the United States, where winners are loved—and one can easily lose fans or the respect of fans by failing to be a winner or to become number 1. Ashe was unaware that some blacks expected him to be "a winner." After he lost a certain televised match, he received a postcard from a black fan that instructed him to get out of the game because "we can't afford to have any losers so visible."[28]

Historian Sterling Stuckey explains, "The black athlete is like the black poet in that he is able to do something—in this case on the field—that the Negro is not able to do off the field, or in life in general." The nation that some black athletes represent has been based on the identity of race, which extends beyond the boundaries of one country. "Behind every victory, every knockout of a white boxer and every new sprint record and every long run from scrimmage, Negroes saw a tiny step forward for Negroes in their everyday relations with the white majority." In short, "they tended to regard individual achievements as progress for the race as a whole."[29]

For most black tennis players, their "racial" identity has been the focus instead of their nationality; of course, Noah had to weather the emphasis on both. Mark Mathabane, a South African player, explains that when Ashe won in South Africa, "blacks all over the country rejoiced, including those who knew nothing about tennis. Ashe's triumphs on the court were becoming triumphs for the black race."[30]

Sociologist Harry Edwards argues, "Sports provide the black fan with the illusion of spiritual reinforcement in his own life struggles. This reinforcement comes from the common values that the general society and sports share. In accordance with these values, which place an exaggerated emphasis on individual achievement, each person is presumed to be accountable for his failures and to deserve rewards and status when he succeeds." He adds that the sports fan has found that the success of a favorite team or athlete "reinforces his faith in those values that define established and legitimate means of achievement. He returns from the game to his job or his community reassured that his efforts will eventually be successful."[31] For black fans, institutionalized racism and discrimination have presented additional obstacles for personal achievement, so they have identified more directly with black athletes. When Jim Crow was blatant and pervasive in the United States, each victory by Johnson, Louis, or Gibson was a victory for blacks.

In tennis, Ashe was exceptional. Other black players attempted to avoid the issue of race or race politics until they were directly affected by racism. Althea Gibson said in an interview, "I was breaking into USTLA tennis, but I couldn't just think of being the first black female to do this. I had to think of playing decently and winning. Winning, to me, is the key. You play to win."[32]

Unlike Ashe, Evonne Goolagong did not welcome this role, although she compared herself to Ashe in that they both were represented in print by their race, not just by their profession. In her memoir, she states, "The press, obviously, has hammered away at my origins: it's a good story. I'm the first Aborigine in tennis and one of a few to win a world championship in any sport. . . . I was very embarrassed by the publicity because I knew I was getting it on the basis of color, not ability. I was a freak."[33] She maintains, "Anybody could see I was aboriginal. I'm honored to have made the Aboriginal breakthrough in tennis, and I hope many more follow, but there comes a time when that constant racial identification should be dropped, as Arthur Ashe, the American black, requested a few years ago. He was always being referred to as a Negro tennis star."[34]

Everyone, however, failed to view her as "black" in the same manner as they viewed Ashe. For example, in the historiography of tennis, Goolagong has not been labeled as "black"; instead, she has been included in the discussion of the white mainstream of tennis. In fact, in 1973 Ashe was credited with being the first black player to compete against whites in South Africa even though Goolagong had competed there in 1971 and 1972 because writers did not view her as "black." In fact, she defeated Virginia Wade in the finals of the South African Open in 1972, becoming the first black player to win that major tournament.

When Noah's critics in Cameroon complained that he never publicly recognized Africa, that he had forsaken his heritage and had "not paid his dues to his people," Noah responded that he "never had a problem being Black," but that the Cameroon Federation had never helped him because his mother was white. He added, "Then they want me to say they helped me. It is too late. I have no responsibility to a race or to a country. Just to my family." Leslie Allen, in contrast, was viewed as an athlete who was "quite conscious of the significant role" she played as a black professional athlete. "Whether I want them or not," she was quoted as saying, "I've got responsibilities to the general public and to the Black public."[35]

Despite the fact that some blacks have refused to play the role of black hero, even if they have been willing to play the role of a general hero, the former role has been a definite factor in sports, especially in those sports with fewer black participants. Examples from the United States, Surinam, Jamaica, and France have included: Tiger Woods in golf; Anthony Nesty and Anthony Ervin in Olympic swimming;[36] Debbie Thomas and Surya Bonaly in ice figure skating; Peter Westbrook in fencing; Cheryl Daniels and Kim Terrell in bowling; Willy T. Ribbs in car racing; the Jamaican bobsled team; and Charles Marks in offshore powerboat racing. Even in the sports where blacks supposedly dominate, the same development occurs. Those blacks who played the quarterback position when it was believed to be a "thinking" and "leadership" position (and thus suited only to a white man) had the pressure of representing the race by proving that blacks could perform well in that role. In short, "the successful black athlete stimulates black people's individual hopes for eventually competing successfully as *equals* in society."[37]

The problem has been compounded even more in sports dominated by whites. Even when some blacks have no interest in a certain sport, they cheer, pray, and hope for the success of any black who wades unchartered waters in that sport. For example, blacks with absolutely no interest in golf began watching televised golf tournaments in which Woods played.

In football, basketball, and even baseball, there have been enough blacks in the leagues so that the burden of representation has not fallen on one or two players. However, that has been difficult in tennis and other sports. Sometimes the burden has been so heavy that black players have had to monitor how they conduct themselves much more so than have white athletes, not just because of racial stereotyping, but also because of race pride.

One writer for *ESPN the Magazine* explained what Cathy Freeman of Australia faced in the 2000 Olympics: "For whites, Freeman is the face of the Olympics, representing an opportunity to resurrect a dismal track and field program on the world's stage. But for Aborigines, who didn't even win the right to vote until 1962, her success means so much more." [38]

Black athletes have also been expected to show some connection with *the* black community by being vocal on social or political issues. White players have had the luxury of ignoring political issues if they desire. Ashe once wrote, "Most of them could care less about apartheid in South Africa; South Africa is just another tennis tournament, like Sweden or Tucson." However, for Ashe, South Africa was an issue. He sensed that "[s]ome blacks—and some whites too—get mad at me because they feel that I don't make enough waves. You'd be amazed how often I hear that I'm not arrogant enough. But how in hell is that going to help—particularly in my situation where I am a single black surrounded by whites. There are many ways of accomplishing things in the white world without compromising integrity." [39]

He also knew that he endured more pressure because he was the only major black player in professional tennis: "My own case is complicated by the fact that I'm the only one. I am *the* black tennis player, a block by myself. Some black basketball player or black minister or black educator can announce a decision much easier than I because he does not carry the weight of his whole community."[40]

In 1968, the image of Tommie Smith and John Carlos on the Olympic medal rostrum raising one black-gloved fist in the air in a black power salute in protest against blatant racism in the United States became the most powerful image of black protest in the world of sport. Later in the games, Larry James, Lee Evans, and Ron Freeman, three black sprinters who swept the four-hundred-meter, also raised their arms in a black power salute when receiving their medals. Smith and Carlos were suspended from the U.S. team, and the reason given was that they made their salute during the playing of the national anthem. Smith and Carlos did not gain from their act, but their actions made a powerful statement to blacks, although most black athletes have lacked the courage to do what they did. The treatment they received after their act of defiance probably did much in guaranteeing that such actions would rarely be repeated on the world stage of sports.

Commenting on the Afro-Caribbean and Asian political struggles in Great Britain in the mid-1990s, several writers argued that "in comparison with the 1968 Black Power demonstrations at the Mexico Olympic Games, political mobilization through sport has not been high on the agenda of community groups in Britain."[41]

Highly visible black personalities have been expected to give their voice to political issues involving blacks. It has mattered little that many have been poorer choices to voice the concerns of black communities. Those highly visible personalities who have failed to voice their opinion on social issues have been criticized, even Michael Jordan. In some instances, other athletes have criticized "the silent majority" in sports. One Chicago-based writer attacked Navratilova because she raised this issue about Jordan in *Conde Nast Sports for Women*. She stated, "He's almost a textbook case of being politically ambiguous, especially when he knows his words are being recorded and his actions photographed. He seems to have the knack of saying little—while collecting big checks—down pat."[42]

Ashe rarely avoided the opportunity to comment on politics in tennis or the world. He not only commented on the racial problems in the United States, but was a leader in the struggle against apartheid in South Africa and vocal about the colonial status in other countries of southern Africa. After his medical condition as it related to AIDS was made public, he became an advocate for AIDS awareness. Although being an advocate for victims of some diseases is not a problem, being an advocate for AIDS awareness might be difficult because of the stigma, stereotypes, and prejudices attached to the disease, causing highly visible personalities to weigh the possible sacrifices they must make for supporting AIDS agencies and victims.

Gibson, however, was the opposite of Ashe. In her autobiography, she carefully attempts to absolve her decision to remain silent on racism:

> I have never regarded myself as a crusader. . . . I don't consciously beat the drum for any special cause, not even the cause of the Negro in the United States, because I feel that our best chance to advance is to prove ourselves as individuals. That way, when you are accepted, you are accepted voluntarily, because people appreciate you and respect you and want you, not because you have been shoved down their throats. This doesn't mean that I'm opposed to the fight for integration of the schools or other movements like that. It simply means that in my own career I try to steer clear of political involvements and make my way as Althea Gibson, private individual.[43]

Gibson's analysis lacks historical accuracy; blacks had already proven themselves as individuals, but that did little to change general racial perception. In addition, being accepted in the world of tennis was far from being generally accepted as an individual by anyone outside of tennis and very far from other blacks being accepted in society. Although some whites might relish hugging a sweaty black athlete after a game or snuggling a dirty, sweaty jersey or shirt worn by that athlete, they may also refuse to touch an anonymous black man, even though he is meticulously dressed and profoundly sophisticated in all of the accepted social graces defined by their society.

Gibson commented that the press took issue with her stance. "I am not a racially conscious person. I don't want to be. I see myself as just an individual. . . . I'm a tennis player, not a Negro tennis player. . . . I try not to flaunt my success as a Negro psyches [*sic*]. It's all right for others to make a fuss over my role as a trail blazer." Perhaps her attitude stemmed from her feeling of inclusion: "As far as the color question is concerned, I have no feeling of exclusion any more," she explained. "At least, I don't feel I'm being excluded from anything that matters." [44]

In a way, black athletes have faced extra pressures to participate in public political conversations on race issues because black points of view have been limited in mainstream media. Blacks feel that the few who have access to public forum have a responsibility to speak for other blacks. Writer Lawrence O. Graham disagrees: "I'm not a rap singer with a tenth-grade education. I'm not a professional basketball player with my own line of sneakers. . . . As black people, we have allowed too many unqualified, ill-equipped individuals to take the reins of authority from intelligent, thoughtful black spokespeople." Graham asserts that the black community's willingness "to make leaders out of irresponsible and thoughtless black celebrities is a character flaw that could continue to undermine our ability to progress beyond media grandstanding and move to a point where our leaders provide intelligent analysis of and practical solutions to our problems." [45] In addition, the media have spotlighted these black personalities more readily than their white counterparts.

The black athlete, then, has had to decide between speaking on the issues and not saying or doing anything that might affect his or her endorsement possibilities. For many who have avoided vocalizing their political views, it has been assumed that endorsement has had much to do with that decision.

Despite the argument that athletes should leave political issues to more qualified individuals, the community has expected to hear their voices. Goolagong has been criticized for refusing to involve herself by becoming a spokesperson for the Aboriginal political movements. She claims that "she is unqualified to discuss the issues and too busy with tennis and her family to afford the time." Even though she was silent about racism in Australia as she played under that banner as a professional, she became more vocal about racism after she retired. Of course, the timing made the shift seem like a professionally expedient thing to do.

Runner Cathy Freeman has taken a different approach. The track and field star has been vocal about the racism in her homeland. Prior to the 2000 Summer Olympics in Sydney, Cathy Freeman and Nova Peris-Kneebone received attention in the international media. Freeman also initially avoided politics in public, but decided to criticize the Australian government for being "insensitive" to the Aborigines in its failure to "formally apologize for the so-called Stolen Generation," referring to the Aboriginal children taken from their parents between 1920 and 1970 and institutionalized in the name of forced assimilation. Peris-Kneebone decided to postpone her involvement in politics, citing, "I want to have more kids. Politics is something you can always get involved in."[46]

In the United States, another political issue brewed in 1999 when southern states insisted on flying the Confederate flag at state buildings. Many blacks feel that the flag is a symbol of white supremacy and slavery, not merely a sign of southern heritage, as southern supporters have claimed, although that very heritage was largely based on racism and slavery. Some black American athletes supported the NAACP in its efforts to force the state governments to remove the flags. Larry Johnson encouraged the New York Knicks not to train in South Carolina, and the team pulled out of a preplayoff draft camp in Charleston. South Carolina collegiate coaches Lou Holt, Eddie Fogler, Tommy Bowden, and Larry Shyatt marched in support of removal of the flag. The National Association of Basketball Coaches joined the Black Coaches Association in calling for the NCAA to remove its men's basketball regional from Greenville in 2000 if the flag was not removed from a state building there. Serena Williams, scheduled to play in the 2000 Family Circle Cup in Hilton Head Island, South Carolina, withdrew from the tournament. "My decision to not play in South Carolina was based on a much deeper issue and one that I feel strongly about."[47]

Larry Johnson added, "Knowing what [the flag] means to people and me being black, I don't need to be in that state." Tennis player Alexandra Stevenson, however, decided to play in the Hilton Head tournament, and the local politicians exploited her presence. For example, she met South Carolina governor Jim Hodges to discuss the issue, which made headlines. She stated, "This could be resolved if more people came and shared their thoughts. I decided to stand up and come to the tournament because I'm coming in to do my job and to have a voice." It remained unclear what that "voice" was, though. She added that she desired to "work alongside all races." Her voice was soon silenced as she lost in the first round. Meanwhile, the WTA decided that "continuing its presence in South Carolina is a more positive approach." WTA tour CEO Bart McGuire argued, "The community has always welcomed our ethnically, racially and geographically diverse roster of players, staff and sponsors. We view the staging of such an event as evidence that people of all walks of live can work and live far better together than they can apart."[48]

Another burden has been whether the black athlete has done enough for the black community. Ashe was criticized for doing too little to help other blacks in professional tennis. Although he was working to maintain a career himself, others expected him single-handedly to promote other juniors. According to journalist Doug Smith, Ashe supported Farrow throughout his junior years, but Farrow felt that the support was insufficient and argued, "I just feel that Arthur feels that I'm not the kind of guy that he would like to see up there. I'm not the one to do the smiling, the patting on the back and going about saying things the way he would. I think that could be the reason why he's not helping me. He probably thinks I get high all the time. . . . Maybe not. I don't know." Coach Sydney Llewelyn argued that Ashe kept the doors closed to blacks and only "gave a handout here or there." Player Horace Reid claimed that "you can't get anywhere with the big corporations unless Arthur OKs you" and reportedly accused Ashe of killing a deal for him with Marlboro. Ashe responded to criticisms that Robert Johnson Jr. levied at him in a 1975 issue of *Black Sports:* "I do feel a tremendous sense of peer pressure and racial ethnic pressure to contribute and I do. It's not so much a debt I owe. That's something I don't adhere to anymore. I don't like being made to feel guilty." He was frustrated by this pressure and attested, "It really burns me up when blacks *expect* me to have certain preordained interests." He felt that blacks (whoever they were) expected him to focus on blacks in junior tennis: "As people outline my life for me, I should spend most of every day sticking rackets into young black kids' hands." And he pointed out that nobody ever asked Stan Smith why he was not helping poor little Presbyterian white kids to play tennis.[49] After his death, his wife, Jeanne Moutoussamy-Ashe, argued, "People criticize athletes today, like Tiger Woods, for not taking a stand on issues. . . . Arthur was criticized too. People wanted him to do more in the '60s, to join the fight."[50]

More recently, black tennis professionals, like several of their white counterparts, have made sure that they have participated in tennis clinics where "minorities" are present, and it has not hurt that pictures of them at the clinics have been posted in tennis publications and on tennis Web sites. It has helped black professional athletes as a group or as individuals to be seen running clinics for white children, although they have rarely been seen doing the same for black children. In addition, images, spread by television and print ads, depicting black athletes with white youths have enhanced public perception of those athletes. For example, a picture of a former black professional doing a clinic in Washington, D.C., featured only young white players, which seems strange given that the city has a majority black population.[51] Oftentimes, these images have been marketed for the benefit of the white fan base, while ignoring how the black fan base will react or taking the black tennis segment for granted.

Pressure concerning strategic images has been related to being a role model. Each individual black athlete in tennis has been automatically selected as a role model regardless of whether he or she wants to assume that role. When black players have been asked about being a role model for the general tennis population rather than functioning as one just for the black tennis population or the black community, the individual answers have differed. Even when athletes in tennis and other sports have refused to accept this role (e.g., Charles Barkley), some whites in the media have still pushed the issue. In a paternalistic fashion, several white journalists have insisted on determining which black athletes have become bona fide "role models" and "leaders," as if blacks are unable to select their own role models and leaders. For instance, Rubin was depicted as such in a leading magazine article: "Rubin is quickly becoming a role model, particularly for African American youngsters." Apparently, this decision was made because "she speaks at as many clinics as her busy schedule permits." [52]

When the white-controlled media have attempted to decide who is to be role models for blacks, rarely have they asked black people. When Charles Barkley argued that he was not a role model to a child he did not know or had not seen, sports journalists criticized him, but he made a valid point. In tennis, the real role models are those teachers and coaches who have worked with black youths on a daily basis, not someone who signed an autograph or conducted a clinic just because he or she won a tournament.

On the other side of the coin has been the trend in the sports media to select certain athletes as heroes or "role models," then to publicize any negative aspect of those athletes' personal lives, so that youths become hyperaware of the negative situations. Role models are expected to win and to be number 1. Other expectations are attached only when the athlete has proven that he or she has the winning formula. In general, journalists allow most top athletes the time to acquire these other essential qualities, but these same journalists will mark a black in tennis as a role model right away merely because he or she is the best black player available. For instance, when Washington and Agenor retired from tennis, Steve Campbell was the top-ranking black player, and he began to get more press. As soon as the Williams sisters began to win on the tour, however, rarely did anyone speak of Campbell anymore, and the Williams sisters were then seen as the formula to bring numbers of blacks into tennis.

8

Racism in Tennis

IN 1991, THE PUBLICATION of an article titled "Charges of Racism Now a Tennis Problem" was ironic because racism had by then already been an old phenomenon in tennis. Racism has existed for a long time in the history of sports—from aggressive segregation to very subtle, institutionalized discrimination. Nevertheless, sports have been credited with improving race relations. In his book *The Black Athlete*, Jack Olsen asserts, "Every morning the world of sports wakes up and congratulates itself on its contributions to race relations. The litany has been repeated so often that it is believed almost universally."[1]

Segregation and Isolation in Tennis

Many in tennis organizations have liked to think that racism has been eroded in the sport. Although these organizations have been unable to monitor the attitudes of each participant, racism has been lodged in the organizations, the players, the fans, and the larger society. For instance, when Doc Johnson took five black juniors to Charlottesville in 1958, rather than the usual two, it was a major step in the South. The following year his team was invited to stay overnight with white players in a campus dormitory and allowed to use campus facilities. Although the organization did its part in effecting change, participants failed to accept change. According to Charles Brown, a member of Doc's team, they arrived late the first night, and the white guys were asleep. "When we woke up the next morning, we were the only ones there. They had moved their beds out." Although the black juniors had passes to the theater, they had to sit upstairs. Sometimes a black junior was the only one in a USLTA event, and white parents cheered when the black player made mistakes and rooted for him to lose. In recent years, class has often overshadowed race. Class has always been a determining factor in tennis, and the sport early became a defining attribute of the upper class. "Even during the depths of the Depression, tennis remained an upper-class game supported by society's elite, not only in the United States, but in other parts of the world."[2] Moreover, "[t]ennis amounts to the sort of outdoor Esperanto perfected by the spry, cosmopolitan bunch of young men and women who in white clothes and becoming suntans buzz around the world to play it."[3] In multiracial societies, where race has historically been inextricably tied to class, blacks have been considered by the very nature of racial identity to be in the lowest rung of society. Therefore, even black elites were barred from exclusive clubs. For example, Ralph Bunche, chief of the United Nation's Division of Trusteeship, and his son were rejected by the West Side Tennis Club at Forest Hills, although the club later grudgingly accepted them.[4]

From the beginning, the USLTA practiced racial segregation. Chapter 1 outlined the racism that Reginald Weir and Gerald Norman Jr. faced. In 1950, Althea Gibson was denied entry in the New Jersey State Championship at the Maplewood Country Club. "Not enough information" was the official explanation. In her autobiography, Gibson laments, "In tennis parlance, that means the applicant hasn't played in enough recognized tournaments to qualify. There was no doubt about that, but the $64 question was how was I going to be able to prove 'enough information' if they didn't let me play in any of their tournaments?"[5]

Player Gladys Heldman argued that Gibson was also denied the opportunity to play at the Essex Country Club in the early 1950s.[6] Although Gibson won two Grand Slam titles, Maidstone Club on Long Island discontinued its tournament rather than accept her entry.[7]

The barring of Gibson from tournaments at exclusive clubs and the USTA National Championships proved that segregation was not a

practice limited to the South. Tennis player Alice Marble wrote an editorial to *American Lawn Tennis* in 1950 questioning USLTA racial
practice. When she asked the USLTA committee about it, they claimed
that Gibson had not "sufficiently proven herself." They admitted that
she was a finalist in the National Indoors, but they also attempted to
downplay this achievement by arguing that the competition had been
weak. Marble's response expressed another view: "It is my opinion that
Miss Gibson performed beautifully under the circumstances. Considering how little play she has had in top competition, her win over a seasoned veteran like Midge Buck seems to me a real triumph." The
committee insisted that Gibson had to make a strong showing in the
major eastern tournaments to qualify for the nationals. However, most
of these major tournaments were by invitation only. The committee
expected that she would not be invited, which would render it impossible for her to prove herself. Marble responded, "If the field of sports
has got to pave the way for all of civilization, let's do it. At this moment
tennis is privileged to take its place among the pioneers for a true
democracy, if it will accept that privilege. . . . The entrance of Negroes
into national tennis is an inevitable as it has proven to be in baseball, in
football, or in boxing; there is no denying so much talent."[8]

In a subsequent issue of the publication, Gibson wrote a response
to Marble's editorial. In part, she wrote,

> I am elated over the opportunity I had to play at Forest Hills, but
> I am sorry for the slurs you received and the friends you lost. I do
> believe you gained more true respectful friends than you lost by
> writing the very fine article you wrote on my behalf in the Tennis
> magazine. . . .
>
> Miss Marble, if you find things really tough, imagine how I find
> them. I wanted to play other tournaments; Mr. Frances and Mr.
> Baker tried to get applications for me to play in them. Some gave ap-
> plications, some promised to send them, but . . . forgot.[9]

Afterward, Gibson was accepted to play at New Jersey's Maplewood Country Club, at Orange Lawn Tennis Club in South Orange,

New Jersey, and in the USLTA National Clay Court Championships in Chicago. ATA officers had worked to get Gibson accepted at Orange and Chicago. Arthur Francis, the assistant to Bertram Baker of the ATA, sent a note to the Maplewood officials who sought to keep Gibson out of the tournament, attacking the association's "snobbishness, prejudice, and bad judgement."[10]

Once the race barrier was broken, the USLTA instituted a "quota system" to control the numbers of blacks participating in the tournaments. However, when this news was revealed at the ATA Nationals, some ATA members strongly objected.[11] In addition, the only way blacks could play at Forest Hills was through a recommendation by the ATA.

In 1952, Gibson was denied entry to the National Doubles at Boston's Longwood Cricket Club. Hal Fenerty, former member and director of the club and member of the National Doubles Committee, argued that Gibson was permitted to play at Longwood and accused Gladys Heldman of making false statements. Heldman, however, maintained that when she entered the National Doubles with Gibson at Longwood in 1952, Gibson was "turned down," and Heldman had to play "with a pickup partner, Jean Clarke." It was not until five years later that Gibson's entry was accepted at Longwood.[12]

The top women's invitation grass tournament in East Hampton, the Woodin Cup Championship, was abruptly canceled in 1953 when Gibson was scheduled to compete. Certain USLTA officials refused to have a black player in the tournament, and it was folded.[13]

Angela Buxton, who played doubles with Gibson, explained that she chose to play with Gibson because of her own experiences as a Jew. "As a winner of the Jewish Olympics, known as the Maccabiah Games, it became public knowledge early in my career that I was of the Jewish faith. . . . I invariably found myself on the receiving end of unexplainable situations. . . . That is one of the reasons I initially befriended Althea Gibson when I saw her isolated, as she was always made to feel in tennis circles."[14]

In discussing continuing racism in tennis, reporter Bob Davis recently asked the question, "How can anyone misinterpret this pattern of behavior that spans more than four decades?" He answered that it is those who attack people who have spoken against the inequities in tennis. He added,

> There is an abundance of proof that black Americans were denied an equal opportunity to play tennis. I don't suggest that any reparations are necessary or that the current administration is accountable to the past. However, the anger of those who have been deprived must be recognized and understood. It should not be beyond the grasp of any present USTA member to recognize that his/her governing body willingly played a role in this discrimination. The USTA was designated by Congress to be the governing body of tennis for all Americans, and in many respects, it failed to represent all of us equally. These are facts, not accusations charged with anger; just historical snapshots.[15]

In 1960, at the Biltmore Hotel in New York, several athletes and journalists convened to discuss blacks in sports: Gibson; Bill Davis, the Negro national tennis champion; Buddy Young, an Illinois professional football star; Sam Lacy of the Baltimore *Afro-American;* and Larry Doby, a baseball player, participated. Davis complained about the fact that merely four blacks played at Forest Hills that year, arguing, "Unfortunately, the USLTA still goes to the Negro Association for their selections. I think of course, Negroes should play their way into the Nationals on merit, the way everybody else does. Now it's more on personal recommendation." He maintained that the USLTA allowed only five blacks to participate in the USLTA Nationals, but added, "But after all, that's good progress. What's more, there are now only about two or three tournaments outside the South that haven't invited Negroes." [16]

According to Gibson's sister-in-law Rosemary Darben, "Althea was the one who got the N-word [*nigger*] hollered at her during matches. She went through hell." Bertram Baker recalled that when Gibson played at the U.S. Nationals against A. Louise Brough, some white fans were shouting, "Beat the nigger, beat the nigger." [17] During her career, Gibson often deemphasized the role of racism in tennis, but she was more vocal when she faced discrimination in the golf world. Administrators at certain courses refused to let her play, and others forbade her to change her clothes or eat in the clubhouses. When Lennie Wirtz, a white director of the Ladies' Golf Association, "made it clear to the golf-course owners that they had to accept all players or none at all," Gibson noticed that "Things have been a little bit better since then." [18]

Arthur Ashe's first experience of racism in tennis came as a youth when he attempted to enter a city tennis tournament in Richmond, Virginia, where he was denied entry. As a pro, he played at clubs that normally admitted "members of his race only as waiters and locker-room attendants." The signs of racism were more apparent beyond the tennis grounds. For instance, he was barred from a Charlottesville movie house when he went there with white players Cliff Buchholz, Charlie Pasarell, and Butch Newman. Ashe said, "What do you want me to do, paint myself with white wash?" All the players promptly walked out behind him." [19]

In 1988, Ashe commented, "Given the same chance as others have had, blacks would dominate our sport as they have done in other sports." Of course, this statement is counterfactual, for it is impossible to demonstrate just how far blacks could have advanced in tennis by the close of the second millennium without segregation, discrimination, and sexism in the process. Even so, it has been argued that one major reason for racial discrimination was that white athletes feared "competing on an equal basis with blacks." Just as "whites only" signs appeared in the South, segregation existed at many tennis facilities in other parts of the country, South Africa, and African "colonies." As one writer argued, the "whites only" sign did not mean tennis clothing. [20]

Racism defined tennis in the segregated United States, segregated Australia, colonial Africa, and apartheid South Africa from the time the sport was introduced in these areas. In an attempt to segregate the races socially and physically, blacks were forced to play tennis at separate facilities, in separate tournaments, and in separate neighborhoods.

As a result, they generally used inferior facilities while attempting to master the game.

In the 1970s, when Jimmie McDaniel was in his sixties, he played at some of the same clubs that had denied entry to him when he was younger. He argued, "It's really ironic. Here are these same people who wouldn't let me into their clubs before. Now I am seemingly accepted. There's no open hostility. But you still know the people feel the same. They haven't changed at all. They don't fool me. I know people, darn it." Moreover, he felt that racism had affected not only his spirits, but his tennis. "I say that I'm not bitter, but I do know that my experience has done something to me. I know it has affected me. Even in my tennis game, when I play and lose, I say 'So what.' Maybe I am conditioned to expect to lose. I don't have the real do-or-die spirit any more."[21]

After Evonne Goolagong-Crawley moved to Sydney and was playing an interclub league match, she heard the word *nigger* for the first time. She and Tricia Edwards, her coach's daughter, defeated two older white women. When they approached the net to shake hands, one of the women "glared . . . , her eyes fierce beneath those plucked eyebrows," and "growled, 'That's the first time I ever lost to a little nigger.' When Tricia started crying, and explained that she was doing so because the woman had hurt her sister, the woman replied, 'She's not your sister!' "[22]

In the 1980s, one writer noted, "While the blatant racism of the past may be gone from tennis—the computer doesn't care about a players' color—the discrimination of today manifests itself in more subtle ways, according to a number of black players." These subtle ways included not selecting a black junior for a traveling team, overlooking a black pro for an exhibition held at a private club, focusing a newspaper article on white players only, and calling out racist names at tournaments. Many tournaments have been played at "old-line, upper-crust clubs where black players may be tolerated rather than welcomed." Player Rodney Harmon claimed, "You get the feeling at some clubs that people just don't want you there."[23]

When Stacey Martin was sixteen and playing in Largo, Maryland, the chair umpire was black. The mother of the white opponent asked the tournament director to remove the umpire because she claimed he was favoring Stacey. Later in the match, "he was rotated out of the chair and into a linesman position," despite a USTA rule that an umpire is to remain in the chair for the duration of a match unless a supervisor finds fault with him or her, in which case he or she should be removed from the match entirely.[24]

Rick Davis realizes that he faced far less racism than his father's generation. He explains, "My father played pro baseball with the Cubs organization. The stories he told me about the things he went through in the 1950s, I didn't have to go through. I can sit in a restaurant now, and he couldn't when he traveled with the team. In situations he had to wait on the bus while the team went to eat and they had to bring him food." Despite social advancements between generations, racist attitudes persisted. Davis recalls white juniors making racist remarks to him while he was on the court. During a match he played when he was around fourteen years old, one white kid asked him questions such as, "I didn't know you people played tennis; did you pay to be in this tournament; do you know who your daddy is?" Davis become so angry that he and the kid got into a scuffle on the court.[25]

Otis Sadler had an experience very similar to Davis's when he was playing the Boys' 16s in a tournament held in Burnie, Texas, in 1987. Sadler was leading the number 1 seed, a Canadian player, who screamed, "I can't believe I'm losing to this fucking nigger!" The players exchanged words, and Sadler wanted to fight, but his mother told him to "shut up and go play tennis."[26]

Rodney Harmon also faced racism on the amateur level, which helped to prepare him for similar situations on the professional circuit. Racism on the professional tour was not a new experience, although it was difficult to "separate racism from the typical coolness of fellow pros." Harmon asked and responded, "Is there racism in tennis? People naturally gravitate to someone who is like them. Someone who is different definitely is an outsider. Unfortunately, with minorities—because the numbers are not as big—someone can feel alienated. I don't think there's out-and-out racism. But things can happen that are insensitive to minorities." Bryan Shelton commented, "When I first started out on tour I found it difficult to get practice partners. . . . I'm not sure if every player feels that way when you first start out. . . . I always gave people the benefit of the doubt. I do know for certain I was helped along by some of the black players out there . . . like Zina Garrison and Lori McNeil." Since integration of the USLTA, institutional racism has replaced overt practices on the professional circuit. Todd Nelson admitted, "Most of the racism I've encountered is under the surface. If you're looking for it, you feel it. It's there in the scheduling of matches, the practice court time and the balls you're given. But if I get a bad break on the court—like a bad line call—I don't think it's because I'm black."[27]

Sports journalists and scholars have often discussed racism. According to Lawrence M. Kahn, professor of economics and labor industrial relations, "Economists and the public at large have become increasingly interested in the issue of discrimination in professional sports."[28] Some sports still have the reputation of being games for whites, including golf, swimming, fencing, offshore boat racing, hockey, and tennis. In 1990, the exclusionary membership policy at the Shoal Creek Country Club in Birmingham, Alabama, created some public awareness of racism in tennis.

Player Katrina Adams sees a difference between Europeans and Americans. "Only in the USA is race a major issue. The Europeans are so diverse that seeing a black is not a threat. In the USA, seeing blacks succeed is a threat."[29] But according to MaliVai Washington, the only times he felt that there were "instances when something occurred that a reasonable person might say there was some racial bias [were] with the press in Germany and South Africa."[30]

Of course, racism has existed in other countries even if it has not concerned black Americans. Blacks in nations such as South Africa and Zimbabwe have continually faced racism although they constitute a majority in those countries. Blacks have accounted for a large segment of the population in Great Britain and France, but their existence in tennis has been almost nonexistent. To date, France has produced one prominent, professional black player, Yannick Noah, and even his entry into the French Tennis Federation was promoted by Ashe. Another French player, Bertrand Liger, who is white, maintains that he has never faced a black player in a tournament in France although he has seen a few blacks play recreational tennis and club tennis.[31] In 1996, at a Reebok junior challenge at the National Training Center at Roland Garros, where Noah supervised a clinic, virtually all of the participants were white.[32] Despite France's terrible record in professional black players, French writers have criticized the United States in discussing the gap between whites and blacks, between rich and poor there, while ignoring the same issues in their own country.

A 1992 *Tennis* (France) magazine feature article about tennis in New York City focused on how poverty affected blacks in tennis. One photo showed a black boy standing by a fire hydrant and holding an old tennis racket. The article mentioned Antonio Garcia Rodriguez, a Dominican, who came to the United States for a better life, but was killed in 1989 by a "drug addict in want of 'crack' and money." Also mentioned was his son, Juan Garcia, who played tennis at the Hoe Community Center.[33] Ironically, this article focused on several negative aspects of neighborhoods close to Flushing Meadows, the premier tennis facility in the United States.

Some black Americans have believed that racism has not existed in France, at least not to the degree that it has in the United States, so that they run to Paris to escape it. There are two ironies in this perception. First, France failed to extend its democratic philosophy to the colonies in Africa, and many Africans living in France have experienced profound racism. However, the black Americans who have insisted that racism has been absent in France apparently never realized that perhaps they were treated differently because they were Americans or because they were celebrities, but that black Africans, especially Muslims, have not been welcomed in the same way. After the war for independence in Algeria in 1962, many white Algerians of European origin migrated to southern France and maintained a negative attitude toward Arabs/Maghrebians. Novelist Leila Sebbar, born in Africa to an Algerian father and French mother, used racist themes in her Sherazade series, outlining generational conflict and social issues faced by children of those from the Maghrib. Azouz Begag, who was born in Lyon to Algerian parents, writes of the racial prejudice and humiliation he experienced at school in France.[34]

Tyler Stovall, author of *Paris Noir*, explains, "The blacks who came to Paris after 1944 were not only different people, but frequently different *kinds* of people. Those engaged in creative endeavors still typified the community as a whole." According to Stovall, many noted the prejudice in France, but it targeted "the poor and unassimilated from the nation's former colonies." The middle-class black Americans appeared to tolerate a racism that placed "greater importance on social class," thereby excluding them from the very base of French racist reaction. Even with the emergence of black pride and global afrocentric philosophies, the racism heaped on the blacks from Africa and on Arabs in France has done little to change the false notion that France has been a hotbed of liberalism and a place of refuge for black Americans, who have received France's version of a "honorary white" policy. Not all black Americans have shared that feeling of total liberty in Paris. According to Jennifer Bullock, who worked for a student exchange program in France, some say that racism "is worse here [in France], and in a way it is, because it is accepted. I mean, if you look at the street cleaners, they're all African."[35]

Stan Franker, former top collegiate tennis player, saw major differences in attitudes between white Americans and white Europeans. "I already had lived in Europe for six years. I could walk into a room and know exactly who was a white European and who was a white American." The key was the body language. "The American would check you out first, and would open up to you only after he realized you were a nice guy or educated. But the European didn't have any experience with blacks so he would treat you without preconceptions." In Franker's eyes, Europeans lacked the racism of white Americans, but in general racism has often been less of a factor when few blacks are present in a particular locale. Even Franker admits that the lack of apprehension about blacks in Holland was because there were few blacks in the country in 1981. "Things have changed now, though, because the increasing black population has altered the attitude of the people. The minorities are getting blamed for the bad economy." [36]

Blacks in Great Britain and France have played football (soccer), and even African immigrants have played on their teams. For several years, blacks have participated on these countries' professional and Olympic football teams. However, Britain has not produced a top black professional tennis player. Even researching black participation in tennis in Britain proves fruitless. Sports historian Wray Vamplew says, "It's a subject which unhappily no one seems to have looked at in this country." [37] Annette Atherton, information officer for the Lawn Tennis Association based in London, maintains, "Tennis is looked upon as a multiracial sport in this country," [38] but few there seem to know anything about black players, and the leading tennis organizations have no information on blacks' participation in tennis. Nick Cheales of Information Sport England admits the difficulty in finding information on black players in the United Kingdom.[39] According to one Brit,

> The spread of black people in this country is far more patchy than in the USA. For example, in the southwest of the country where I lived until I was eighteen there were no more than one hundred (yes, one hundred) nonwhites living. In fact, I was eighteen and at college before I met a black person in the flesh! However, in places like some London districts there are far larger concentrations. . . . I must admit I cannot think of one black person from this country that has appeared on, say, the television playing the game [tennis].[40]

Great Britain was once a power in tennis, but fell on hard times with the retirement of Virginia Wade, Sue Barker, Jo Durie, and John Lloyd. It was almost two decades before fans could hope that a major championship could be won by Tim Henman or Greg Rudseski. Unlike the United States, where a private tennis organization has taken steps to find the next generation of tennis greats, the British approach to producing better athletes has been through a government-sponsored project. Whereas USTA strategies have included the search for "minorities" who might fill the void left by white players, the British government has used different terminology, focusing on *social background* instead of on racial identities.

Professional black tennis players have been lacking in Britain although the country has opened doors to blacks in other sports such as boxing, football, and track and field. Even within these sports, however, racism has been an obstacle. In 1977, people shouted "Kill the fucking nigger" at a football match at Elland Road in which black player Viv Anderson was participating.[41] Black athletes such as Learie Constantine, a black cricketer, and Billy Boston, the black rugby player from South Wales in the 1950s and 1960s, were accepted as heroes by working-class whites in northern towns.[42] Until recently, being black and being northern "were considered incompatible. Constantine in the 1930s was an exception, an exotic attraction and a familiar Northern figure."[43]

In 1991, a series of sports programs focused on Afro-Caribbean and Asian communities in Britain, suggesting that "while sport played a significant part in the life of some groups of people, sport itself was not free from racism."[44] The London Strategic Policy Unit, the London Council for Sport and Recreation, the Local Government Training Board, the West Midlands Council for Sport and Recreation, the Stirling District Council, and the Commission for Racial Equality addressed "the assertion that British sport reproduces forms of racism."[45] Much of this discussion centered on the absence of Asians in the football leagues (because blacks made up 20 percent of the twenty thousand professionals playing football)[46] as opposed to the absence of blacks in tennis.

The "Sport for All" campaign in June 1997 attempted to recoup the spirit of yesteryear in the sport history of Great Britain. A German visitor wrote in the 1920s, "All peoples have their play, but none of the great modern nations has built it up in quite the same way into a rule of life and a national code [as Great Britain has]." In a speech in Parliament about the campaign, Culture Secretary Chris Smith argued in part, "The Government will take the lead in extending opportunities for participation in sport through a national strategy for sport, which will embrace all sections of the community, regardless of where they live or what their social background, age or ability might be." Historically, the government has had little direct responsibility for the nation's sporting life, which has been left to local authorities, working with the private and voluntary sectors. However, "The central Government is responsible for the legislation and policy framework within which all sports and sporting activities take place."[47] A 1997 government publication featured blacks competing in track and field, football, swimming, boxing, and gymnastics. But Daley Thompson, an Olympic decathlete, was the only black athlete included in the "Champions of Sport" section, which featured twelve other athletes.

Great Britain has recently placed the pressures of a winning tennis tradition on the shoulders of Tim Henman and, to a lesser degree, of Greg Rudseski, who played for Canada before becoming a British citizen. Ironically, no one from the British Davis Cup team approached James Blake to play for Britain although his mother, Betty Blake, is a native of Oxfordshire, England.

A similar scenario has existed in South America. According to Joseph L. Arbena, who has researched sport in Latin America, "No doubt, sport can also reflect, express, and even encourage class and/or racial cleavages. Despite the recent success of darker players such as Pelé, Brazilian soccer was marred in its early days by overt racism and discrimination; even today, critics contend, the black player earns less while playing and has little carry over into his retirement years." In fact, Arbena points out, it was argued that Brazil's decline in international football in the late 1970s was due to the military regime's wanting to "whiten" the national team for a "superior European model."[48]

In contrast, more blacks playing football in Peru had other ramifications. The team Alianza, with mostly black players, became the most popular club in the 1920s, "put[ting] a positive value on blackness, on the particular qualities of society's traditionally lowest racial stratum."[49] "Soccer is the sport of the blacks" became a popular "refrain," much like references to basketball and football in the United States.

The Professional Tour in the Open Era

Recently, racism has become more subtle, and most white tennis players have failed or have refused to acknowledge many racist acts. When some have been interviewed on the subject, their response has been that racism is currently only minimally present in tennis, if at all. For example, in 1997 Gigi Fernandez was reported as saying, "There's no racism on the women's tour. I adamantly deny that. We've had Zina and Lori." That statement is one that would make most blacks cringe, especially because it has been all too common to point to the presence of one or two blacks to prove that racism no longer exists in a particular venue. Garrison responded, "That's Gigi's opinion. . . . It's an all-white sport; you feel it, are made to feel it, like you don't belong. So you protect yourself." Martina Hingis, Lindsay Davenport, and Pam Shriver, all white, have insisted that racism has not existed on the professional tour in the open era. When Venus Williams stated, "If anyone thinks there isn't racism, they should think again," Hingis was the "first player to call such talk 'absolutely ridiculous,' " and Davenport stated flatly, "There isn't any racism."[50]

Like so many, Fernandez was living in denial. As sociologist Jonathan Warren argues, "In not discussing race, in working to not recognize it, many U.S. whites also, of course, tend to direct their attention away from racism. That is, in being race-evasive there is a concomitant pull toward being power-evasive with regard to race." Jennifer Simpson observes that many "educated whites" attempt to "ignore, forget, or deny racism" through "selective hearing," "creative interpreting," and "complicitous forgetting." Therefore, "white talk" has been based on learning "*not* to acknowledge or perceive the links between phenotype and power."[51] White players have not had to perceive racism, for they see what has been "normal." It is ironic that many white female players have readily recognized gender inequities, but not racial ones, whereas many black players have focused on race, but have failed to recognize gender problems.

When McNeil and Garrison were excluded from a doubles draw at a Houston tournament even though both had signed up to play singles, Bonnie Gadusek, a white player, responded to the idea that they were excluded because of racism, "That's laughable! Mix-ups happen to everybody. I could see this being more of an issue in junior tennis and in clubs, but here, we're all professionals and behave that way, on and off the court." [52]

Other instances of racism are more subtle. A security guard can allow ten players to pass unidentified into a facility before stopping a black player to ask for identification, or a tournament director might fail to reserve a place in a draw for a black player who has registered. Garrison commented, "At some tournaments, if I didn't have the badge on, [officials] stopped me. It was subtle, but I didn't see them checking the badges of others. And I knew that comments were made." [53] "Each incident may seem hardly noticeable until you look at the cumulative effect of hundreds of microaggressions. Psychologists call it 'institutional racism.' " Barry Barnes, of Oliver Group, who represented Garrison and McNeil, argued, "Tennis has traditionally been an aristocratic sport, and I think there's a hard-core establishment who'd like to keep it that way and who view minorities as a threat to that establishment." [54]

The most recent incident of perceived racism came in the 2001 U.S. Open when in the second round against James Blake, Lleyton Hewitt wanted to remove a black linesperson, who had called two foot faults against him, and commented on the similarity between the black linesperson and Blake. Hewitt denied any racial intent and claimed that he was referring to "the similarities between the two foot faults for which he had been called." [55] He later apologized to Blake in private, although the outburst was public, and there was no mention of his apologizing to the linesperson.

Hewitt's winning the title overshadowed the comment, and several journalists were careful to avoid flatly accusing him of racism. For instance, one wrote, "Hewitt stirred up controversy when his on-court remarks to the umpire were construed by some to be racist." [56] The incident was conveniently omitted from the coverage of the Open by *Tennis* magazine. One writer praised Blake for failing to make a major issue of the incident, arguing, "The world would be a much happier place if everyone reacted to moments of trauma in the same way."[57] Black athletes have historically been praised for being passive even when facing racism or perceived racism.

Oftentimes, it has been difficult to distinguish personal dislike from racism. For example, when Venus and Serena Williams played their first Wimbledon together in 1998, several female players left soiled underwear and dirty sneaker insoles by the sister's lockers. This act could have been perceived as a dislike for them based on their personalities or some aspect other than race, but even the dislike could be perceived as being constructed in part by race ideologies.

In 1999, Mike Lurie, a sports journalist, argued that tennis "has been typecast as a game played by white-skinned people with dark tans, oblivious to the 'real world' as they traipse around with cotton sweaters hanging over their shoulders. Such is the stereotype." In response, he cited the facts that the new stadium at Flushing Meadows was named after a black player (Ashe), that Althea Gibson was "one of the most inspirational and accomplished champions of women's tennis," and that the emergence of the William sisters was revolutionizing how women play the sport owing to their "sheer power and athleticism" in tennis.[58] Whether such instances might be viewed as major advances has often been determined by the observer, who is generally a white writer. These "advancements" have in reality amounted to little in the more than one hundred years of tennis being played in the United States.

As critical a role as race has played in every facet of society in nations such as the United States and South Africa, many have refused to admit it. When *Tennis Week* published a three-part article on racism in tennis by Linda Pentz in 1997, it was not well received. One reader, Leif Wellington Haase, accused Pentz of writing a very subjective article. Despite the particulars of the article, Wellington Haase argued that unfair treatment in the United States has been "more likely to stem from the impersonal workings of capitalism and greed and nepotism lodged in human nature than from racism."[59] But the truth is that race has played and continues to play a significant role in tennis and in other aspects of society the world over; it has been lodged not merely in human experience, but also in capitalism itself.

After two conflicts between black players and club personnel at the Vertical Club in New York during the Virginia Slims Championships in November 1986, Ella Musolino, the tournament director, stated, "I would imagine that in traveling from city to city, they [black players] must encounter some [racism], and I'm sure their guard is up and it's very easy for any incident to be misconstrued. I think that's very unfair, particularly in New York, one of the last places you'd find that kind of situation."[60] Apparently, Musolino has not had the experience of being black and trying to flag a cab, particularly at night in New York! Ashe argued that even in New York he had not been immune to racism despite his popularity: "I may have trouble getting a taxi because white cab drivers automatically assume I'm going to Harlem and won't pick me up."[61]

When Leslie Allen-Selmore (now her married name) won in Detroit in 1982, she earned a spot in the Avon Championships in New York. Barry Lorge assessed this event: "It is because she is making an impact in a still predominantly white game that Allen received far more attention than six other first-time qualifiers" for the Avon Championships. He argued that her color should have been irrelevant because she came "from a middle-class, well-educated background, and is in no sense a child of the ghetto."[62] In effect, Lorge was focusing on class issues, suggesting that Allen-Selmore's life experience mirrored that of a white player. Just because Allen-Selmore came from a middle-class background, however, does not mean that racism was not a factor in her tennis career or in her life. Lorge suggested that only a black child "from the ghetto" could possible be the object of racism. In reality, the fact that upper-class blacks have also faced racism demonstrates that wealth has failed to "whiten" blacks and instead underlines that race and class have remain blurred phenomena. The history of blacks in the United States shows repeatedly that middle-class status has failed to shield blacks from racism and, in fact, has sometimes heightened it. For example, prior to and during the modern Civil Rights Movement, a middle-class neighborhood where blacks resided in Birmingham, Alabama, was the target of many bombings by racist whites.

Although black athletes can often cross the line of racism and segregation because of their money and fame, many will periodically be reminded that money "whitens" them only when people recognize them. When black athletes leave the insular world of sports, they enter a different arena. Occasionally, when they are not recognized, they have a glimpse of what other blacks face in racist societies. For example, a sales clerk once looked at Lori McNeil in disbelief and said, "Are you sure you want this? It's $200!" One of Zina Garrison's experiences exemplifies not only racism, but sexism as well. When she took a fur jacket to the checkout counter at a Houston store, a white female clerk told her, "Gee, you look familiar. What famous black athlete are you married to?"[63]

One such incidence of a tennis player's exposure to racism in the larger society occurred in the 1960s. In 1969, player Phyllis Konstam wrote of her travels in the South with fellow player H. W. "Bunny" Austin and black actor-singer Muriel Smith, who had a role in a musical in Atlanta:

> In Atlanta, we stayed with Muriel in the home of a gracious white Southern family and experienced real Southern hospitality. But we could not eat together in the restaurant, nor go to the cinema, nor even ride in a taxi together. It was a painful experience.
>
> Many of the cast, white and coloured, were living in a hotel run by a coloured man. It was a hotel lived in normally only by coloured people. The cast had not been there long before a cross was burning outside the front door.[64]

Some black professionals have adeptly avoided discussing race. Noah remained virtually silent about racism when he was a young player, and it was not until later in his career that he spoke out against racism. In 1983, he insisted, "I live in a world where people judge me on the basis of my performance on the tennis court, not on the color of my skin."[65] Actually, many, if not all, black athletes could make this claim, but the question has been whether they are shielded from racism by their fame. Noah was not totally shielded; once when attending a football game, he was called "dirty nigger." The name calling lasted until he removed his sunglasses and the taunters saw that he was Noah instead of just an unidentified black man.

Bryan Shelton overheard "comments" toward him and his mother while he played tournaments in the South. Despite this, he stated, "I've done the same interview a number of times. Growing up in the South and playing tennis, there weren't a lot of black kids out there playing with me. I don't feel one way or the other about it. I just happen to be an African-American who loved the game of tennis and who pursued it."[66]

Ashe, of course, was one of the few who fielded the question. In addition, he became an activist, standing up for his causes regardless of what the media or advertisers thought. That has been a difficult feat for most black athletes, particularly for those who have learned to say nothing that could jeopardize their endorsement opportunities.

Venus and Serena Williams have also generally avoided discussing the issue of racism in professional tennis. In one interview when asked about racism on the circuit, Venus replied, "I don't know. Do you, Serena?" Serena's response was, "I don't know. We're not here to talk about that."[67] Later, in a taped interview with Robin Robins, Venus tacitly acknowledged racism among the players. Similarly, Chanda Rubin's mother did not like stressing the race issue. "We don't want to stand out from everybody else. We just want to be like everyone else, and we are, if you look past our color."[68]

Venus and Serena's father, however, has been more outspoken about race. He remembers when Venus was younger and competing in a tennis tournament in the Southern California area and the only thing "all the other players knew was that she was Black and poor." He explained, "I overheard some people say we shouldn't even be there. 'They are from Compton.' 'What are they doing here. They can't play.' People would pick at us all the time. They should be glad that I am a good man because if I wasn't a good man, I would have picked up a stick and knocked the hell out of somebody. There comes a time when you get tired of people picking on you."[69]

Richard Williams recalls when he would greet white tennis parents at junior tournaments, but they "rarely said hello back." The Williams family began receiving racially threatening letters when the daughters started to win on the pro tour. The letters opened with "Dear Nigger." His daughter Isha confirmed that they received hate mail.[70] Some journalists have often discounted Williams's discussion of race, but before doing so, they should take another look at the life of Hank Aaron, who received more than threatening letters when he was on the verge of breaking Babe Ruth's home-run record. And years later, Barry Bonds's feat of breaking the new record of home runs in a season set by Mark McGuire, although less profound, was tainted with racist reception.

Another interesting point concerns the relationship between one's ranking in a sport and racism. According to Haitian tennis player Ronald Agenor, "My ranking in the top twenty was my protection against racism. When you're number twenty in the world, you can do whatever you want, but once I lost that ranking, I became a regular person. Then I started to see racism."[71] This might explain why so many black players claim that racism has not been a major factor in their careers: with a high ranking and high visibility, they have been seen as "crossover" personalities. Horace Reid echoed this sentiment, "If you're a winner, you're special. All of a sudden, I had no color. Most of my help came from the white community because I was such a novelty."[72]

Blacks have also composed a small percentage of nonplayer positions in professional tennis. Only very few have slowly entered the domain of umpiring. For instance, in 1968 Marion Rice served as an umpire at the Western Championships in Indianapolis. Dexter C. Adams served at the U.S. Open and at the ATP Championships in Mason, Ohio. Claranelle Morris has worked as an umpire since 1973. In 1996, Bernard Chavis was the first black to referee at the USTA Nationals tournament. Tony Nimmons finally chaired a major match, a semifinal match, at the 2003 U.S. Open, but in that same year Cecil Hollins accused the USTA of discrimination. Hollins had been a certified tennis official for eleven years, holding a gold badge, the highest certification, but at that time had never been assigned a final at the U.S. Open. He argued that no minority had been assigned a men's final and only one, Sandre French, a black woman, had umpired a women's final in 1993. He also maintained that the USTA discriminated against women by not allowing them to serve as umpires for men's matches except at the lowest level of competition.[73] Norman Fitz has been one of the few black officials who has chaired a nationally televised match, but he has worked at a stadium match only twice in twelve years of working at the U.S. Open. In 1983, he had been a certified official for twenty years, but his most highly publicized act was his default of Nastase in 1975, an act that he maintains was justified, but that affected his assignments at the U.S. Open. He had only six chairs in an eleven-year period and never chaired a final.

Racism and the elitist character of tennis have remained intact despite the presence of some "blue-collar" professional players (e.g., Jimmy Connors). In 1992, Lawrence Otis Graham, a corporate lawyer and graduate of Princeton University and Harvard Law School, "invented a completely new résumé," portraying himself as a young college dropout, and applied to the position of "busboy" at the Greenwich Country Club, one of the most prestigious clubs in the United States, but with no black members. He was told that the term *busboy* was demeaning and that the club preferred to use *busmen*. Nevertheless, the members called him "busboy." One woman called out, "Here, busboy. Here, busboy. Busboy, my coffee is cold. Give me a refill." After the woman heard him speak, she remarked, "My goodness. Did you hear that? That busboy has diction like an educated white person." Graham was later informed why one building where workers lived was called "the Monkey House": "it got that name since it's the house where the workers have lived at the club. And since the workers used to be Negroes—blacks—it was nicknamed the Monkey House. And the name just stuck—even though Negroes have been replaced by Hispanics." Speaking of O. J. Simpson playing on the course, one waiter commented, "It never occurred to me before, but it seemed so odd to see a black man with a golf club here on this course."[74]

Natural Talent

Another racist perception is that blacks are naturally athletic. This view has remained so pervasive among Americans that scholars have conducted research for more than a century to prove the difference between whites and other constructed races, in particular blacks. Todd Boyd, professor in the School of Cinema-Television at USC, explains, "[T]he old racially coded debate in sports . . . describes African American athletes as 'natural' and white athletes as 'hard-working.' It is assumed that African American athletes are born with the skills to play and excel at sports, a clear reference to an assumed physical prowess that defies mental capacity, while white athletes are regarded as industrious, in keeping with the ideology of the American work ethic."[75]

Sadly, many black athletes have accepted and internalized this perception, while not realizing the racist component of what has appeared to be a compliment. Harry Edwards, renowned sociologist, has fought this stereotype for more than thirty years.[76] Despite the fact that Jimmy "the Greek" Snyder lost his job at CBS for saying exactly what many whites and blacks have always believed (that blacks are "natural" athletes), it has not changed the perception of the black athlete. One man lost his job, even though others have emphasized the same stereotype.

The need to justify the trade in human cargo caused whites in Europe and the Americas to develop stereotypes about Africans and those of African descent. In the late nineteenth and early twentieth centuries, scholars and writers attempted to "prove" why and how blacks were inferior. Historians Paul Bohannan and Philip Curtin argue that the myth of savage Africa has been part of Western thought since the seventeenth century, "created out of philosophical necessity, not out of observations."[77] Race theorist bell hooks adds, "They [white supremacists] constructed images of blackness and black people to uphold and affirm their notions of racial superiority, their political imperialism, their will to dominate and enslave."[78]

Between 1890 and 1930, numerous essays in various fields were published to prove that blacks were inferior to whites. For example, James Bardin of the University of Virginia, wrote, "Mental characteristics are as distinctly and as organically a part of a race as its physical characteristics, and for the same reason: both depend ultimately upon anatomical structure."[79] In 1906, Robert Bennett Bean, professor of anatomy of the University of Virginia, argued that blacks had inferior brains.[80] Nathaniel Southgate Shaler, son of a Kentucky slaveholder and head of Harvard's Lawrence Scientific School, which was dedicated to "Scientific truth and Negro uplift," argued that racial characteristics were "innate, inherited," and altered by "paternal racial policies."[81] As I. A. Newby concludes in his book on "segregationist thought," "In the final analysis, one's attitude toward race and related subjects rests upon initial assumptions and value judgments concerning such debatable things as human nature, heredity and environment, the relationship of the individual to society, the nature of American democracy, the meaning of race itself."[82]

The "breeding" or genetic theory has also continued to find support. For example, Martin Kane notes that scholars have argued that "outstanding athletic performances in particular sports were based on racial characteristics indigenous to the black population."[83] J. M. Tanner photographed and X-rayed 137 track and field athletes and a number of weightlifters and wrestlers at the 1958 British Empire and Commonwealth Games and the Rome Olympics in 1960 and concluded that "there were large significant racial differences in leg length, arm length and hip width" between black and nonblack athletes.[84] Anthropologists Edward E. Hunt Jr. and Robert M. Malina have made similar contributions. Hunt maintains that the black athlete has "hyperextensibility—or what the layman might call being double-jointed," and Malina asserts, "Animals living in hot climates tend to have longer extremities and a lesser body mass in order to dissipate heat. With their long legs and arms, blacks have a greater surface areas from which to dissipate heat through the skin."[85]

Even athletes have commented as if they were authorities on the history of the Atlantic slave trade and slavery. Lee Evans, Olympic and world four-hundred-meter record holder, insisted, "We were bred for it. Certainly the black people who survived in the slave ships must have contained a high proportion of the strongest. Then, on the plantations, a strong black man was mated with a strong black woman."[86]

The problem with such assertions is that relationships among slaves were more complex. For example, not all blacks were slaves, and not all slaves lived on plantations. Also absent in these theories is the role slaves themselves played in selecting their own mates. Furthermore, slave children who had white fathers are omitted from the equation, and it is assumed that slaves who survived did so because of physical strength rather than because of mental and spiritual attributes. Finally, the assumption that the fittest slaves were bred assumes that weaker slaves failed to reproduce.

John Hoberman maintains that in "tabloid-style fascinations that dress up irrational drives as scientific theories, racial science is the game that virtually anyone can play," adding, "The black intelligentsia has had so little to say about the ruinous consequences of making athletic achievement the prime symbol of black creativity."[87]

Other researchers have arrived at different conclusions. For instance, T. E. Reed points out that "[t]he American individual to whom the term Negro (Black, African American) is applied is almost always a biracial hybrid. Usually between 2 and 50 percent of his genes are derived from Caucasian ancestors, and these genes were very probably received after 1700."[88] And Claude Bouchard argues, "It is now generally recognized that the majority of genetic variants are shared by all humans and that only about 10% of the genetic variations is specific to populations or races," emphasizing that "[g]enetic difference between various racial groups tend to be small, particularly when one looks beyond skin colour and facial characteristics."[89] According to David W. Hunter, "It is important to recognize that Africans and African Americans do not come from some 'magical' common gene pool. . . . [O]ver 98% of the captured Africans for slavery came from a very extensive area of West Africa and West-Central Africa, from Senegal to Angola, a distance of more than 3,000 miles."[90]

Racist ideology perceived slaves to be muscle and no brains. Once blacks were allowed to participate in professional leagues, this attitude transferred to sports. After years of exclusion, blacks were more readily welcomed in track and field, basketball, and (American) football, where it was perceived that speed and strength were of great importance. For years, blacks in football were placed mainly in "speed positions." According to Edwards, blacks began to dominate "speed" track and field events mainly because whites, fearing they would be unable to compete with blacks in such events, moved to other events.[91] For example, the eight hundred meters was considered an endurance event until a black athlete, Alberto Juantorena, won it in the 1976 Olympics. Afterward, it began to be viewed as a speed event. Whites' abandonment of such events contributed to the impression that blacks were better in those events.

So-called thinking positions in a sport, such as quarterback, were reserved for white males, who were considered "natural leaders." But when black quarterbacks such as Warren Moon (who refused to be play another position and therefore was forced to play in the Canadian Football League), Doug Williams, Randall Cunningham, and others began to emerge, sport announcers began to discuss the position more in terms of "mobility," "athleticism," and "size," instead of "intelligence," "sensibility," and "leadership."

Racial genetics, or racial science, first developed in the 1890s, has attempted to explain the "superior" black athlete. Apparently, most more recent racial geneticists have forgotten Hitler's similar claims of the "superior white, Aryan athlete." "The most creative of all races was the Aryan, the 'archetype' of Man, responsible for 'every manifestation of human culture, every product of art, science and technical skill.' "[92]

Although Lindsay Davenport's father played for the USA volleyball team in the 1968 Summer Olympics, journalists have avoided using racial genetics to explain her rise in tennis. Although a "sport gene" has been mentioned when discussing second-generation white athletes in tennis, it has not been tied to the concept of race, and no one has claimed such a gene for the Maleeva sisters, whose mother was a professional tennis player. "Athletes' kids have a sporting chance of greatness, but inheriting genes of the strong and the speedy is no guarantee." In fact, "nobody can offer exact odds on the importance of genes in athleticism, but everyone admits that they are important—to some degree."[93]

In May 2001, tennis fan Jim Irish wrote in a letter to a leading tennis magazine, "Whites could take exception to the fact that 80 percent of NBA players are black when they comprise only 15 percent of the U.S. population. The bottom line is that blacks are better basketball players and if a white man makes it to the NBA, he is exceptional."[94] This type of racist thinking essentially argues that the few blacks who have made it in tennis constitute the norm as mirrored by another sport, deemed a black sport, and that blacks should not complain about the lack of blacks in tennis, which is a "white" sport.

The perception of the black superior athlete has been fed commercially. For example, the Fila commercial featuring Jerry Stackhouse running to the court to slam dunk as a baby when his parents were merely trying to get him to walk is clearly racist, indicating that Stackhouse did not work hard to become a top player, but was instead born to it. On the other side of the fence, another commercial features a white boy in his driveway shooting the basketball in the summer heat, snow, and rain, indicating that he became good because he worked hard. Jackie Jenkins of Atlanta, who has six children—three of them adopted—playing tennis, maintains, "A lot of people think my biological sons are just talented, that they ain't had to work at being great tennis players. But people's going to find out that I got three [adopted kids] I took out of the shelter with no talent. . . . All three of them's going to get a college scholarship. My goal is to make them better than my biological kids."[95]

The stress on athleticism is a relatively new component in producing a top tennis player, largely owing to Navratilova and Lendl. Despite new emphasis on physical fitness, however, some have excelled without being in great physical shape. For example, Seles, Hingis, Sampras, Agassi, and Davenport, among others, reached the top echelon of professional tennis without defined physical prowess, although they later worked to keep pace with competitors. If tennis is supposedly a thinking game, can physical athleticism compensate for an absence of the mental aspects of the game or great strokes? It is one thing to say how fast Graf or Navratilova, both white, were in their prime, but it is another to say that Garrison, a black woman, was one of the fastest on the tour, but she never reached number 1 like Graf or Navratilova.

Too often the first comment about the potential of a black tennis player has been his or her natural athleticism. For example, Althea Gibson was defined as a "natural," who "developed a ball sense which she never wanted to waste."[96] Another reporter wrote of Goolagong's "rare natural talent and instinctive flair for match play."[97] Columnist David Gray made this distinction between Chris Evert and Evonne Goolagong: "Evonne's talent had been discovered accidentally, and luckily, in Australia. Chris had been brought up to be a champion. Concentration and cool precision were the virtues of her game. When the two women met that first year, it seemed like a perfect encounter between the most natural player in women's tennis, and the best-schooled competitor America has produced since Maureen Connolly."[98]

For sport journalists beginning in the late 1990s, *power* became the key adjective to describe Venus and Serena Williams's game.[99] Chris Evert stated at the State Farm Evert Cup, "They're exceptional athletes, first of all. So far, that's gotten them to where they are, just because of their athletic prowess. I don't think they've even begun to use their heads out on the court yet. . . . These girls are incredible athletes, they're genetically natural athletes."[100] One response to this comment was, "I realize that Evert's idea was to compliment the sisters on their playing ability and she was probably subconscious [*sic*] of the connotations. However, these comments about the stereotype[d] 'natural athletic prowess' of a particular group subtly reinforce the concept of eugenics. In the wake of the diversity of today's professional athletes, it behooves commentators and the like to reconsider making such comments."[101]

Radio reporter Sid Rosenberg lost his job after commenting on Don Imus's syndicated show that Venus Williams was an "animal" and that she and Serena had "a better shot at posing nude for *National Geographic* than for *Playboy*. Program director of WFAN, Mark Chernoff, stated that Rosenberg apologized and "showed he understood he was wrong" in addition to sending a written apology to the Williams.[102]

Aleta Haynes, executive director of Sportsman Tennis Club, stresses, "It is annoying when the commentators suggest that Martina Hingis is bright and intelligent. However, the Williams sisters are deemed physically fit. It gives the impression that whites are smart, and blacks are physically fit."[103] William Redd, director of Tennis and Things, agrees that this is the general trend of some commentators' descriptions of the Williams's success. "Sometimes commentators and others suggest that it is purely physical, and not mental. As anyone who plays tennis knows, it is definitely a mental game."[104]

One journalist wrote of Yannick Noah, "Noah's size dwarfs the racquet in his hand, and pure athleticism so dominates his game that the racquet seems no more conspicuous than a hammer or saw in the hand of a carpenter."[105] A number of white players have been larger than Noah, however. Sport announcers credited hard work for the physical sculpturing of Navratilova and Lendl. Even when Pete Sampras leaped for one of his famous overheads, sport announcers commented on his jumping ability, but did not tie it to racial genetics. Did Sampras's Greek antecedents contribute to his ability to do what announcers have called a "slam dunk smash"? When a black tennis player does likewise, however, the "genetic" view often comes into the vocabulary used to describe his or her feats. A major question to be answered in the near future is: As more blacks continue to move into the upper echelon of professional tennis, will tennis suddenly be perceived as less of a thinking sport and more of a physical one?[106]

One writer described Noah as "[p]acing restlessly about the back of the court between points like a tiger impatient for dinner."[107] Another described him as he "prowled around the court, muscles coiled up, just waiting for the opportunity to spring."[108] In the 1983 French Open final, Wilander was graced with such descriptions as having an "implacable nature," whereas Noah was portrayed as "aggressive" in terms of his "physique" and "instincts." It was "fire [Noah] against ice [Wilander]."[109] However, Wilander, too, charged the net during the match, but print journalists spared him from such "accolades." Not just their games, but Noah's African heritage and Wilander's Scandinavian background played major roles in the depictions of them in print. How often have white serve-volleyers been described like an animal in the wild?

When black athletes work hard to make it to the top, their work is negated because of their supposed athletic superiority based on "race." But John Madden said it best, "Great players tend to work harder than the average ones."[110]

Blacks and Tennis Organizations

Another problem has been the absence of black administrators in tennis organizations. The upper echelon of national and international tennis organizations has been dominated by whites. In 1991, there were no blacks on the twenty-four-member U.S. Open Committee. In addition, the USTA Board of Directors included no blacks.[111] However, nonwhites were included on the USTA Executive Committee: Virginia M. Glass and Dwight A. Mosley were presidential appointees. In 1997, the USTA Board of Directors included no blacks, although Mosley had served on the board from 1993 to 1996. He was elected secretary-treasurer in 1995 when the board was realigned. That year the USTA had 18 blacks on a staff of 156; the ATP tour had 86 U.S. employees and only one black, Erika Green, who worked in player services. The WTA tour had approximately 25 full-time U.S. employees, but refused to reveal if any were black.[112]

In 1998, Eugene L. Scott, editor of *Tennis Week,* argued, "Minority representation at the game's highest leadership levels is pitiful. No blacks sit on the U.S. Tennis Association's 14 member Board; not one black has a place on the International Tennis Hall of Fame's 22 member Executive Committee; no blacks are among the hierarchy of the ATP's top 15 Board and Executive staff members; none are [sic] on the USPTA [United States Professional Tennis Association] Board; and none on the USPTR [United States Professional Tennis Registry] Board."[113] In addition, no black entrepreneur has risen to be a tournament director of the eighty men's ATP tour events or of the fifty-three WTA tour events. Moreover, few blacks hold management positions at the principle tennis manufacturing companies.

Scott explained that golf has been worse because it has continued to be played at private clubs, whereas tennis events have generally been held at public facilities. He added that golf "has insulated itself from criticism almost solely on the back of Tiger Woods." Consequently, he challenged the USTA announcement of the $50 million Plan for Growth, which would include everyone. "Nonsense. It is not enough to be inclusive in the abstract. In order to attract minorities to the Plan's free lesson feature, a strategy must be developed to reach out boldly to the inner-city and literally pull blacks into the fold." He added, "It's foolhardy to believe that any of today's pioneering black coaches or administrators could slog their way anytime soon onto the USTA Board. Why? The grisly record shows that there has never been a black president even of any of the 17 USTA sections."[114]

Other hidden issues have affected blacks' participation in tennis organizations. For example, the USTA is a volunteer organization, but fewer blacks have salaries that will allow them to volunteer. "If you live in Albany, N.Y., it takes a day away from work to participate in meetings that take place in Harrison, New York."[115]

A few blacks have worked within the USTA, but nonwhites who have been recommended for positions of leadership in the USTA usually have been turned down because, according to Pat Koger, former head of the Minority Participation Committee, "the USTA felt that they need training, they did not know the USTA well enough to be effective, they needed to be educated as to how the USTA does things, they probably would not fit in, not our kind of folks, not from the USTA family, etc. Then the USTA turns around and says it cannot find suitable, qualified and credentialed people of color to fill these positions."[116]

In 1997, Leslie Allen-Selmore gave another example showing why more black people are needed in staff positions. While working as USTA staff, she went to the Breakers Hotel in Palm Beach, Florida, where it was suggested that the uniforms of the U.S. Open maintenance workers reflect a red, white, and blue theme. One member suggested that the uniform consist of denim bib overalls, a white shirt, and a red bandanna. Allen-Selmore argued, however, that such a uniform could be perceived a "slave uniform" and would be politically incorrect because 99 percent of the maintenance workers were "dark-skinned minorities."[117]

Wanted: Coaches—Blacks Need Not Apply

Becoming a coach or teaching pro at prestigious clubs has also been difficult for blacks. It was a major breakthrough when Benny Sims Jr. was hired as a teaching professional at the prestigious and all-white Longwood Cricket Club in Boston in 1982. The club had never had a black member, but, according to Bud Collins, no black had ever applied. One club member explained, "The place is a lot broader than it once was. We have quite a few Jews, even though there was a time when Arthur Fiedler had a difficult time getting in. I feel certain blacks could be accepted now. Technically, we did have one black, an infant that was adopted by a member." [118]

Jack Crawford, chairman of the committee that selected Sims, argued, "I'll probably get some flack once some people realize that the new pro is black, but who cares? He was the most qualified of nearly 50 applicants, a likeable guy with a fine record. So we hired him. No big deal. It wouldn't be anyway." It *was* a big deal, though, considering the racial history of the club. Sims himself commented, "I would be angry if color kept me from getting a good job. It never has. Boston is the best and the worst, so much to do and be part of. I feel great getting a job at a place that means so much in tennis. But I know a couple of miles away I could get killed just for being black."

When Arthur Ashe was asked the following question in an interview in 1968, "How does it feel to win a title at a club that would never have you as a member?" he annoyed club members by responding, "I don't like the situations in these clubs. I'm uncomfortable, but right now they're the only places where I can play important tournaments." When Ashe heard about Sims's new position, he laughed, "You've got to be joking!"

According to Bob Moseley, it is necessary to have a greater number of black coaches in order to produce more black players, an angle that has been neglected in the discussion of getting blacks to play tennis. The USTA, the USPTR, and the USPTA began making efforts to produce more black coaches in the early 1990s.

Stanley Franker's attempt to get a coaching job reveals a common scenario. Ashe remarked, "He's a gifted minority coach who had to leave the U.S. to become fully employed."[119] When Franker applied for a coaching job at a Southern California country club, management never responded. When he called to follow up on the letter of application, he learned that the position had been filled. Two days later he had a friend call the club about the job, and the friend was told to apply. Meanwhile, many of Franker's white USC teammates were approached for jobs at other clubs.

Franker taught "backyard tennis" to celebrities in Beverly Hills while searching for a permanent coaching position. Finally, in 1981 he went to Europe and became the national coach of the Austrian Tennis Federation in 1983 and then the technical director of the Royal Dutch Lawn Tennis Association in 1986. His response to not getting the position at the California country club was that it was "[b]ecause of race, what else? I realize it's easy to say that, but I don't know what other explanation there could be. The guy the country club picked was no more qualified than I was."

On the professional tour, black coaches have worked mainly for black players. Sims eventually coached Chanda Rubin. Washington, Garrison, McNeil, and other black players have hired black coaches. Increasingly, young players of any race began having a parent serve as their coach. An important question is whether the absence of black coaches on nonprofessional levels has affected the pool of black players on the professional tour?

Media

The media has also played a role in the racism in sport. Little exposure has been given to black athletes who have not been in the mainstream sports. Of course, many sports journalists might argue that they have not been racist in that they cover many black athletes. In fact, black athletes who are celebrities have come under intense scrutiny. It has been argued that

> [t]hese well-known black figures have served as grist for the mill of cultural spectacle, fodder for the programmers of television and talk

radio, and subjects for seemingly limitless column inches in print media and magazine covers. Why does there seem to be a growth industry in African-American celebrity? . . .

Although not the only group of people who function as objects of intense media scrutiny, African Americans who find themselves displayed so spectacularly in public serve as prisms through which the nation views issues of race and gender.[120]

Beyond professional black athletes, the media has covered mainly black athletes in predominately white collegiate programs while virtually ignoring athletic programs at predominately black colleges unless there is a negative spin to the story. For example, rarely does ESPN show highlights of basketball games of black collegiate programs. However, when a big brawl occurred at a game at a historically black university, camera crews were on hand, and the videos were shown repeatedly on ESPN. The only time Prairie View A&M, a predominantly black college, has received any press of note was when it threatened to become the holder of the longest losing streak in NCAA football.[121] The other times when these programs get major press is when something extraordinary happens. For instance, when legendary coach Eddie Robinson of Grambling University broke the NCAA all-time winning record in football, a number of photographers and television cameras were present. The next game, however, it was back to the norm.

During the parade of nations at the 1996 Olympics, the announcers commented on the many negative situations in African and other third-world nations as the representatives of these nations marched in the stadium. Meanwhile, when the teams from the major Western nations entered the stadium, comments were limited to the lives and performances of the competing athletes.

This trend has extended to tennis. Herb Joseph Provost, tennis coach at Texas Southern University, believed that the news media "failed to provide well-deserved exposure to the development of black tennis."[122] Although athletic programs at many small colleges have received less national press, athletic programs at predominately black universities have been omitted even from local media reports.

When Venus Williams was on course to her final in the 1997 U.S. Open, many in the media wanted gossip about her. Linda Pentz, writer for *Tennis Week,* wrote, "The eagerness of media covering the U.S. Open to seize on negatives when reporting on Venus Williams was sickening to see. The same people who whine constantly for a Tiger Woods of tennis, couldn't wait to join the chorus of lockerroom schoolgirl sniping about Venus not consorting with her peers and her father Richard's absence." *Sports Illustrated* reporters, without identifying themselves, followed the family, attempting to get information, but "The press largely refused to focus on the actual story of a 17-year-old who came from nothing, competing in her first U.S. Open, reaching the final. . . . The whole thing was disgusting, and, whether they meant it or not, racist."[123]

Some writers in print journalism have strived to become more "politically correct," but others have remained insensitive. In the past, sport writers were less mindful of their descriptions of black players. For instance, in the 1950s, one article in an Australian newspaper referred to Gibson as a "negress."[124] When Noah claimed that a healer was responsible for curing his nagging knee injuries, that person was pejoratively called a "witch doctor" in Western print media. Despite the skepticism, Noah insisted that the cure worked.[125]

When the United States faced Zimbabwe in the 2000 Davis Cup tie, insensitive comments surfaced. For example, long-time tennis commentator Bud Collins wrote, "[T]he final day of the best-of-five series commenced with the American surrounded by jungle drum-beaters, gyrating dancers." Collins quoted Zimbabwe president Robert Mugabe, who stated that the encounter was "the dwarfs against the giants"; then Collins added that "the dwarfs looked like rain forest pygmies with poison darts." Collins's language could easily have been lifted from an early-nineteenth-century European traveler's account. Furthermore, he took the opportunity to point out several of the negative aspects of Mugabe and the situation in Zimbabwe:

> The importance of the U.S. visit was underlined by President Mugabe's presence. . . . He could have used a win. This Prez of 20

suspect years is in a slump, what with an AIDS epidemic on his graspy hands, 50 percent unemployment, 57 percent inflation, a fuel shortage and his eager participation in a foolish, expensive war in the Congo. Moreover he was recently rebuffed at the polls in an attempt to re-write the constitution so that lands owned by whites might be seized by the government.[126]

Apparently, Zimbabwe's Constitution does not warrant a capital "C" as in the United States. More important, when have negative aspects about the U.S. president and government ever been included in articles about Davis Cup tennis held in the United States?

Sports analysts discuss many stereotypical images of blacks. A prime example occurred when sportscaster Ted Robinson made a sweeping generalization about black fathers. During the 2001 French Open, he argued that Richard Williams was an "African American" man who raised his children, commenting that the absence of black fathers "has been a problem in the past." He added that for raising his children, "Williams should be given a massive amount of credit."[127] He failed to apply this stereotype to white men even though some of them have not raised their children. In addition, Williams has not been the only black father in tennis to raise his children. Many other black players have had wonderful relationships with their fathers, including Ashe, Noah, the Blakes, the Washingtons, Rubin, and others. Lori McNeil was close to her father, who traveled with her to tournaments, gave her advice, and made sure he was the one to drop her at airports. She explained, "It was very important to him that I go out and give everything I have. He taught me about sports." After her father's death, she stated, "I really believe that I just know that he's here in spirit, and that helps me every day. I think about him. I always think about him."[128]

Even the black-owned media have failed to cover blacks in tennis adequately. For instance, when Agenor was in the final of the 2000 Eddleman USTA Challenger in Birmingham, Solomon Crenshaw Jr., a reporter for the *Birmingham News,* was the only black reporter at the tournament. He felt that Agenor's becoming the first black and first Haitian to make the finals was a story.[129]

• • •

A few people have periodically raised the question of racism in sports in general and in tennis in particular. It has become increasingly more difficult to address issues of race in a period when much of the scholarship has shifted to class analyses. However, the politics of race has continued to be an underlying question in such scholarship, especially in periods when overt racist expression has increased. As a result, the absence of real discussions about racism has continued to plague tennis and other sports, and many continue to deny even the possibility that racism exists in sports.

9

USTA Minority Participation

THE USTA HAS TAKEN STEPS in expanding its presence in "minority" communities, particularly after charges of racism were levied at the organization. The USTA formed the Player Development Program in 1987 in order to make sure that other players followed the success of Jimmy Connors and John McEnroe. Although the rankings have been based on individual performance, nationalist, patriotic, and jingoist jargon have infiltrated professional tennis beyond the Davis Cup format, which is supposed to be the home of such expressions. As a result, tennis federations in France, Sweden, Spain, and the United States, for example, have attempted to secure a new generation of players who can gain tennis supremacy within the professional ranks. In an effort to compete with national programs of other countries, the USTA has sought means to insert into its program some attributes of a team concept, using a notion akin to nationalism.

The emergence of Andre Agassi, Michael Chang, Jim Courier, and finally Pete Sampras on the professional tour boosted the hopes of those wanting players from the United States to dominate professional tennis. However, these players' rise in professional tennis had little to do with the USTA Player Development Program.[1] In addition, the focus of the concern for "American" tennis was men, not women, even when the top "American" women were players who formerly represented other countries, such as Martina Navratilova and Monica Seles.

199

Within this context, the issue of "minority" players and what they could do for "American" tennis was fostered.

The USTA has defined *minority* as "people of Hispanic, African American, Asian, and Pacific Island descent."[2] If the USTA wanted supremacy, it was asked, why not tap the resources of "minority" youths and look beyond the traditional means of producing top tennis players? Some believed that if the type of talent among black athletes, for example, that has existed in football, basketball, and track and field could be harnessed for tennis, then "American" tennis could again reign supreme.

More than 150 players have participated in the Player Development Program. But several years ago writer Mark Winters argued that the success of players such as MaliVai Washington, Todd Martin, Jennifer Capriati, Lindsay Davenport, and Chanda Rubin has been overshadowed by limited achievements of players such as Long Phan, Nicole Hummel, Lex Carrington, Jill Brenne, Kim Kessaris, Will Bull, and J. J. Jackson.[3] Winters was careful to include a multiracial list to show the diversity that the program has attempted to achieve. Nonetheless, the examples of limited success have loomed over the program.

In 1989, twenty-four of the "most talented and promising" twelve- to sixteen-year-olds attended a five-day USTA developmental training camp, working with Stan Smith, USTA director of coaching, and two black coaches—Benny Sims and Jean Desdunes, a USTA summer coach.[4] An important question concerning the program was the number of black youths reached.

The USTA established the Minority Participation Committee in 1991 to "reflect its commitment to minority players and volunteers." The mission was "to ensure that everyone—regardless of age, sex, race, social or economic circumstances—has the opportunity to experience the lifetime benefits of tennis."[5] Dwight A. Mosley became the first chair of the committee.

The USTA has publicized its general efforts in tennis and the work of "minorities," particularly in local programs. Those who have been instrumental in USTA-affiliated organizations have included Bob

Bynum, the president of the USPTA Eastern Division; Joe White, the USTA Midwest minority participation chairman in Illinois; Dave Abrams, USTA Missouri Valley executive director; May Hines, regional volunteer for the USTA Western Division in 1998; Jerome Simmons of Tennis Players Without Partners, winner of the USTA/NJTL Chapter of the Year in 1998; Emily Moore, receiver of a 1998 Special Service Award for more than twenty years of service to the Eastern Division; and Carl McDonald, who has held clinics for youth.

Jenny Schnitzer, Eastern Division director of junior programs, has taken tennis pros to school assemblies. Milton Parker, vice principal at Thurgood Marshall Elementary School in Asbury Park, New Jersey, runs tennis programs at the school and has seen his numbers jump owing to USA School Tennis.

Linked to the specific programs have been USTA-sponsored events. A Multicultural Parents Forum was held in Philadelphia in March 2000, where parents of local juniors who competed in USTA tournaments attended the question-and-answer session. Also present were Rodney Harmon; Larry Shippen, Middle States board member and Multicultural Participation Committee member; and Linda Mann, USTA/MS Multicultural Participation and Philadelphia District liaison.

In cooperation with other organizations, *Tennis Industry Magazine* published *Tennis in Public Places* in 1997, a informational publication about various aspects of tennis in the United States from team tennis to grassroots tennis. According to contributors, public-parks facilities were growing more sophisticated in their efforts at promoting tennis participation. Some of them were running "grassroots" programs such as Play Tennis America (PTA), which provided new players with a package of group lessons.[6]

According to 1996 Minority Participation Committee reports, Pat Koger, then chair of the committee, the original mandate had been expanded "to place greater focus on economics, marketing, sports industry and careers, along with player programs, communications and volunteer development." USTA administrators were urged to increase recruitment and support of talented minority athletes, collaborations with minority tennis and corporate leaders, and marketing efforts within minority communities. In addition, Koger outlined the activities of 1996.

• letters of endorsement reinforcing MP [Minority Participation Committee] goals
  • $2K grants to each section for diversity training
  • survey and analysis of ranked minority juniors
  • input on Junior Task Force
  • Florida and Hawaii sections and Native American open forums
• funding and service support for North American Indian Tennis Association
• Native American, Hispanic/Latino and general sessions and forums/presentations at USTA Recreational Tennis Leadership Workshop
  • input to player Development
  • input on U.S. Open TV ads, print ads in minority publications
  • strengthening of MP volunteer/staff network[7]

One question asked is whether the USTA's mission has been to develop college players or top pros? The question of education—how much to obtain and how to go about obtaining it—has become a crucial decision for juniors. Of the 1997 USTA national team, two players continued to attend school, one being Alexandra Stevenson. The other members took correspondence courses or home study.[8]

Dan Middleton, father of team member Melissa Middleton, argued that there was confusion regarding the National Team's goals. "First they were supposed to develop future number ones. And then last year, their team members ended up going to college. The USTA has to decide right now what its objective is. Is it to develop college players or top pros? If it wants to produce top pros, it has to go the whole way like the other countries are doing. It can't have one foot in and one foot out."[9]

How does a program to increase tennis participation affect "minorities"? Will greater participation across the United States result in greater opportunities for "minority" coaches and head pros? According to the USTA, in 1995 roughly thirty thousand people were introduced to tennis through the Player Development Program. The goal was to establish five hundred thousand new tennis players by the end of 1997.[10]

The USTA/NJTL kept more than 160,000 youths in tennis at more than twenty-five thousand sites nationwide. In addition, the USTA/NJTL had an increase of more than 30 percent in the number of its programs between 1995 and 1997. The USTA Tennis 1-2-3 Program introduced "approximately 160,000 people to tennis in 1998. In the Eastern Division, 17,450 new players were introduced to the game," including the following groups: "Caucasian 29 percent, Hispanic-American 27 percent, African-American 25 percent, Asian-American 10 percent, American-Indian 1 percent, and Other 8 percent."[11]

The language used for the program has also created discussion. Oftentimes the terms *minority* and *inner city* have been used to mean *black*. Other times *minority* is stereotypically assumed to mean *black* or *Latino* or both. Much of this connection is owing to images these terms have created in general population. However, the USTA has also fostered this notion. For example, generally when there has been an article on inner-city tennis, there have been photos of black youths. When the USTA spokespersons have been asked about minority participation, they generally first comment how the program has worked within black communities, or "inner-city" areas, before addressing what is being done for other groups as well. Such responses are part of a broader media problem of what phrases have essentially become synonyms for *black*.

In 1998, William Washington, MaliVai Washington's father, argued that *minority participation* and *multicultural participation* have been confusing terminology. "When people of color think of minorities, they do not think it means Afro-Americans. That's what the white man thinks when he hears minority." In addition, he maintained that the USTA Minority Participation Committee "has been an absolute waste of USTA Money. They have not accomplished an initiative from 1994 to 1998." Furthermore, he criticized Bob Davis, head of the tennis organization Black Dynamics, Inc., who was trying to "resurrect an operation that died under the leadership of Bollettieri and it would be a mistake for minority tennis athletes to [participate]."[12]

A debate ensued over the change of the name from "Minority Participation" to the broader "Multicultural Participation." Wendell Willis supported the change, arguing, "Changing the name from minority to multicultural would do a couple of things. One is when you have the name 'minority' most people think only of African-Americans. Our committee is for all kids." Committee chair Koger admitted that she was "on the fence about this issue when Dwight Mosley was the chairman. . . . The name change is a way of talking about it differently and minimizing it." She viewed the change as looking at "minority participation less closely so that anything controversial might go away." Bob Davis added, "I see a further diffusing of the MP initiative by the multiculturalism. Over the last few years it has been diffused. Many of the sections have done it already, but what does multicultural mean? It means Bosnian, Croatian, Russian. It means everything but what the designers intended it to be."[13]

• • •

There has been further disagreement on the positive role of the USTA. The USTA began a campaign for print and television ads to show that tennis was a lifetime sport for everyone. Presenting top tennis stars such as Chris Evert, Pete Sampras, and Andre Agassi, the USTA promotion was astounding. One commercial even featured a black youth pretending to be Sampras, hitting against the wall, which represented Agassi, and his dog serving as the ballboy.

Whereas some blacks are very critical of the USTA, others have praised it for its effort in fostering tennis among black youths. Those blacks who have criticized the USTA have worked both inside and outside of the organization; however, most of those who have praised the USTA have worked for the organization or have benefited from the program. Of course, high-ranking officials and members of the organization have praised their own efforts in the minority program.

The USTA has also been touted for its more recent role in reaching "inner-city" youths. For instance, in 1990 there were fifteen blacks on the USTA's working list of twelve- to sixteen-year-olds with "exceptional potential." That year Ashe declared, "The USTA has really started to grab the problem by the throat." [14]

Rodney Harmon, former professional player, has been a part of the USTA's $35 million investment plan, labeled "Plan for Growth," to make the game more accessible. In three years, 260,000 people participated in clinics and recreation programs, of which 50,000 "were believed" to be minorities. [15] Another report claims that of the 202,000 who participated in USTA programs in 1998, 28 percent were black, 8 percent were Hispanic, 6 percent were Asian American, and 2 percent Native Americans. According to Julia Levering, USTA president and chairperson of the Board of Directors, "It brings people together in a way that transcends race or sex or financial means. It's just people getting together from all sides of town to play tennis and have fun." [16]

Harmon stated, "I want to have kids in the inner cities playing tennis. Arthur Ashe started the [N]ational Junior Tennis League in the late 1960s to include those kids. We're spending nearly $2 million this year to fund programs and train coaches." [17] According to Harmon, 408 ATA clubs participated in the Plan for Growth in 1998. [18] Nevertheless, Harmon contended that the USTA missed a big opportunity when MaliVai Washington reached the 1996 Wimbledon final. "It would have been a tremendous shot in the arm for multicultural development if we had had a structure in place at the time. What MaliVai did was unbelievable, but there should have been people and programs in place so everyone could build on the energy he created. I've told him that once we get everything going, I need him to get back to the final. Then we can seize the moment." [19] This hypothetical argument could be taken further. If Washington's success in 1996 could have been instrumental for USTA minority development if a "structure" had been in place, what of the many other missed opportunities, such as Garrison's appearance in the 1990 Wimbledon final?

In 1997, former *Black Tennis* editor Ed Freeman argued that 99 percent of the top black tennis players and coaches had come through the ATA or through the black community. The USTA, he maintained, had identified the "elite minority athletes" for the national programs, but "the grassroots start at home on the old beat up public park courts."[20]

Tour player James Blake asserted, "I couldn't be happier with the USTA. They've helped me out a lot. I appreciate what they've done." Regarding those who criticize, he added, "People take the same situation different ways a lot of times. I try to look on the bright side."[21]

Despite the claim by the USTA that it has been doing a more than adequate job at reaching minorities, others disagree. Virginia Glass, longtime ATA member, has been unimpressed with USTA efforts. She maintains,

> If you're talking about developing grass roots with the USTA, that's not impressive. There are three outstanding women coming up, but what's behind those three? They weren't the result of a concentrated effort by the USTA. They had very select and unusual parents, who knew what they were doing. If the USTA could open its eyes and offer more support, then they would open up the coffers instead of [doing] all this talking. They need to step up. It's the organization for the country, but not for minorities.

Willis Thomas alleges that the USTA minority effort had so far been "worse than nothing because it gives us false hopes while still giving the money to the establishment." That is the fundamental key: How has the USTA dispensed funds in the various programs?

Whereas James Blake has praised the efforts by USTA, Mashiska Washington, another tour player, thinks otherwise. "We have to speak up, there is no other way. I don't feel I have been given the same chances and funding to succeed. This is another chapter in the struggle for equality." In addition, he places this struggle within the historical context of combating racism: "If somebody hadn't spoken up about past injustices, we wouldn't be drinking from the same water fountain today."

Houston instructor John Wilkerson argues that USTA has given little money to support established minority programs. The USTA instead has taken a "comprehensive approach that installs it at the controls and provides some independent operators with carefully rationed support. Limited funds is the main reason given for that approach, but it seems to derive equally from a philosophy of centralized authority."

The USTA hired Alexander & Associates, a Washington, D.C., consulting firm to study ways to encourage minority participation. One idea was to expand the minority applicant pool for jobs in the sectional offices. The firm rejected the suggestion of a national USTA training camp for blacks. The camp was to be held in Indianapolis with twenty-four of the most promising young black players. Ron Woods, USTA director of player development, explained, "The consultants told us that kind of 'separate but equal' arrangement would send the wrong message." Instead, it was suggested that working with blacks in small groups as part of regular development programs was better.[22] Of course, that would still be separation, but under the umbrella of "integration."

More recently, the awarding of wild cards at the U.S. Open has become a volatile issue. In 1997, several black players from the United States received wild cards. In addition to Steve Campbell, who received a wild card into the main draw, James Blake, Mashiska Washington, Phil Williamson (who had retired), Mashona Washington, and Katrina Adams received wild cards for the qualifying rounds. Some felt that great strides were being taken to increase the number of blacks in the most important tournament in the United States. Cesar Jansen, minority tennis activist, proclaimed, "They're starting to listen."[23]

When William Washington received permission in July 1999 from the New York office of the Equal Employment Opportunity Commission to file a civil suit against the USTA for discrimination, it was highly publicized. The Washingtons and their lawyer, Ellis Rubin, faced Eugene L. Scott, *Tennis Week* publisher, and David Jasinski, a labor and employment attorney, on *Johnnie Cochran Tonight,* which aired on Court TV and Black Entertainment Television.[24]

William Washington accused the USTA of "withholding career opportunities from his son and other black tennis players." Although, according to Washington, there were many instances of racism by the

USTA, ATP, and WTA, a specific event at the 1998 U.S. Open had provided the impetus for the lawsuit. Six players were placed ahead of Mashiska Washington in the draw. Of those six, two were black, James Blake and his younger brother, Thomas. But Mashiska's not getting a wild card was "the straw that broke the camel's back," according to Washington, who argued that other events before 1998 also supported his accusations.

Eugene Scott conceded that racism had existed in the sport, but not in the case of how the wild cards were awarded. He argued that the players who received wild cards in the U.S. Open men's main draw were ranked above Mashiska. As for the qualifying rounds, there were some with rankings below Mashiska, but "they're in categories." He added, "If the USTA is guilty of discrimination, or racial bias, they're doing a very bad job of it because three out of the eight wild cards in the qualifying were given to minorities." Those were the Blake brothers and Kevin Kim, who is of "Asian" descent. Also, Scott argued that Washington's other daughter, Mashona, received a wild card into the main draw in 1998 even when three women ranked above her failed to get into the main draw.

Washington responded by explaining that in 1998 white player Taylor Dent was ranked lower than 500 and received a main draw wild card, and white player Scott Humphries received a main draw wild card even though ranked number 1,245 between 1995 and 1996. "That has never happened to a minority person," he stated. He added that Mashona only got a wild card because "she was the first alternate out." He also maintained that the six players placed ahead of Mashiska had lower rankings.

Scott explained that wild cards were awarded for any purpose, called peremptory challenge in the legal profession. He agreed with Washington that the "wild cards have enormous economic impact" because if a player gets into the first round of the U.S. Open, he or she gets a ranking point and $10,000 even if he or she loses.

David Jasinski argued that the Washingtons were confusing "discrimination" with "entitlement." He insisted that if the USTA were discriminating, the Blakes would have been denied wild cards. Washington challenged Jasinski to explain why Bryan Shelton, Steve Campbell, Mashiska Washington, and Mark Foster failed to get any wild cards on the tour, whereas players such as Justin Gimelstob and Luke Jensen did. Jasinski's refutation was that there were probably hundreds of white tennis players who were not awarded wild cards either.

Lawyer Ellis Rubin contended that the basic premise of awarding wild cards is wrong. "It is discretionary. . . . There's no guidelines; no rules; no required fairness; you can't earn a wild card." He added that he knew of no other sport that awards wild card.

The courtroom was an improper venue to settle the issue, according to Jasinski. Washington maintained, however, that he had written former USTA presidents Les Snyder and Harry Marmion, but neither had ever responded. In fact, Marmion once walked out of the room while Washington spoke at a USTA national meeting. Rubin asserted that he had also attempted to arrange a meeting to no avail. Nevertheless, Scott agreed to arrange a meeting at Cochran's asking.

When Mashiska, Mashona, and MaliVai received wild cards in the main draw of the 1999 U.S. Open, the decision drew censure. One tennis fan argued that it was possible that USTA "sold out to the pressure it has been put under by unfounded claims of prejudice by Mr. Washington."[25] Julia Levering, then USTA president, however, maintained that these players deserved the wild cards. She argued, "The committee felt the Washingtons earned those wild cards because they show potential. We are not in the business of handing them out idly or without merit. We have made it our emphasis to get more minorities into this game. I want people like William Washington and Richard Williams to be involved in our programs."[26]

James Blake said that he failed to understand anyone's expecting a wild card, except maybe in extreme cases. For him, wild cards were a privilege.[27] William Washington disagreed: "It is expected for French players to get most of the wild cards at the French Open, or the same for Australians at the Australian Open, but the USTA will give wild cards to white foreign players while overlooking black American players. Wild cards drive the system."[28]

Washington had a list of twenty black tennis players "now unaccounted for." He claimed," Rodney Harmon made it to the quarters of the U.S. Open. The man died because the system didn't give him no wild cards, no help. The system has done the same thing to all of them. Chewed them up. Didn't help them. Stopped them." Harmon, who was the newly appointed director of multicultural development for the USTA in 1997, professed, "I did get some wild cards. And there were times I didn't get them but felt I should have." He believed that the "current exclusion may be what Washington described as unintentional but habitual racism."[29]

Washington was not the only one who felt that racism still existed in the USTA. Albert Tucker, the executive director of the ATA in 1997, argued that he and his organization had no voice in the USTA decision-making process. In addition, it was stressed that Wendell Willis, USTA Minority Participation Committee chairperson, could not devote all of his energies to the post because he had a full-time job with Honeywell. This decision questioned the USTA's commitment to increase opportunities for "minorities." Tucker also charged that the Tennis Industry Association (TIA) was out of touch with the problem: "The TIA keeps making comments that they want to make changes but they don't change people on the board who will make the decisions." He argued that the TIA Free Lesson Blitz program in Washington, D.C., had failed. He asked, "Why send someone like Kurt Kamperman who has no clue about the inner city? Send somebody who can relate to the leaders."[30] Kurt Kamperman, president of the TIA, maintained that the ATA was ineligible for USTA board membership because it had not joined the TIA, a problem that was rectified later.

In a letter to *Tennis Week* in 1998, William Washington insisted that there was no minority participation in the USTA and that the TIA Free Lesson Blitz program was an example. "No blitz captains or coaches are minorities. The program has not been brought to the inner-city, yet the USTA has appropriated $3.6 million over the last three years to grow the game through this process." He further asserted that the USTA should take the programs to the "ghettos," instead of the opposite approach: "Don't try to bring them out of there and expect them to come to Key Biscayne [USTA player-development headquarters]. They're not going to pay that dollar toll and go way out there to Key Biscayne to play tennis. Put the facility in the community. And don't try to entertain us. You go in and talk stroke production and skill development and after that we'll say goodbye, get out of here, I'll handle the fun part." [31]

In August 1999, Richard Williams presented a plan to the USTA for increasing inner-city programs. He explained, "Venus and Serena take pride in where they come from. We want to come back and lead others out of the ghetto. I want to be the Pied Piper of the ghetto and use tennis and education to get people out." But ATA president Tucker warned against the use of the "race card." "We have to stop believing that every time something doesn't happen it is because of the color of our skin. I know a lot of white folks who have the same problems. I don't always buy the race card. It's more of a business card than anything." [32]

Doug Smith, columnist for *USA Today*, affirmed in 1998 that there was at that time a consistent pattern of discrimination in the management of tennis. As an example, he pointed out that black player J. J. Jackson was overlooked in USTA national team selection when Jackson was number 1 in Boys' 14s. Previously, the number 1 had been automatically selected to the national team. Another case involved James Blake, who had won the Boys' 18s Clay Court Championships and was a finalist in the Hard Court Championships, but was not selected to the national team.

Racism has existed in the upper echelons of tennis, and white males have dominated the administration of tennis organizations, with the USTA being no exception. In 1998, Steve Milano of Lawrence, Kansas, urged blacks to nominate and vote for a qualified black USTA board candidate, possibly with the help of the ATA. [33] In June 1998, former committee chair Koger wrote in a letter to *Tennis Week,*

Many people who are in the sport of tennis (as well as some of the other national sport governing bodies in this country) cannot help but notice the lack of color in the leadership positions. The few people of color who have slipped through the cracks to leadership in the USTA and have fought for increased presence of people of color are usually labeled militant or rabble-rousers. They are usually given a letter of thanks and excused from whatever position of leadership they had and replaced by others who will go along with the status quo. The few who are in positions of leadership in the ranks have taken some soft-peddling approaches to getting people of color in the sport of tennis. To look at their efforts to date, there are few to none in the many USTA programs.

Koger argued that the "lack of presence of people of color, particularly black, Asian and Latino" also meant the lack of a "diverse perspective in the decision-making processes" within tennis. She added that the problem of leadership was found at the sectional and district levels.

She suggested that the USTA add a clause to its constitution stipulating that it would be an equal opportunity and affirmative action organization. In addition, it must set policies and programs for recruitment and retention in its appointment and hiring practices. Moreover, it should seek expertise from those outside of the USTA in "nontraditional places." Finally, it should offer "training facilities and programs in the neighborhoods which are accessible to average families."[34]

About a month later, Bob Davis of Black Dynamics asserted:

There are people of goodwill involved in the MP [Committee] now, but to me the question will always be whether or not minority participation is in fact allowed to grow. And it is oxymoronic to think that you are going to get some of the most influential people in the business, people of color of particular influence in their region who sit on MP committees, and they are not able to act with autonomy. The USTA controls the purse strings. But I can't tell you if our committee is doing what it set out to do because we don't have a device by which we can measure the increases and decreases in participation, or a mechanism to measure our successes and failures.[35]

The chairperson who replaced Koger was Wendell Willis, who had worked for Honeywell for twenty-five years. He explained, "My hope is to take this into the 21st century with a lot of positive programs and actions." Then new USTA president Harry Marmion placed Willis in the chair position. He argued, "Wendell had a totally different background. He has a corporate background and he has been in mainstream white America. He is very capable and has gone after wealthy African-American executives to get them involved." Koger maintained that her posture cost her the position as committee chair. "I might have been perceived as too outspoken. I am a person who has always been willing to keep certain tough issues on the table and address things that need to be addressed. Maybe the organization of the board wanted to have minority participation handled differently."[36]

Davis confirmed, "Many of us . . . knew during Pat's tenure that she would be replaced. We knew that Pat was pressing for some real serious accomplishments out of the MP initiative. And we knew she was ruffling some feathers. I remember meeting Pat at an MP meeting and I said to myself that this girl is dead on target, but she is going to self-destruct because she is saying too many things that are dead on, and they are going to get her. And they did."[37]

In terms of funding, $288,900 was allocated directly to the Minority Participation Committee. In addition, "minority tennis" benefited indirectly from the $548,800 allocated to the USTA/NJTL Program, the $570,000 given to the Schools Program, and the $400,000 budgeted to the Player Development Program. However, considering the overall USTA budget, the funding for the committee was minuscule.

USTA vice president Joy Rodenberg, also the liaison with the Minority Participation Committee, felt in 1998 that the committee had up to that point performed as well as it could. Rodenberg stated: "Obviously, I am impatient in some ways and would like to wave a wand and have it be business as usual, but our society isn't like that right now. So it would be very difficult to do something society hasn't worked out yet. But I do think we are headed in the right direction."[38]

Correcting a *Tennis Week* article about the Player Development Program, William Washington argued in a letter to the editor that his son MaliVai did not participate in the USTA Player Development Program as had been publicized and that the USTA had merely paid MaliVai's entry fees to play USTA events. He added, "We were not a part of USTA, and I will not be a part of USTA as long as it continues its exclusionary discriminatory racist practices against tennis athletes of color. . . . Racism permeates USTA from top to bottom. The Nominating Committee, governing board and Player Development Committee have been all white for over one hundred years."[39]

In response to learning of former New York City mayor David Dinkins's involvement in the USTA, the elder Washington maintained, "Well, Mr. Dinkins is a politician, not a tennis player. We don't expect Mr. Dinkins to attack the racism issue in tennis; that wouldn't be politically expedient." His letter continued with a challenge to Julia Levering, then the newly elected president of the USTA:

> Several writers have said Ms. Levering cast her vote to name the National Tennis Center after Arthur Ashe and that she feels strongly about tennis being an inclusive sport; however, the two are not related. We want to know what Ms. Levering plans to do about the thousands upon thousands of youngsters in the New York area who will never be invited to the National Tennis Center to learn to play tennis. In fact, there are thousands of kids who live within walking distance of the National Tennis Center and don't even know Arthur Ashe's name is written upon it.

As for Arthur Ashe Day at the National Tennis Center, to be held just before the opening day of the 1999 U.S. Open, he suggested, "The Arthur Ashe Day is nothing more than a picnic/funeral for white folks to try and resurrect a dead lifestyle for blacks in tennis that we all reject. Black tennis athletes cannot follow Arthur Ashe and survive pro tennis in America today. We blacks today demand to be treated with balance, fairness and equality from the USTA, WTA and ATP." Washington even challenged whether the USTA's Plan for Growth was really implemented to help "people of color." "I want to be the first to declare that the $50 million, five-year USTA Plan for Growth is a whites-only project and should be stated as such. It's not designed to incorporate people of color. The plan has no arm that reaches out to the minority community." Finally, he asserted, "We do not need a USTA Minority

Participation Committee. Such a committee is tantamount to the separate but equal system that existed to keep schools segregated in the South. It's an excuse for the USTA Player Development Committee to not do its job. It's a smoke screen for the USTA president and governing board to hide behind."[40]

According to writer Julianne Malveaux, the Williams sisters' successes "energized women's tennis, attracting millions of new viewers to televised tennis, and millions of dollars in new revenue to the U.S. Tennis Association." In her September 15, 2000, article, she questioned whether the USTA had given enough to develop a new group of black players. Rodney Harmon cited the positive efforts of the USTA's multicultural development program because of its $2.2 million annual budget, which had developed new players such as Jamea Jackson, Natalie Frazier, Jewel Peterson, and Megan Bradley. However, Malveaux stressed that the $2.2 million represented a mere one percent of USTA's total budget. Finally, she questioned whether the sisters' successes happened "in spite of—not because of—the tennis association."[41]

Conclusion

THE HISTORY OF BLACKS IN TENNIS is a long one that has witnessed many developments. An interest in the history of blacks in tennis and in sport in general has created recognition of the achievements of certain individuals. For example, at the 2003 Federation Cup tie, held in Washington, D.C., Margaret and Roumania Peters were honored and inducted into the USTA Mid-Atlantic Hall of Fame (they were inducted into the Tuskegee University Athletic Hall of Fame in 1977). The 2003 Federation Cup team made history when three of the four players named to the squad were black: Venus Williams, Serena Williams, and Alexandria Stevenson. Chanda Rubin had to pull out of the tie, but Zina Garrison served as assistant coach to Billie Jean King and later replaced her as head coach.

Historically, black fans have attended tournaments in greater numbers when black players have participated. According to *World Tennis* writer Gladys M. Heldman, blacks had not attended the tournament at Forest Hills until Althea Gibson competed in the U.S. National Championships. "The handful of black fans who came out to watch her the first year she played got almost as much attention as the competitors."[1]

TIA data in 2000 showed that of 20.8 million people in the United States who play tennis, 1.5 million are black (7.2 percent). In comparison, 26.4 million people play golf, and 880,000 are black (3.3 percent), according to the National Golf Foundation.[2] More blacks might watch a sporting event but still not actually play the sport. Many blacks have watched tennis or golf when the Williams sisters or Tiger Woods have played, but have continued otherwise to ignore these sports. Even at the height of the Williams's publicity, white audiences continue to predominate, and high ticket prices exclude many minorities.

The issues of race and gender have remained constant. Despite the Williams sisters' success, many overlook the fact that there are fewer black professionals on the tour at the start of the new millennium than there were in the 1970s. As has been the case in many formerly all-white institutions, the presence of one or two blacks has satisfied the goals of diversity and has prompted the belief that racism no longer exists.

In 2001, William Washington warned against the belief that the sisters' success would somehow eradicate other obstacles:

> The inference that the Williams sisters will have a big impact upon the black community and that there is going to be a mad rush of young black females into tennis is very unlikely. There is a big price to be paid to become a world class player and most families aren't willing to pay the price. . . . So, forge the notion that we need someone with flair or he must have the looks of Koby Bryant to survive the pro circuit. That's a non-tennis perception of things. . . . This business is about hard work and soul, not gimmicks and rock 'n' roll. That coupled with equal access to developmental opportunities to make it. Right now, in America, that's not the case for most blacks.[3]

While work on this book was being completed, blacks had achieved additional accomplishments in tennis. A black player from Great Britain, Justin Lagne, as well as two from Germany, Ibrahim Kimmerling and Junior Ghedina, were on the pro tour. Algeria's Lamine Ouahab, Senegal's Khady Berthe, South Africa's Raven Klassen, and Kenya's Yvette Akoth lead a new generation of African players who hope to enter the domain of professional tennis. In the United States, collegiates Alexis Gordon, Megan Bradley, and Raquel Kops-Jones vied for the 2004 NCAA Women's Championships. The new professional focus is Donald Young, who turned pro at age fourteen. The fact that Levar Harper-Griffith and even James Blake have already ceased to be "the next hopeful" exemplifies how the media move on to other black hopefuls when success by current black players fails to develop quickly enough or well enough. Time will tell whether Young will be the next recipient of the "Ashe syndrome." However, the biggest story in tennis now is France's Gael Monfils, top ranked among junior boys, winning the Junior Boys' Australian, French, and Wimbledon championships in 2004.

Although much of this work has focused on professional tennis, blacks on all levels continue to provide interesting stories. Many have a passionate love for the game. For example, one black player loved tennis so much that he continued to play each Saturday despite a physical limitation and died on the court. Dallas player Sarah Ward regularly played tournament matches after working all night. In one match, she fell asleep on the court while waiting to receive serve. Slightly injuring herself as she fell on the asphalt court failed to stop her from winning the match, however. It is this type of passion that many in the world have never witnessed because they are not professionals.

Appendixes

•

Notes

•

Glossary

•

Bibliography

•

Index

ATA Championship Singles

	Men's	Women's
1917	Tally Holmes	Lucy Slowe
1918	Tally Holmes	M. Rae
1919	Sylvester Smith	M. Rae
1920	B. M. Clark	M. Rae
1921	Tally Holmes	Lucy Slowe
1922	Edgar Brown	Isadore Channels
1923	Edgar Brown	Isadore Channels
1924	Tally Holmes	Isadore Channels
1925	Theodore Thompson	Lulu Ballard
1926	Eyre Saitch	Isadore Channels
1927	Theodore Thompson	Lulu Ballard
1928	Edgar G. Brown	Lulu Ballard
1929	Edgar G. Brown	Ora Washington
1930	Douglas Turner	Ora Washington
1931	Reginald Weir	Ora Washington
1932	Reginald Weir	Ora Washington
1933	Reginald Weir	Ora Washington
1934	Nathaniel Jackson	Ora Washington
1935	Franklin Jackson	Ora Washington
1936	Lloyd Scott	Lulu Ballard
1937	Reginald Weir	Ora Washington
1938	Franklin Jackson	Flora Lomax
1939	Jimmie McDaniel	Flora Lomax

1940	Jimmie McDaniel	Agnes Lawson
1941	Jimmie McDaniel	Flora Lomax
1942	Reginald Weir	Flora Lomax
1944	Lloyd Scott	Roumanie Peters
1945	Lloyd Scott	Kathrn Irvis
1946	Jimmie McDaniel	Roumania Peters
1947	George Stewart	Althea Gibson
1948	George Stewart	Althea Gibson
1949	unfinished	Althea Gibson
1950	Oscar Johnson	Althea Gibson
1951	George Stewart	Althea Gibson
1952	George Stewart	Althea Gibson
1953	George Stewart	Althea Gibson
1954	Earthna Jacquet	Althea Gibson
1955	Robert Ryland	Althea Gibson
1956	Robert Ryland	Althea Gibson
1957	George Stewart	Gwendolyn McEvans
1958	Wilbert Davis	Mary E. Fine
1959	Wilbert Davis	Gwendolyn McEvans
1960	Arthur Ashe Jr.	Mimi Kanarek
1961	Arthur Ashe Jr.	Carolyn Williams
1962	Arthur Ashe Jr.	Carolyn Liguori
1963	Wilbert Davis	Ginger Pfiefer
1964	George Stewart	Bonnie Logan
1965	Luis Glass	Bonnie Logan
1966	Wilbert Davis	Bonnie Logan
1967	Wilbert Davis	Bonnie Logan
1968	Robert Binns	Bonnie Logan
1969	Marty Gool	Bonnie Logan
1970	Gene Fluri	Bonnie Logan
1971	John Wilkerson	Bessie Stockard
1972	Horace Reid	Lorraine Bryant
1973	Arthur Carrington	Mimi Kanarek
1974	R. D. Guedes	Jean Burnett
1975	Benny Sims	Diane Morrison
1976	Terrance Jackson	Kim Sands
1977	Terrance Jackson	no one

1978	Rodney Harmon	Joann Jacobs
1979	Warrick Jones	Zina Garrison
1980	Kelvin Belcher	Zina Garrison
1981	Kelvin Belcher	Lori McNeil
1982	Warrick Jones	Luch Bacerra
1983	Adrian Clark	Lisa de Angeles

World Rankings of Black Players, 1979–1992

Men	'79	'80	'81	'82	'83	'84	'85	'86	'87	'88	'89	'90	'91	'92
Agenor						48			44	28	37	29	73	129
Ashe	7													
Belcher					214									
Bourne				71	146	97	144		158					
Doumbia										93			228	
Foxworth	167			143		234								
Freeman					142	95			160					
Harmon				70	117	94								
Hooper				32	55	83	112		146					
Mmoh						220			187					
Nelson						106	166		111	123				
Noah	28			9	4	10	7		8	12	16	40	190	
Odizor				81	64	116	76		101		185	184		
Shelton											162	122	71	100
Smith									155	194				
Washington											216	91	49	13
Wekesa										170		250		

Women	'79	'80	'81	'82	'83	'84	'85	'86	'87	'88	'89	'90	'91	'92
Adams									223	102	86		93	143
Allen	41			25	46	151			205					
Benjamin				64	50	29	58		64	90	93	137	216	247
Blount				102	135	241	161							
Buchanan	114													
Garrison				15	11	7	8		9	9	4	10	12	18
Jones					220									
Martin										88	82	105	163	204
McNeil					144	85	92		11	13	37	52	19	15
Morrison	62													
Rubin													83	83
Sands	110			108	66	108								

USTA Circuit Winners and Runners-Up

USTA Men's Circuit Singles, 1981–2000

	Winner	*Runner-Up*
Belcher, Kevin		1984 Annandale, Va.
Blake, Thomas		1998 Kansas City, Mo.
Campbell, Steve	1993 Los Angeles, Calif.	
	1994 Bakersfield, Calif.	
	1994 South El Monte, Calif.	
	1994 Los Angeles, Calif.	
	1995 Elkin, N.C.	1995 Macon, Ga.
	1996 Fairfield, Calif.	
Farrow, Juan		1979 Wichita, Kans.
	1980 New Haven, Conn.	1980 Wall Township, N.J.
	1980 Abilene, Tex.	1980 Midland, Tex.
	1981 Hilton Head, S.C.	
	1982 Greensboro, N.C.	1982 Washington, D.C.
Foxworth, Bruce	1979 Hilton Head, S.C.	1979 Clemmons, N.C.
	1979 Wall Township, N.J.	
	1982 Augusta, Ga.	
	1982 Midlothian, Va.	
	1982 New Haven, Conn.	
	1982 Washington, D.C.	
		1983 Waco, Tex.
Freeman, Marcel		1979 Wilton, Conn.
		1979 Wall Township, N.J.
	1982 Dallas, Tex.	1982 Houston, Tex.

Harmon, Rodney	1981 Greensboro, N.C.	
Hooper, Chip	1981 Sioux City, Idaho	1981 Rockwall, Tex.
	1988 Sarasota, Fla.	
Ismail, Haroon	1979 Hialeah, Fla.	
Ladipo, Sule	1996 Lauderhill, Fla.	1996 Vero Beach, Fla.
	1996 Tallahassee, Fla.	
N'Goran, Clement		1989 Springfield, Mo.
Smith, Roger	1987 Lawrence, Kans.	1987 Lake Ozark, Mo.
Washington, MaliVai		1988 Litte Rock, Ark.
	1989 Fort Worth, Tex.	

Men's Challenger Series Singles, 1984–2000

	Winner	Runner-Up
Agenor, Ronald	2000 Birmingham, Ala.	
Blake, James	2000 Spring, Tex.	
	2000 Rancho Mirage, Calif.	
Shelton, Bryan	1990 Tampa, Fla.	
		1991 Aptos, Calif.
Washington, MaliVai	1989 Seattle, Wash.	

USTA Men's Futures Series Singles, 1998–1999

	Winner	Runner-Up
Agenor, Ronald	1998 Delray Beach, Fla.	
	1998 Vero Beach, Fla.	
	1998 Boca Raton, Fla.	
Blake, James	1999 Altamonte, Fla.	
	1999 Haines City, Fla.	
	1999 Clearwater, Fla.	
Blake, Thomas		1998 Phoenix, Ariz.

(continued)

USTA Women's Circuit Singles, 1981–1999

	Winner	*Runner-Up*
Adams, Katrina		1987 Lebanon, N.J.
	1991 New Braunfels, Tex.	
Benjamin, Camille		1982 Warrensville Heights, Ohio
		1982 Houston, Tex.

USTA Women's Circuit Singles, 1981–1999 *(continued)*

	Winner	*Runner-Up*
Jones, Cheryl	1987 Fresno, Calif.	1987 Key Biscayne, Fla.
McNeil, Lori		1983 Baltimore, Md.
Rubin, Chanda		1991 Mission, Tex.
Washington, Mashona		1994 Indianapolis, Ind.
		1995 Hilton Head, S.C.
		1998 San Antonio, Tex.
Washington, Michaela		1983 Birmingham, Ala.
	1984 West Palm Beach, Fla.	1984 Chatham, N.J.

Women's Challenger Series Singles, 1985–1999

	Winner	*Runner-Up*
Benjamin, Camille	1994 Salisbury, Md.	
Martin, Stacey		1986 Bethesda, Md.
McNeil, Lori	1998 Rochester, Minn.	
Rubin, Chanda	1995 Midland, Mich.	
Washington, Mashona		1998 Clearwater, Fla.

Source: Adapted from USTA, Circuit Office, *2000 Eddleman USTA Challenger Program* (Lynn, Mass.: H. O. Zimman, May 2000).

Some of the Best Matches by Black Players, 1957–2001

Althea Gibson defeated Louise Brough 6-3, 6-2 in the final of the 1957 U.S. Open.

Arthur Ashe defeated Tom Okker 14-12, 5-7, 6-3, 3-6, 6-3 in the final of the 1968 U.S. Open.

Arthur Ashe defeated Jimmy Conners in the final of the 1975 Wimbledon.

Evonne Goolagong defeated Chris Evert 6-1, 7-6 in the final of 1980 Wimbledon.

Leslie Allen defeated Hana Mandlikova 6-4, 6-4 in the 1982 Avon Championship in Detroit.

Leslie Allen lost to Chris Evert 6-3, 3-6, 7-6 (7-3) in the quarterfinals of the 1982 Avon Championship in Oakland.

Yannick Noah defeated Mats Wilander 6-2, 7-5 7-6 (7-3) in the final of the 1983 French Open.

Nduka Odizor defeated Guillermo Vilas (4) 3-6, 5-7, 7-6, 7-5, 6-2 in the 1983 Wimbledon.

Lloyd Bourne defeated Nduka Odizor 6-7, 6-1, 6-1, 4-6, 7-6 in the first round of the 1983 U.S. Open.

Camille Benjamin defeated Lisa Bonder (13) 7-6, 5-7, 6-3 in the quarterfinals of the 1984 French Open.

Nigeria (Nduka Odizor and Abdoulahi Sadiq) defeated Senegal (Yaya Doumbia and Thierno Amidou Ly) 4-6, 9-7, 7-5, 6-3 in 1986 Davis Cup tie.

Yannick Noah defeated Ivan Lendl 6-3, 7-5 in the semifinals and Guillermo Vilas 7-6, 6-0 in the final of the 1986 Tournament of Champions.

Lori McNeil defeated Chris Evert 3-6, 6-2, 6-4 in the quarterfinals of the 1987 U.S. Open.

Ronald Agenor defeated Yannick Noah 4-6, 6-2, 6-3 in the 1988 Grand Prix Passing Shot, Bordeaux.

Zina Garrison defeated Monica Seles 3-6, 6-3, 9-7 in the quarterfinals of the 1990 Wimbledon.

Ronald Agenor defeated Wayne Ferreira (2) 6-3, 5-7, 6-1 in the quarterfinals of the 1995 Grand Prix Passing Shot, Bordeaux.

Yaya Doumbia defeated David Prinosil (5) 6-3, 6-2 in round 16, Lionel Roux (8) 6-4, 6-2 in the semifinals, and Jakob Hlasek (7) 6-4, 6-4 in the final of the 1995 Grand Prix Passing Shot, Bordeaux.

Chanda Rubin defeated Jana Novotna (5) 7-6 (10-8), 4-6, 8-6, coming from a 5-0 deficit in the 1995 French Open.

Chanda Rubin defeated Patricia Hy-Boulais 7-6, 6-7 (5-7), 17-15 in three hours and forty-five minutes in the 1995 Wimbledon, establishing Wimbledon records for longest final set (two hours, four minutes), games in a set (thirty-two), and games in a match (fifty-eight), and almost for most games in a women's Grand Slam singles match.

James Blake lost to Jeff Morrison 6-7 (2), 6-2, 4-6 in the 1999 NCAA Championships final.

Venus Williams defeated Martina Hingis 6-4, 1-6, 6-4 in the semifinals and Mary Pierce 6-7 (1), 6-2, 6-4 in the final of the 1999 Italian Open.

Serena Williams defeated Julie Halard-Decugis 6-4, 6-4 in the 1999 Acura Classic in Manhattan Beach.

Younes El Aynaoui (6) defeated Mariano Zabalata (3) 6-0, 6-3 in the 1999 Grolsch Open, Amsterdam. He also defeated countryman Karim Alami 1-6, 6-1, 6-1 in the second round.

Chanda Rubin defeated defending champion Martina Hingis 6-3, 7-6 (7-2) in the quarterfinals of the 1999 Evert Cup.

Ronald Agenor defeated Paradorn Srichaphan 7-5, 6-2 in the final of the 2000 Eddleman USTA Challenger in Birmingham, Ala.

Hicham Arazi defeated Lleyton Heweitt (5) 6-1, 6-4 at the 2001 Tennis Masters Series–Canada (Montreal).

Ronald Agenor lost to Gustavo Kuerten (1) 6-4, 4-6, 3-6 at the 2001 Tennis Masters Series–Canada (Montreal).

Younes El Aynaoui defeated Magnus Gustaffsson (6) 6-4, 7-5 in the semifinals and lost to Alex Crretja (2) 6-3, 5-7, 7-4 (0), 3-6, 6-4 in the final of
  2001 ATP Tour Energis Open in Amsterdam.
Dally Randriantefy lost to Eva Bes 6-4, 5-7, 6-4 in the first round of 2001
  Casablanca Grand Prix.

The Results of the First Annual Southern Tennis Championships, July 9–11, 1930

Men's Singles Edward Ramsey (Tuskegee) defeated Dr. H. O. Matthews (Tuskegee U.A.) 7-5, 6-3, 6-4

Men's Doubles Edward Ramsey and F. D. Patters (Tuskegee) defeated J. J. Harper and A. B. Harper (Atlanta) 6-4, 6-4, 6-2

Women's Singles Vivienne Hollis (Tuskegee) defeated Lonie Curtis (Fort Benning) 6-2, 6-2

Women's Doubles Almeta Hill (Atlanta) and Lonie Curtis (Fort Benning) defeated C. L. Abbott and C. G. Bevans (Tuskegee) 6-2, 5-7, 7-5

Mixed Doubles A. B. Harper and Almeta Hill (Atlanta) defeated Vivienne Hollis and F. D. Patterson (Tuskegee) 6-3, 3-6, 6-4

Notes

Caveats

1. Dwight A. McBride, "Can the Queen Speak? Racial Essentialism, Sexuality, and the Problem of Authority," in *The Great Taboo: Homosexuality in Black Communities* (Los Angeles: Alyson, 2000), 27.

Introduction

1. "Will Have No Colored Member," *Chicago Tribune*, Sept. 9, 1892.
2. "Tennis Tournament," *Chicago Inter-Ocean*, May 28, 1893.

1. The American Tennis Association and the Early Years

1. Robert W. Henderson, *Ball, Bat, and Bishop: The Origin of Ball Games* (New York: Rockport, 1947), 3–4.

2. Ibid., 5, quoting Malcolm D. Whitman, *Tennis: Origins and Mysteries* (Detroit: Singing Tree, 1968). See also Edna Rust and Art Rust Jr., *Art Rust's Illustrated History of the Black Athlete* (Garden City, N.Y.: Doubleday, 1985), 399.

3. Heiner Gillmeister, *Tennis: A Cultural History* (New York: New York Univ. Press, 1998), 5.

4. Henderson, 3–4.

5. Irene Sommers, "Who First Brought Tennis to America?" *Tennis*, Sept. 1994, 128. See also Martha Summerhayes, *Vanished Arizona: Recollections of My Army Life* (1908; reprint, Chicago: Lakeside, 1939); Bishop William Lawrence, *Memories of a Happy Life* (Boston: Houghton Mifflin, 1926); George Alexander, *Lawn Tennis: Its Founders and Its Early Days* (Lynn, Mass.: H. O. Zimman, 1974); and Rust and Rust, 399.

6. "Lawn Tennis 1872–1972," *World Tennis*, Aug. 1972, 22.

7. Sommers, 128.

8. Benjamin G. Rader, *American Sports: From the Age of Folk Games to the Age of Televised Sports* (Englewood Cliffs, N.J.: Prentice Hall, 1996), 64.

9. See Rust and Rust, 134–35; Rader, 69. Very few sports played in colonial North America, such as wrestling, were played in West Africa.

10. Donald Mrozek, *Sport and American Mentality, 1880–1910* (Knoxville: Univ. of Tennessee Press, 1983), 103–35.

11. "History of Tennis at Tuskegee University," unpublished manuscript, Tuskegee Univ. Sports Information Office, 1977, 6.

12. Bertram Barker, "A Black Tennis Association: Active since 1916," in *American Tennis Association National Rankings 1983–1984* (Philadelphia: American Tennis Association, 1984), 60.

13. The ATA was formed out of racial segregation like many black institutions, including a golf tour for black players called the Universal Golf Association, formed by Bill Spiller.

14. Barker, 60.

15. Druid Hill Park became the site of the Netman Coed Annual Tournament, an ATA event.

16. There is a discrepancy in the spelling of Dr. Hoage's name in different documents.

17. Barker, 60.

18. Rader, 190.

19. Ibid., 191.

20. "History of Tennis at Tuskegee," 6.

21. Douglas A. Noverr and Lawrence E. Ziewacz, *The Games They Played: Sports in American History 1865–1980* (Chicago: Nelson Hall, 1983), 132.

22. Steven M. Tucker, "Against all Odds," *Racquet,* fall 1991, 58.

23. "Tolan's Success on Track Recalls Deeds of Negro Sports Stars of Other Days," *New York Times,* Aug. 17, 1930.

24. "Wilberforce Wins Tennis Tournament," *Chicago Defender,* May 1930.

25. "History of Tennis at Tuskegee," 2–3.

26. Roumania died in 2003 at age eighty-five after a bout with pneumonia. See "Sisters Blazed Trail for Venus, Serena," *Wichita Eagle,* July 20, 2003; John Krawcqynski, "Trailblazing Black Tennis Sisters 'Pete' and 'Repeat' Finally Getting Their Due," *The Call,* July 14, 2003; Larry Gross, "Tuskegee Legends Honored," *Chicago Defender,* July 26, 2003; and Louis Estrada, "Matilda Walker, Tennis Champ," *Washington Post,* May 22, 2003.

27. Tucker, 58, emphasis in original.

28. Interview of Chris Scott, black tennis coach at the University of Chicago and tennis pro at Southside Racket Club, in Helen Logan Watson, "Project Serve: A Junior

Development Project in an Inner City Area," master's thesis, Northwestern Illinois State College, 1970, 2.

29. Parke Cummings, *American Tennis: The Story of a Game and Its People* (Boston: Little, Brown, 1957), 17.

30. Tucker, 60.

31. Al Laney, "2,000 Negroes," *New York Herald Tribune,* July 30, 1940.

32. Other articles report that the crowd numbered three thousand. See Peter Horner, "ATA: The Best Kept Secret in Tennis?" *Tennis USTA,* July 1991, 11; and Tucker, 60. Tucker claimed that three thousand more looked on from apartment windows and fire escapes.

33. Ed Hughes, [no title], *Brooklyn Daily Eagle,* July 30, 1940.

34. Horner, "ATA," 11.

35. Laney.

36. Barry Meadow, "Jimmie McDaniel: Never Allowed to Be a Legend," *World Tennis,* Oct. 1979, 56.

37. Laney.

38. Ibid.

39. Meadow, "Jimmie McDaniel," 52.

40. Quintard Taylor, *In Search of the Racial Frontier: African Americans in the American West 1528–1990* (New York: W. W. Norton, 1998), 251–52. For a full discussion of proletarianization of black workers, see Joe Trotter Jr., *Black Milwaukee: The Making of an Industrial Proletariat, 1915–1945* (Urbana: Univ. of Illinois Press, 1985), chaps. 2, 7.

41. Taylor, 252–53.

42. In 1930 Los Angeles, 86.7 percent of black women worked in domestic service, 4.7 in manufacturing, 1.5 in trade, and 4.5 in professional service. See U.S. Bureau of the Census, "Occupation by States," in *Population,* vol. 4 of *Fifteenth Census of the United States, 1930* (Washington, D.C.: Government Printing Office, 1933).

43. Later this park was the site of the Los Angeles Sports Arena.

44. Meadow, "Jimmie McDaniel," 57.

45. William "Wild Bill" Johnson, letter to *World Tennis,* Jan. 1980, 8.

46. Meadow, "Jimmie McDaniel," 56.

47. Ibid., 57.

48. Darlene Love, *My Name Is Love: The Darlene Love Story* (New York: William Morrow, 1998), 12, 17. Love was a member of the Blossoms, and Wright was the lead singer of Honey Cone prior to their solo careers. La Jolla, California, was a mecca for tennis players in the 1930s and 1940s, and some of the world's best players played there. When actor Cliff Robertson attended La Jolla High, one black player was on the

tennis team. See Cliff Robertson, "Remember the Good Times," *World Tennis,* Oct. 1980, 49.

49. Barry Meadow, "What's White . . . and White . . . and White . . . and Why?" *World Tennis,* Mar. 1984, 58.

50. Brief, *World Tennis,* Apr., 1956, 36.

51. Meadow, "What's White," 58.

52. Interview of Oscar Johnson in Arthur Ashe Jr., *A Hard Road to Glory: A History of the African American Athlete since 1946* (New York: Warner, 1988), 161.

53. Ibid., 160.

54. Alice Marble, editorial, *American Lawn Tennis,* July 1, 1950. See also chapter 2 of this volume.

55. Allison Danzig, "Negro to Compete for First Time in a National Tennis Tournament," *New York Times,* Mar. 9, 1948.

56. Ibid. Weir, a physician, was inducted into the Eastern Tennis Hall of Fame posthumously in 1999.

57. Brief, *Tennis Week,* May 21, 1998, 59. Alleyne died in 1998 at age seventy-seven.

58. Brief, *World Tennis,* June 1957, 64.

59. Brief, *World Tennis,* Oct. 1956, 56.

60. Brief, *World Tennis,* Aug. 1957, 61.

61. Brief, *World Tennis,* June 1958, 20, 75. According to Christy Helsinger, Ryland turned pro in 1959. See "Tennis, the Sport of a Life Time," *Tennis Week,* Apr. 24, 2001, 64.

62. Kenny Lucas, "First Black Pro Makes a Racket," *B T Magazine,* spring 2001, 13.

63. Other sources report that Ryland began playing at age seven. See Lucas.

64. Ibid.

65. Robert E. King, "Trendsetter of the Nineties: Bob Ryland," *Black Tennis,* spring 1996, 24.

66. George McGann, " 'Doc' Johnson, Dedicated to Medicine and Junior Tennis, Wins July Marlboro Award," *World Tennis,* July 1965, 32.

67. Ibid., 33.

68. Interview of Robert Walter Johnson Sr., May 5, 1985, in Ashe, *A Hard Road,* 166; and Doug Smith, *Whirlwind: The Godfather of Black Tennis: The Life and Times of Dr. Robert Walter Johnson,* (Washington, D.C.: Blue Eagle, 2004), 8–35.

69. Ashe, *A Hard Road,* 166; Smith, *Whirlwind,* 37–54.

70. Ashe, *A Hard Road,* 166.

71. Ibid.

72. For this section, see Larry Simpson, "A Royal Tennis Presence in New Orleans," *Tennis USTA,* Apr. 1997, 22.

73. Victor Lee, "Atkinson's Light Shines Brightly," *Black Tennis,* 1985 (no season listed), 7.

74. Touchstone, architect of River Hills, died in 1965, and the award has been given in his honor for outstanding contribution to tennis in the South.

75. "Atkinson First Sugar Classic Chairman," *Black Tennis,* spring 1991, 26.

76. Joseph R. Wheeler, "Triple Match Point: The Story of Branch Curington . . . Tennis Pro," *Black Tennis,* summer 1983, 19.

77. Author's interview of Branch Curington, Atlanta, Ga., Oct. 11, 2000.

78. Earnest Reese, "Caring Curington: Washington Center Pro Teaches More Than Teaches," newspaper and date unknown; clipping held at Branch Curington Library, Atlanta, Ga.

79. Wheeler, "Triple Match Point," 19.

80. Joseph R. Wheeler, "Triple Match Point: The Story of Branch Curington . . . Tennis Pro," unpublished manuscript, Branch Curington Library, Atlanta, Ga.

2. Althea Gibson: "The Jackie Robinson of Tennis"?

1. Althea Gibson, *I Always Wanted to Be Somebody* (New York: Harper and Brothers, 1958), 9.

2. Sue Davidson, *Changing the Game: The Stories of Tennis Champions Alice Marble and Althea Gibson* (Seattle: Seal Press, 1997), 97–98; see also Tucker, 61.

3. Gibson, 31.

4. Ibid., 40. Gibson trained at Johnson's during the winter months, and Eaton supervised her tournament play during the summer.

5. Ibid., 43, 45.

6. Julie M. Heldman, "Distinguished Women of Tennis: Althea Gibson Darben," *World Tennis,* Apr. 1969, 68.

7. Gibson, 55.

8. As described in Davidson, 113.

9. Rust and Rust, 311; Oscar Dixon, "NBA Not Forgetting Barrier-Breakers," *USA Today,* Oct. 20, 2000.

10. See Arnold Rampersad, *Jackie Robinson: A Biography* (New York: Knopf, 1997), 242.

11. Tucker, 61.

12. Marble cited in Davidson, 114.

13. "Ladies & Gentlemen . . . ," *Time,* July 17, 1950, 74.

14. [No title], *Time,* Apr. 3, 1950, 60.

15. Davidson, 116.

16. Brief, *Tennis,* Sept. 1955, 46.

17. Jeanette Chappell Kalt, "The Women's Rankings," *Tennis,* Feb. 1956, 10.

18. See brief in *World Tennis,* July 1956, 18.

19. Ibid., 42; see also p. 18.

20. Ibid. In 1956, she participated in a U.S. State Department–sponsored tour of Asia and Europe, winning sixteen tournaments. See "Althea's Odyssey," *Life,* July 2, 1956, 88.

21. J. Heldman, 68.

22. Bill Clothier, "The Pennsylvania State," *World Tennis,* Sept. 1956, 46.

23. Ibid., 48.

24. Mary Hardwick, "The Women's Singles," *World Tennis,* Sept. 1956, 63.

25. Gardner Mulloy, "Larsen and Gibson Take Colorado State Titles," *World Tennis,* Nov. 1956, 42.

26. Brief, *World Tennis,* Oct. 1956, 70.

27. Edward C. Potter, "The World's First Tens," *World Tennis,* Nov. 1957, 42.

28. Jeannette Chappell Kalt, "The Women's Ranking," *World Tennis,* Feb. 1958, 34.

29. "The Power Game," *Time,* July 15, 1957, 61.

30. Gibson, 131–32.

31. Michael Bamberger, "Inside the White Lines," *Sports Illustrated,* Nov. 29, 1999, 115.

32. Joan Bruce, "Althea the First," *Sports Illustrated,* July 15, 1957, 12.

33. Ibid.

34. Brief, *World Tennis,* Sept. 1957, 31. According to biographers Francis Clayton Gray and Yanick Rice Lamb, Gibson sang "If I loved You" and "Around the World." See *Born to Win: The Authorized Biography of Althea Gibson* (Hoboken, N.J.: John Wiley and Sons, 2004), 99.

35. Bamberger, 115.

36. Brief, *World Tennis,* Apr. 1958, 22.

37. Brief, *World Tennis,* June 1958, 26.

38. Billy Talbert, "The Serve," *World Tennis,* June 1958, 29. See p. 28 for photos. See also Smith, *Whirlwind,* 61.

39. Brief, *World Tennis,* Oct. 1958, 22.

40. "Where Are They Now?" *Newsweek,* Sept. 1, 1969, 8.

41. Gibson, 155.

42. "Where Are They Now?" 8.

43. Quoted during Wimbledon final, broadcast on NBC, July 8, 2000.

44. "Where Are They Now?"

45. Gwen Knapp, "Ailing Legend Gibson Rich with Dignity," *Atlanta Journal-Constitution,* Nov. 14, 1996.

46. Ken Kamlet, "Going It Alone," *Tennis,* Sept. 1999, 37.

47. Ibid.; Doug Smith, "Ailing Gibson Receives $8,500 Worth of Aces," *USA Today,* Nov. 25, 1996.

48. See Doug Smith, "Seles Forced to Exit U.S. Hardcourt with Fever and Sore Throat," *USA Today,* Aug. 22, 1997.

49. Kamlet, 37.

50. Ibid.

51. L. Jon Wertheim, *Venus Envy: Power Games, Teenage Vixens, and Million-Dollar Egos on the Women's Tennis Tour* (New York: Perennial, 2002), 182.

52. Melissa Isaacson, "She Blazed Trail on the Court for Blacks," *Chicago Tribune,* Sept. 29, 2003.

53. Doug Smith, "Gibson First to Break Many Barriers," *USA Today,* Sept. 29, 2003.

54. Howard Frendrich, "Tennis Legend Broke Down Barriers, Opened Doors," *Chicago Tribune,* Sept. 29, 2003.

55. Isaacson, "She Blazed Trail."

56. Bruce Schoenfeld tells the story of two friends considered outsiders on the tour in *The Match: Althea Gibson and Angela Buxton* (New York: Amistad, 2004).

57. "Tribute: Althea Gibson," *Tennis,* Nov.–Dec. 2003, 96.

3. Arthur Ashe: Citizen of the World

1. Frank Deford, "Service, but First a Smile," *Sports Illustrated,* Aug. 29, 1966, 49.

2. Ibid.

3. Ibid.

4. "Interview with Beverly Coleman," *B T Magazine,* spring 2001, 7.

5. Murray Janoff, "In July 1959 a Shy 26-Year-Old Black Tennis Player Made His First Trip to Forest Hills," *Tennis USA,* July 1975, 31.

6. Ron Bookman, ""Arthur Ashe: Sill Classy after All These Years," *World Tennis,* Aug. 1980, 26.

7. Arthur Ashe Jr., *Days of Grace: A Memoir* (New York: Alfred A. Knopf, 1993), 61–62.

8. "First Negro Davis Cupper," *Ebony,* Oct. 1963, 151.

9. Ibid., 32.

10. Brief, *World Tennis,* Nov. 1964, 31.

11. Frank Deford, "An Understudy Takes Charge," *Sports Illustrated,* Aug. 9, 1965, 18.

12. Joe Jares, "Arthur Was King for a Day," *Sports Illustrated,* Sept. 20, 1965, 36. Ashe lost the following day to Spain's Manuel Santana.

13. "Australia: The Victorian Championships," *World Tennis,* Jan. 1966, 16–17.

14. "Newcombe Downs Ashe at NSW," *World Tennis,* Jan. 1966, 25.

15. Arthur Ashe Jr., "The Western Australian State Championships," *World Tennis,* Mar. 1966, 61.

16. Ashe had proposed to Diane Seymore of Stanford, Connecticut. See *World Tennis,* Apr. 1966, 72, for photo of Seymore.

17. Bookman, 26.

18. David Gray, "The U.S. National Amateur Championship," *Tennis,* Oct. 1968, 18.

19. Ibid., 20.

20. Ibid., 21.

21. Bookman, 26–27.

22. "Around the World," *World Tennis,* Dec. 1968, 62.

23. "U.S. National Open," *World Tennis,* Nov. 1968, 19.

24. Arthur Ashe Jr., *Arthur Ashe, Portrait in Motion: A Diary* (1975; reprint, New York: Carroll and Graf, Richard Gallen, 1993), 37.

25. Richard Evans, "Wimbledon: Ashe Authors a Thinking Man's Guide to Victory," *World Tennis,* Sept. 1975, 25; and Ashe, *Days of Grace,* 72.

26. Evans, "Wimbledon," 25.

27. Ibid.

28. Rex Bellemy, "Ashe Crowns Wimbledon Drama with a Schoolboy-Fiction Victory," *London Times,* July 7, 1975.

29. Ibid.

30. See John Ballantine, "Glory for No-Chance Ashe," *London Times,* July 6, 1975, for an additional review of the match.

31. Rex Bellamy, "Connors Played in Pain during Wimbledon," *London Times,* July 8, 1975.

32. Steve Flink, "The 10 Best Men Plus One," *World Tennis,* Feb. 1976, 27.

33. Ibid.

34. Evans, "Wimbledon," 25.

35. Arthur Ashe Jr., "Catching Connors in the Stretch," *Sports Illustrated,* July 21, 1975, 20.

36. Ibid.

37. Brief, *World Tennis,* Feb. 1976, 38.

38. Ibid.

39. Barry Lorge, "Arthur Ashe: In the Right Place," *World Tennis,* Dec. 1976, 47.

40. Arthur Ashe Jr., "Shifting Gears," *World Tennis,* Sept., 1981, 117–18.

41. Susan B. Adams, "Memories and Mileposts," *World Tennis,* June 1980, 9.

42. Ashe, *Days of Grace,* 62.

43. Ibid.

44. Ibid., 99.

45. Ashe, *Portrait,* 73.

46. Frank Deford, "A Momentous Occasion," *Tennis,* Sept. 1993, 103.

47. Harry Gordon, "Pioneer in Short White Pants," *New York Times Magazine,* Jan. 2, 1966, 5.

48. "I'm Simply Me," *Newsweek,* Sept. 7, 1964, 53.

49. Gordon, 7.

50. Peter Bodo, "Growing Up with Arthur," *Tennis,* June 1992, 19–20.

51. Barry Lorge, "Lessons in Living," *Tennis,* Apr. 1993, 114.

52. Bob Moseley, "He Will Grow with History," *Tennis USTA,* Apr. 1993, 6.

53. Bodo, "Growing Up with Arthur," 20.

54. Benjamin Quarles, *The Negro in the Making of America* (New York: Touchstone, 1987), 324.

55. Other participants included Jack Javits, Herb Fitzgibbon, and Jim Brown, and the event was held in New York's Central Park.

56. Brief, *World Tennis,* Sept. 1968, 84.

57. Neil Amdur, "Conversations with Lt. Arthur Ashe, Part III," *World Tennis,* July 1968, 36.

58. Barry Lorge, "The Taste of Champagne," *World Tennis,* Jan. 1977, 33.

59. Geoffrey Green, "Breakfast with Arthur Ashe," *London Times,* July 5, 1975.

60. Neil Amdur, "Conversations with Lt. Arthur Ashe, Part IV," *World Tennis,* July 1968, 52.

61. Ibid., 52–53.

62. "International Stars," *World Tennis,* Oct. 1969, 90.

63. Ashe, *Portrait,* 1.

64. Ibid., 2.

65. Ashe, *Days of Grace,* 66.

66. Lorge, "Lessons," 114.

67. "Professor Arthur Ashe: Tennis' Class Act Moves into the Classroom," *Ebony,* July 1983, 80.

68. Author's interview of Sue Fawn Chung, Las Vegas, Feb. 18, 2001.

69. Arthur Ashe Jr., "Send Your Children to the Libraries," *Negro Heritage,* 1977 (no month or season listed), 98–99.

70. Steve Flink, "Ashe Goes Ivy," *World Tennis,* May 1983, 55.

71. All quotations in this paragraph are from Moseley, 5; Williams participated in the 15-Love Program in Rochester, which Ashe helped to start.

72. Steve Wilstein, "His Legacy Lives On," *Dallas Morning News,* Feb. 5, 2003.

73. Arthur Ashe Jr., "Life Goes On," *Tennis,* July 1992, 41. Doug Smith discusses the meeting with Ashe in a bonus chapter in *Whirlwind,* 173–78.

74. Ashe, *Days of Grace,* 9.

75. Ibid., 21.

76. Jim Baker, "Ashe: Still Angry after All This Year," *T. T. Guide,* June 27, 1992, 22.

77. The material in this paragraph and in the next two paragraphs comes from Donna Doherty, "Did We Do the Right Thing?" *Tennis,* June 1992, 123.

78. Bodo, "Growing Up with Arthur," 19.

79. Baker, 22.

80. For instance, *B T Magazine* published "The Contemporary Posture of Arthur Ashe," 1993 (no month or season listed).

81. Lorge, "Lessons," 110.

82. Doug Smith, "Statue Saluting Ashe Unveiled on Historic Avenue in Hometown," *USA Today,* July 11, 1996. A few people protested the statue with signs and Confederate flags. Citizens for Excellence in Public Art also disapproved. Ashe's wife, Jeanne, hoped that the statue would instead be placed in front of a proposed African American sports hall of fame.

83. Doug Smith, "Notes," *USA Today,* June 26, 1998.

84. Rhonda K. Miller, "Ashe Legacy Lives on in City of Brotherly Love," *USTA Magazine,* July–Aug. 1999, 3.

85. Bonnie Desimone, "Home-Grown Talent Gets Featured Roles inside New Stadium," *Chicago Tribune,* Aug. 26, 1997.

86. Kevin O'Keefe, "King Arthur's Gift," *Tennis Match,* Feb. 1999, 12.

87. Lorge, "Arthur Ashe," 43.

88. This paragraph and the next paragraph are based on Lorge, "The Taste of Champagne," 29.

89. John Rosengren, "On Court with Michael Jordan," *Tennis,* Dec. 1999–Jan. 2000, 20.

90. Green.

91. Mike Lupica, "Ashe Is Back," *World Tennis,* Apr., 1979, 44.

92. Yannick Noah, "Arthur mon ami," *Afrique Magazine,* July–Aug. 1993, 65, 66.

4. A New Horizon

1. Brief, *World Tennis,* Feb., 1960, 49.

2. Other top juniors in 1965 included Lendward Simpson and Robert Binns. Some black youths had success on teams as the Southeast All-Stars in Houston, such as Craig Peterson, Horace Jackson, James Strambler, Steve Roy, and Darrick Jackson. See *World Tennis,* Sept. 1970, 100.

3. Author's interview of Branch Curington.

4. For winning the title, tennis great Tony Roche took Farrow to the movies. See brief, *World Tennis,* Nov. 1968, 82.

5. "Farrow Has Had Fill of Net Losses," *Black Tennis,* spring 1992, 20.

6. Ibid., 21; see also Lenard Jackson, "Juan Farrow, Tennis Champ," *Black Collegian,* Nov.–Dec. 1977, 79.

7. Ashe and Farrow quoted in "Farrow Has Had Fill," 21.

8. Reese.

9. Todd Holcomb, "Park Started Reid to Hall of Fame," *Atlanta Journal-Constitution,* Apr. 15, 2001.

10. After retiring, Reid won five USTA senior national titles and worked as a pro at Cross Creek Golf Club, Beltsville, Md.

11. Author's interview of Keith Allen, Atlanta, Ga., June 19, 2000. Other important tennis figures in Atlanta were Willie Whited, Turner Sibley, Albert Huntley Sr., and Sammy Bacote.

12. Author's interview of Rick Davis, Atlanta, Ga., Nov. 10, 2000.

13. Bud Collins, "Longwood's New Pro: From Broken Glass to Bent Grass," *World Tennis,* June 1982, 11.

14. Susan B. Adams, "The A.T.A.: The Base of the Pyramid," *World Tennis,* Dec. 1975, 43.

15. See *The Tiger,* Texas Southern Univ. yearbook, vol. 27, (Houston: Texas Southern Univ., 1975).

16. Zina Garrison was a high school senior who competed on the tour but was unranked.

17. Brief, *World Tennis,* Mar. 1982, 58.

18. Susan B. Adams, "Around the World," *World Tennis,* Dec. 1979, 24.

19. The material here and in the next two paragraphs comes from the author's interview with Leslie Allen-Selmore, New York, Nov. 2, 2000.

20. For Ashe quote, see Joy Duckett, "And the Women Shall Lead Them," *World Tennis,* Mar. 1982, 58.

21. "Comeback Queen," *World Tennis,* May 1982, 82.

22. Author's interview with Leslie Allen-Selmore.

23. "Comeback Queen," 82.

24. Mark Mathabane, *Kaffir Boy in America* (New York: Collier, 1989), 66.

25. Adams, "The A.T.A.," 44–45.

26. "Tennis Surprise, Benjamin Gets Her Shot at Lloyd," *USA Today,* June 6, 1984.

27. The material on Benjamin comes from Arthur S. Hayes, "Camille Benjamin: The Jigsaw Girl," *Tennis,* Mar. 1985, 97.

28. The material on Katrina Adams comes from the author's interview of Adams, Atlanta, Ga., Oct. 6, 2000.

29. See brief, *World Tennis,* June 1970, 62.

30. "Chip Hooper," *Tennis,* Sept. 1982, 147.

31. Barry Lorge, "Blue Bloods, New Bloods," *World Tennis,* Jan. 1982, 37.

32. Ibid.

33. "Hitting Out," *World Tennis,* Nov. 1985, 9.

34. Joel Drucker, "Catching Up with Chip Hooper," *Tennis USTA,* Feb. 1988, 26.

35. Author's interview of Rodney Harmon, Miami, Oct. 2000.

36. Ray Kennedy, "Then Zing Go the Strings," *Sports Illustrated,* June 6, 1983, 102.

37. Lorge, "Blue Bloods," 38–39.

38. David J. Higdon, "Rodney's Search for Tennis Harmony," Tennis Magazine Online, no. 1197, n.d. Prior to that, Harmon served as a USTA national coach and head tennis coach at the University of Miami.

39. Peter Bodo, "The Education of Martin Blackman," *Tennis,* Dec. 1997, 24.

40. Ibid., 25.

41. S. Djata, "Chip Dorsey: A Crest Wave of Talent," *Black Tennis,* winter 1983; and author's interview of Chip Dorsey, Baltimore, Nov. 1982.

42. David J. Higdon, "Meet an Ivy League Bum," *Tennis,* Jan. 1991, 23.

5. The Houston Triumvirate

1. Peter Bodo, "The Miracle of MacGregor Park," *Tennis,* Aug. 1987, 50.

2. Tommy Thompson, "This Pro Turns Out a Professional Product," *Texas Tennis,* Mar. 1987, 5.

3. Ibid.

4. Bodo, "The Miracle," 52.

5. Thompson, 4.

6. Ibid.

7. Ibid., 5.

8. Ibid. This story varies in other sources. See, for example, Susie Woodhams, "At Zenith, Garrison Electrifies," *Dallas Times Herald,* July 7, 1998.

9. For quote, see Ish Haley, "Garrison Finds Strength to End Seles' Streak," *Dallas Times Herald,* July 4, 1990. For Eastbourne, see "Black Tennis Teen Reaches Semifinals of $150,000 Tourney," *Chicago Defender,* June 18, 1983.

10. Cindy Shmerler, "Under Control," *World Tennis,* Sept. 1985, 55.

11. Ibid.

12. Ibid., 56.

13. Ibid.

14. David J. Higdon, "Zina on Her Own," *Tennis,* Mar. 1989, 37.

15. "Lloyd Upset," *New York Times,* Apr. 22, 1985.

16. The Virginia Slims in Dallas started in 1972 as the Maureen Connolly Briner Memorial Professional Women's Tennis Tournament.

17. Marilyn Marshall, "Zina Garrison Aiming for the Top in Tennis," *Ebony,* June 1986, 86.

18. Susan Festa, "The Eight-Year Itch," *World Tennis,* May 1990, 41.

19. Woodhams.

20. Higdon, "Zina on Her Own," 34.

21. Ibid.

22. David J. Higdon, "Tennis Husbands Also Serve," *Tennis,* Oct. 1993, 14; see also Festa, 40.

23. "In Brief," *Dallas Times Herald,* July 8, 1990.

24. Festa, 39.

25. Andrew Longmore, "Besieged Garrison Holds Out for Victory," *London Times,* July 4, 1990.

26. Robin Finn, "Garrison Stuns Graf in Wimbledon Semifinal," *New York Times,* July 6, 1990. See also Jean Couvercelle, Guy Barbier, Yannick Cochennec, and Patrick Meltz, "Wimbledon: Simple Dames," *Tennis* (France), Aug. 1990, 48–52.

27. Andrew Longmore, "Graf's Reign Is Cut Short," *London Times,* July 6, 1990.

28. Ish Haley, "Inspired Zina Ready for Giant-Killer Role," *Dallas Times Herald,* July 7, 1990.

29. Ibid.

30. Steve Flink, "I've Never Zina Better," *World Tennis,* Sept. 1990, 16.

31. Ibid., 19.

32. Cindy Shmerler, "Luck Be a Lady," *World Tennis,* Sept. 1990, 76.

33. Ish Haley, "Garrison Has Fun Despite Finals Loss," *Dallas Times Herald,* July 8, 1990.

34. Alex Ramsey, "Garrison-Jackson Restores Faith in Women's Game," *London Times,* June 29, 1994.

35. "Sampras, Garrison-Jackson Win," *USA Today,* June 19, 1995.

36. Longmore, "Besieged Garrison."

37. Karima A. Haynes, "Zina Garrison-Jackson: Tennis Star's Battle with Bulimia," *Ebony,* June 1993, 88.

38. Ibid., 88, 90.

39. All material in this paragraph comes from *Sports Century: Zina Garrison,* ESPN, 2002.

40. See *Virginia Slims Legends Tour 1996,* program (St. Petersburg, Fla.: WTA, 1996).

41. Bodo, "The Miracle," 53.

42. Don Markus, "Sloppy Play, McNeil Closes Evert Open Era," *Baltimore Sun,* Sept. 10, 1987.

43. Doug Smith, "McNeil: Youth Is Served . . . and Returns Well for Victory," *USA Today,* Sept. 10, 1987; see also Markus, "Sloppy Play," and Doug Smith, "McEnroe, Evert Out of U.S. Open," *USA Today,* Sept. 11, 1987.

44. Peter Bodo, "Navratilova & Lendl Defend Their Titles," *Tennis,* Nov. 1987, 112.

45. Markus, "Sloppy Play."

46. Smith, "McEnroe, Evert."

47. Don Markus, "Newest Celebrity McNeil Faces Graf Today," *Baltimore Sun,* Sept. 11, 1987.

48. Ibid.

49. Don Markus, "Navratilova, Graf Reach Open Final," *Baltimore Sun,* Sept. 12, 1987.

50. Don Markus, "Round 3 for Top Women," *Baltimore Sun,* Sept. 12, 1987.

51. Bodo, "Navratilova & Lendl," 112.

52. S. L. Price, "London Blitz; Lori McNeil Shocked Steffi Graf to Start an Explosive Week of Wimbledon Upsets," *Sports Illustrated,* July 4, 1994, 40. Bryan Shelton defeated number 2 seed Michael Stitch after McNeil's win.

53. Stuart Jones, "Graf Loses Crown in Gathering Gloom," *London Times,* June 22, 1994.

54. John Goodbody and Lin Jenkins, "McNeil Emerges from Shadows at Last," *London Times,* June 22, 1994.

55. Stuart Jones, "McNeil Seeking to Fly in the Face of Tradition," *London Times,* June 30, 1994.

56. David Miller, "Martinez Edges Out McNeil in Classic," *London Times,* July 1, 1994.

57. David J. Higdon, "Talking about Lori McNeil," *Tennis,* Sept. 1994, 53.

58. Doug Smith, "Graf Suffers Wimbledon Upset," *USA Today,* June 22, 1994.

59. Price, "London Blitz," 42.

60. Ibid.

61. Doug Smith, "Refocused McNeil Continues Serving Notice of Her Revival," *USA Today,* June 24, 1994.

62. See Roger M. Williams, "Lori McNeil," *Tennis,* Sept. 1994, 16.

6. The "Post-Soul Era"

1. These juniors included J. J. Jackson, Quentin B. Huff, Mashiska Washington, Mashona Washington, Donald Evans, Christin Hill, Marcus Fluitt, Johnathan Glover, Ry Tarpley, Martell Buford, Damu Dee Bobb, Kawanish Ross, Darly Wyatt, Arthur Carrington Jr., Silas Bouer, Emmett Braxton, Malcolm Bufford, Erik M. Graves, and Omar Ahmed. See the glossary for a definition of the "Post-Soul era."

2. Peter Bodo, "Easy Does It," *Tennis,* Aug. 1996, 18.

3. Brian Cleary, "Talking about Chanda Rubin," *Tennis,* Sept. 1995, 136; see also the interview with Chanda Rubin by Yannick Cochennec (entretien avec Chanda Rubin par Yannick Cochennec), *Tennis* (France), Aug. 2003, 66.

4. Cochennec's interview with Chanda Rubin, 67. For quote, see Bodo, "Easy Does It," 27.

5. Stephen Wilson, "Novotna, up 5-0, Eliminated with French Open Collapse," *Dallas Morning News,* June 4, 1995.

6. Bill Scott, "Unheralded Rubin Joins Elite Group in Quarterfinals," *Dallas Morning News,* June 5, 1995.

7. Bodo, "Easy Does It," 28.

8. "Rubin Gaining Reputation as Women's Marathon Winner," *USA Today,* Jan. 12, 1996.

9. Linda Pentz, "Rockin' Rubin," *Tennis Week,* Apr. 4, 1996, 11.

10. See Andre-Jacques Dereix, "Chanda, Chere Rubin" *Tennis de France,* June 1996, 17.

11. All quotations in this paragraph come from Bodo, "Easy Does It," 28, 30.

12. Dereix, 17.

13. See Doug Smith, "Rubin Ready to Continue Rebound from Wrist Injury," *USA Today,* Jan. 10, 1997.

14. Cochennec's interview with Chanda Rubin, 64, 65.

15. Author's interview of MaliVai Washington, Ponte Vedra Beach, Fl., Oct. 2000.

16. "Talent Scout," *World Tennis,* July 1989, 9.

17. Peter Bodo, "Mal's Content," *Tennis,* Oct. 1993, 50.

18. Ibid., 49.

19. "Washington Rallies Past Martin, Faces Krajicek in Final," *Chicago Tribune,* July 7, 1996.

20. Jennifer Frey, "Heir to King Arthur's Court," *Washington Post,* July 7, 1996.

21. Doug Smith, "Krajicek's Serve Proves Too Much for Washington," *USA Today,* July 8, 1996.

22. Stephen Tignor, "A Mal-Function," *Tennis,* June 1999, n.p.

23. Bodo, "Mal's Content," 52.

24. "Advantage U.S. in Davis Cup," *Chicago Tribune,* Feb. 8, 1997.

25. Sandra Harwitt, "At 30 MaliVai Washington Calls It a Career," *USTA Magazine,* Apr. 23, 1998, 4.

26. "XL Bermuda Open," *Tennis Week,* Apr. 23, 1998, 25.

27. Laurie Casaday, "Washington Won't Make Wimbledon," *Florida Times-Union,* June 18, 1998.

28. Mike Bianchi, "MaliVai Doesn't Fit the Mold," *Florida Times-Union,* Nov. 13, 1996.

29. Horace W. Rice, "Bryan Shelton's Latest Racket," *Black Tennis,* Jan. 1986, 3.

30. See Brian Moran, "The Life of Bryan," *World Tennis,* Jan. 1990, 51–52.

31. In 1991, Shelton won the Cairo Open; in 1992, he captured the River Oaks International and the Abilene Regional Medical Center Pro Indoor titles. He won the latter again in 1994.

32. Doug Smith, "Shelton Pulls Upset of Krajicek: 'This Place Lifts You Up,' " *USA Today,* June 27, 1995. That same day Paul Wekesa of Kenya lost to Henman, and Washington lost to Alexander Volkov.

33. Material in this paragraph and the next three paragraphs comes from Peter Bodo, "Motown's Surprise Hit," *Tennis,* July 1998, 18.

34. Diane Bennett and Matthew Jordan Smith, *Sepia Dreams* (New York: St. Martin's, 2001), 40.

35. Raquel Cepeda, "Courting Destiny," *Essence,* June 2001, 182.

36. Tom Friend, "Break Point," *ESPN the Magazine,* June 11, 2001, 70.

37. Jon Saraceno, "Tennis' Real No. 1, Venus, Is Rising," *USA Today,* Aug. 8, 2000.

38. Interview with Nick Bollettieri, *Tennis Week,* Jan. 15, 1998, 32.

39. William D. Rhoden, "The Father Really Did Know Best," *New York Times,* Sept. 8, 2001.

40. Bruce Schoenfeld, "Who Is Jamea Jackson?" *Tennis Match,* Apr.–May 1998, 50.

41. Ibid.

42. "Richard Williams: Venus and Serena's Father Whips the Pros and Makes His Family No. 1 in Tennis," *Ebony,* June 2000, 94.

43. Paul Fein, "King Richard" (interview), *Tennis Week,* Apr. 23, 1998, 18.

44. Paul Fein, "The Invisible Man," *Tennis Week,* Nov. 20, 1997, 10.

45. Mark Winters, "Grassroots Start," *Tennis USTA,* Dec. 1997, 24–25.

46. Andrea Leand, "Time to Grow Up," *Tennis Match,* Sept. 1999, 45–46.

47. Bud Collins, "Romancing the Romans," *Tennis Week,* May 21, 1998, 20.

48. Bud Collins, "Signorina Tentalcoli," *Tennis Week,* May 27, 1999, 12.

49. Peter Fink, "William's Wimbledon," *Tennis Week,* July 20, 2000, 15.

50. Andrea Leand, "Earth to Venus: What's Up?" *Tennis,* June 2000, 16.

51. Chip Brown, "Venus Thunders to Repeat," *Dallas Morning News,* July 9, 2001.

52. Rhoden.

53. Michael Hiestand, "Star Power Dictates Rise, Fall of Tennis Ratings," *USA Today,* Aug. 23, 2001.

54. The women's final was moved to Sunday when CBS lost the NFL in 1994, but then it was moved back to Saturday in 1998 and placed after the men's semifinals. Daniel Kaplan and Langdon Brockinton, "Prime Time for Women's Open Final," *SportsBusiness Journal,* March 19–25, 2001, 41.

55. Steven Wine, "Prime-Time Final: Sister, Sister," *Chicago Tribune,* Sept. 8, 2001.

56. Joel Stein, "Williams Wins!" *Time,* Sept. 17, 2001, 91.

57. "Venus and Serena Williams Live Up to the Hype," *Tennis Week,* Sept. 20, 2001, 16.

58. Manuela and Magdalena Maleeva lost in finals on the same day in Apr. 1991.

59. "Serena Williams: Wins at U.S. Open; First Black Female Champion since 1958," *Jet,* Sept. 27, 1999, 54.

60. "Venus and Serena Williams Live," 16.

61. Melissa Isaacson, "Big Sister Does It Again," *Chicago Tribune,* Sept. 9, 2001.

62. Carl Fussman, "Serene Queen," *ESPN the Magazine,* Aug. 19, 2002, 43.

63. L. Jon Wertheim, "Serena Show," *Sports Illustrated,* Mary 26, 2003, 38.

64. Bruce Schoenfeld, "The Venus Trap," *Tennis,* July 2003, 43.

65. Idowu Oke, "William's World," *West Africa,* July 17–23, 2000, 38.

66. Andrea Leand, "U.S. Dream Team," *Tennis Week,* Aug. 5, 1990, 24.

67. Ibid., 86.

68. See brief, *Tennis Week,* Apr. 3, 2001, 49.

69. Vanessa Grigoriadis, "Like a Virgin," *Spin,* Apr. 2001, 133, 135.

70. E. Lynn Harris, *Any Way the Winds Blows* (New York: Doubleday, 2001), 154.

71. "Venus and Serena Come to DC," *Sister 2 Sister,* July 2001, 77.

72. "Love Game: Serena and Internet Shopping," *USA Today,* Aug. 10, 2001.

73. See Devin Friedman, "Sister Act," *Elle,* Jan. 2001, 148.

74. Allen St. John, "Father Knows Best," *Tennis,* May 2003, 20.

75. Joel Stein, "The Power Game," *Time,* Sept. 3, 2001, 57–58.

76. Rachel Nichols, "The Supremes," *Tennis,* Nov. 2001, 22.

77. Although Holcomb uses the term *minorities,* he focuses on blacks. See "Converted by the Williamses," *Atlanta Journal-Constitution,* Apr. 15, 2001.

78. S. L. Price, "Simply Super," *Sports Illustrated for Women,* Nov.–Dec. 2000, 85.

79. Joel Drucker, "Venus Rediscovered," *USTA Magazine,* Nov.–Dec. 2000, 7.

80. Price, "Simply Super," 87.

81. "Sister Slam," interview with Serena Williams by Roy S. Johnson, *Savoy,* Nov. 2002, 53.

82. Tom Friend, "Break Point," *ESPN the Magazine,* June 11, 2001, 70.

83. Allison Samuels, "Life with Father," *Newsweek,* July 2, 2001, 46.

84. See Warren Florence and Andrea Leand, "Battle over Wounded Knee," *Tennis,* June 2001; Doug Smith, "Dad Denies Fixing Daughters' Matches," *USA Today,* Mar. 26, 2001; Joel Drucker, "Desert Disarray," *Tennis Week,* Apr. 3, 2001.

85. Smith, "Dad Denies Fixing."

86. Drucker, "Desert Disarray," 9, 10.

87. Ibid., 10.

88. Selena Roberts, "The Williams Sisters Have a Date with History," *New York Times,* Sept. 8, 2001.

89. J. Stein, "Williams Wins!" 91.

90. Judge Greg Mathis, speaking at the Rainbow/Push Rally, Chicago, Ill., Mar. 31, 2001.

91. Fussman, "Serene Queen," 43.

92. See Mitch Rustad, [no title], *Tennis,* June 2004, 14; Adam Sachs, "Red, White & Williams, *Tennis,* Sept. 2003; Elliott Harris, "William Sisters to Be the Focus of Reality TV Show," *Chicago Sun-Times,* Apr. 7, 2005; and Melody K. Hoffman, "The Williams Sisters: How They Inspire Each Other to Score in Tennis, Design, & Life," *Jet,* Dec. 20, 2004, 55, 59.

93. Doug Smith, "Stevenson Finds Being in Spotlights' Glare 'Fun,'" *USA Today,* Aug. 4, 1999.

94. Doug Smith, "Cash Registers," *USA Today,* June 29, 1999.

95. The team included Jerry Tucker, Iris Liang, Nicky Hedge, and Ellenoira Featherston.

96. Cindy Shmerler, "Alexandria the Great?" *Tennis,* July–Aug. 2000, 46–47.

97. Doug Smith, "Stevenson Tries to Back Up Some Big Talk," *USA Today,* June 27, 2000.

98. Greg Garber, "Blake Picks up Where Ashe, Washington Left Off," ESPN.com, Feb. 29, 2000; and Peter Bodo, "Stepping Up," *Tennis,* Apr. 2002.

99. Peter Horner, "Sharing the Gift," *USTA Magazine,* May 1999, 31.

100. David Thorpe, "Changing the Game," *Bullseye,* spring–summer 2003, 20.

101. Thomas Hackett, "The Dream Seekers," *Tennis,* July–Aug. 2000, 36.

102. Mike Szostak, "Blake Brothers Make Their Mark at Miller Hall of Fame Tennis," *Providence Journal,* July 6, 1999.

103. Hackett, 38.

104. Doug Smith, "Blake Falls to Rafter but Still Aces Big Test," *USA Today,* Aug. 10, 2001.

105. For quote, see "A Cut Above," an interview with James Blake by Eddie Taylor, *Deuce,* 2002 (no month or season listed), 139. See also Bodo, "Stepping Up," 47.

106. Hackett, 34, 36.

107. Joel Drucker, "Confidence Game," *Tennis,* June 2004, 13.

108. Tim Curry, "Home, Sweet Home," *USTA Magazine,* Apr. 2000, 4.

109. "Young American Gets Eye-Opening Experience," *USA Today,* Feb. 7, 2000. See also Levar Harper-Griffith, "On the Job Training," *USTA Magazine,* Apr. 2000, 27.

7. The Additional Burden of the Professional Black Player

1. Pentz, "Rockin' Rubin," 11.

2. Djata, 18.

3. Author's interview of Rick Davis.

4. Meadow, "What's White," 58.

5. Gibson, 37.

6. Ibid., 80.

7. Leslie Allen-Selmore, "Althea, Arthur, Then Me," *Tennis,* Sept. 1997, 114.

8. Pentz, "Rockin' Rubin," 25.

9. Bodo, "Mal's Content," 50.

10. Actually, they were braids, not dreadlocks. Marilyn August, "Noah Faces Stardom," *World Tennis,* Oct. 1983, 35.

11. Pamela Andriotakis, "Between the U.S. and Another Davis Cup Stands a Formidable Frenchman Named Yannick Noah," *People,* Nov. 29, 1982, 113.

12. Donna Doherty, "Yannick Noah: Is He Too Laid Back to Become No. 1?" *Tennis,* Nov. 1982, 42.

13. Richard Evans, "Vive la France," *World Tennis,* June 1981, 83.

14. Ibid.

15. Peter Bodo, "Yannick Noah: A Champion in Turmoil," *Tennis,* June 1984, 35.

16. Ibid., 36.

17. Ibid., 38.

18. Marilyn August, "The French Kiss of Fate," *World Tennis,* June 1984, 66.

19. Yannick Noah, *Secrets, Etc.* (Paris: Plon, 1997), 65.

20. Ibid., 66.

21. Ibid., 81.

22. "Pride Spurs a Haitian," *New York Times,* Dec. 29, 1983.

23. "Farrow Has Had Fill," 21.

24. Frey.

25. Author's interview of MaliVai Washington; and "ChatReel: James Blake," CNNSI.com, May 3, 2001.

26. Meadow, "What's White," 58.

27. Ibid.

28. Ashe, *Portrait,* 174.

29. Stuckey cited in Jack Olsen, *The Black Athlete: A Shameful Story* (New York: Time-Life, 1968), 18–19.

30. Mark Mathabane, *Kaffir Boy: An Autobiography* (New York: Signet, 1989), 271.

31. Harry Edwards, "The Black Athletes: 20th Century Gladiators for White America," *Psychology Today,* Nov. 1973, 44.

32. Joy Duckett, "And the Women Shall Lead Them," *World Tennis,* Mar. 1982, 57.

33. Evonne Goolagong, *On the Move* (New York: E. P. Dutton, 1975), 66; see

also an updated memoir, Evonne Goolagong-Crawley, *Home: The Evonne Goolagong Story* (East Roseville, Australia: Simon and Schuster, 1993).

34. Goolagong, *On the Move,* 67.

35. "Rising Tennis Stars Leslie Allen, Yannick Noah Show Promise," *Ebony,* June 1981, 84.

36. Nesty won two Olympic Gold medals before Ervin did, although the latter was called the "first swimmer of African American descent" to compete in the games. In reality, Ervin was the first from the United States, not the first from the Americas.

37. Edwards, "The Black Athletes," 44.

38. John Gustafson, "Sister Girl; One Win for Cathy Freeman Would Be Worth All the Gold in Sydney," *ESPN the Magazine,* Sept. 18, 2000, 108.

39. Ashe, *Portrait,* 40, 151.

40. Ibid., 173, emphasis in original.

41. Brian Holland, Lorna Jackson, Grant Jarvie, and Mike Smith, "Sport and Racism in Yorkshire: A Case Study," in *Sport and Identity in the North of England,* edited by Jeff Hill and Jack Williams (Keele, Staffordshire: Keele Univ. Press, 1996), 168.

42. Steve Rosenbloom, "Foulline," *Chicago Tribune,* Oct. 27, 1997.

43. Gibson, 61–2.

44. Ibid., 158,157.

45. Lawrence Otis Graham, *Member of the Club: Reflections on Life in a Racially Polarized World* (New York: HarperCollins, 1995), 136–37, 173.

46. Michael Hiestand, "Still in the Running: Australia's Freeman Using Her Prowess on the Track to Leap over to Politics," *USA Today,* Aug. 21, 2000.

47. Pete Iacobelli, "Williams Withdraws, Backs Boycott," AP Wire-News, Apr. 22, 2000.

48. Tom Wier, "Racism Issue on Center Court," *USA Today,* Apr. 19, 2000.

49. Ashe, *Portrait,* 172–73.

50. Wilstein, emphasis in original.

51. See photo in *Tennis,* Apr. 2000, 16.

52. "Star Profiles: Chanda Rubin," *Third Annual Black Enterprise/Pepsi Golf and Tennis Challenge,* special supplement of *Black Enterprise,* Sept. 1996.

8. Racism in Tennis

1. Olsen, 6.

2. Noverr and Ziewacz, 132.

3. "Wimbledon," *Time,* July 13, 1936, 46.

4. Gordon, 25.

5. Gibson, 66–67.

6. "Gibson and Longwood," Gladys Heldman replies to letter from Hal Fenerty to *World Tennis,* Mar. 1982, 76.

7. Gladys Heldman, "Rating Yourself," *World Tennis,* Sept. 1981, 78.

8. Alice Marble, editorial, *American Lawn Tennis,* July 1950, cited in Gibson, 62–66.

9. *American Lawn Tennis,* Feb. 1951, reprinted at www.usta.com.

10. Gibson, 68.

11. Ed Fitzgerald, ed., "Round Table Discussion: The Negro in American Sport," *Negro History Bulletin* 24 (1960), 28.

12. "Gibson and Longwood," 76.

13. Edward T. Chase, "Player's Dilemma: Savor College Education or Go for Pro Dough?" *Tennis Week,* Apr. 15, 1999, 37. It is reported that the club and its members were prepared to welcome Gibson.

14. [No title], *New York Times,* Sept. 10, 1997, quoted in Bob Davis, "A Search for Sanity?" *Tennis Week,* Nov. 20, 1997, 19. See a detailed discussion of their relationship in Bruce Shoenfeld, *The Match: Althea Gibson and Angela Buxton* (New York: Amistad, 2001), 147–50.

15. Davis, 19.

16. Fitzgerald, 28.

17. Kamlet, 37.

18. "Where Are They Now?" 16.

19. Gordon, 25.

20. Paul Fein, "20th Century Retrospective," *Tennis Week,* Nov. 18, 1999, 15.

21. Meadow, "Jimmie McDaniel," 56.

22. Goolagong, *On the Move,* 99. The club president apologized, and the team, White City, vowed never to play again if the offending woman was on the team. The woman reportedly left the team because "she was no longer welcomed." See p. 100.

23. Meadow, "What's White," 57.

24. Mary Witherall, "Winning Is Only Half the Battle," *World Tennis,* May 1987, 41.

25. Author's interview of Rick Davis.

26. Author's interview of Otis Sadler, Houston, Aug. 22, 2001.

27. The material in this paragraph comes from Mike Lurie, "Racial Net Gains on Court Come with a Price," *CBS Sportsline,* at www.sportsline.net, May 9, 1999.

28. Lawrence M. Kahn, "Discrimination in Professional Sport: A Survey of the Literature," *Industrial and Labor Relations Review* 44 (Apr. 1991), 395.

29. Author's interview of Katrina Adams.

30. Author's interview of MaliVai Washington.

31. Author's interview of Bertand Liger, DeKalb, Ill., Apr. 11, 2001. Liger generally played in Montesson, a suburb of Paris.

32. See Reebok supplement in *Tennis,* June 1996.

33. Bruno Cuaz, "Balles perdues à New York," *Tennis* (France), Sept. 1992, 46, 48.

34. See Leila Sebbar, *Sherazade,* translated by Dorothy Blair (London: Quartet Books, 1999); and Azouz Begag, *Le gone du Chaaba* (Paris: Editions du Seuil, 1986). A film by the same title was made of the latter. See also Paul A. Silverstein, *Algeria in France: Transpolitics, Race, and Nation* (Bloomington: Indiana Univ. Press, 2004), for a discussion of the Algerian presence in France in history, which includes discussion of contemporary cultural forms, immigration policy, colonial governance, urban planning, corporate advertising, sports, and songs.

35. Tyler Stovall, *Paris Noir: African Americans in the City of Light* (Boston: Houghton Mifflin, 1996), 131, 288, 293.

36. Christopher Clarey, "Expatriate Games," *Tennis,* Feb. 1993, 51.

37. Author's interview of Wray Vamplew, author, London, Oct. 18, 2000.

38. Author's interview of Annette Atherton, information officer of the Lawn Tennis Association, London, Oct. 26, 2000.

39. Author's interview of Nick Cheales, London, Oct. 18, 2000.

40. Author's interview of Tony Kneebone, Merseyside, England, Aug. 15, 2001.

41. Leeds Trades Union Council and Anti-Fascist Action, *Racism in Leeds and West Yorkshire* (Leeds, England: Leeds Trade Council, 1987), 4.

42. Jeff Hill and Jack Williams, "Introduction," in Hill and Williams, 9.

43. Richard Holt, "Heroes of the North: Sport and the Shaping of Regional Identity," in Hill and Williams, 159; see also Jeff Hill, "Reading the Stars: A Post Modernist Approach to Sports History," *The Sports Historian* 14 (May 1994), 48; and Marshall, 25.

44. Holland et al., 165.

45. Vivek Chaudhary, "Asians Can Play Football Too," *The Guardian,* Sept. 7, 1994.

46. Holland et al., 165.

47. Hayden Middleton, *Sport in Britain* (London: Foreign and Commonwealth Office, Sept., 1997), 2, 8.

48. Joseph L. Arbena, "Sport and the Study of Latin American Society: An Overview," in *Sport and Society in Latin America,* edited by Joseph L. Arbena (New York: Greenwood, 1988), 4.

49. Steve Stein, "The Case of Soccer in Early Twentieth-Century Lima," in Arbena, 76.

50. Harvey Araton, "Talking about the Country Club," *New York Times,* Sept. 9, 1997.

51. Jonathan W. Warren, "Masters in the Field; White Talk, White Privilege, White Biases," in *Race: Researching Race in Critical Race Studies,* edited by France

Winddance Twine and Jonathan W. Warren (New York: New York Univ. Press, 2000), 146.

52. Witherall, 40–41

53. Florence and Leand, 14.

54. Witherall, 40.

55. Richard Evans, "Tough Guy," *Tennis Week,* Sept. 20, 2001, 21.

56. Selena Roberts, "Hewitt Sprints Through Generation Gap," *New York Times,* Sept. 10, 2001.

57. Evans, "Tough Guy," 21.

58. Lurie, 1.

59. Leif Wellington Haase, letter to the editor, *Tennis Week,* Dec. 18, 1997, 31.

60. Witherall, 41.

61. Ibid.

62. Barry Lorge, "A Late Charge: Leslie Allen Has Yet to Reach Her Peak," *Washington Post,* specific date unknown, 1982.

63. Witherall, 38, 40.

64. Bunny had chaired a meeting when Mrs. Bethune was present, and an elderly white southern woman, whose family had owned slaves, apologized to Bethune for the superiority of a family like hers. Smith played Emma Tremayne, a part based on the life of Bethune. H. W. "Bunny" Austin and Phyllis Konstam, *A Mixed Double* (London: Chatto and Windus, 1969), 216.

65. August, "Noah Faces Stardom," 33–34.

66. Todd Holcomb, "Shelton a Success in College, as Pro," *Atlanta Journal-Constitution,* Apr. 15, 2001.

67. Georges Homsi, "Mirror, Mirror on the Wall," *Tennis Week,* June 24, 1994, 60.

68. Cleary, 136.

69. "Richard Williams," 94–95.

70. Cepeda, 184.

71. Author's interview of Ronald Agenor, Birmingham, Ala., May 13, 2000.

72. Holcomb, "Park Started Reid."

73. Lynn Zinser, "Discrimination Complaint Filed," *New York Times,* Sept. 3, 2002.

74. Graham, 8, 10–11, 12, 17.

75. Todd Boyd, *Am I Black Enough for You? Popular Culture from the 'Hood and Beyond* (Bloomington: Indiana Univ. Press, 1997), 7.

76. See Harry Edwards, "The Myth of the Racially Superior Athlete," *Black Scholar* 3 (Nov. 1971): 16–28, reprinted from *Intellectual Digest* 2 (Mar. 1971): 59–60; and Edwards, "The Black Athletes," 43–52.

77. Paul Bohannan and Phillip Curtin, *Africa and Africans* (Prospect Heights, Ill.: Waveland, 1995), 8.

78. bell hooks, *Black Looks: Race and Representation* (Boston: South End, 1992), 2.

79. James Bardin, *The Psychological Factor in Southern Race Problems* (New York: Science, 1913), reprinted in *The Development of Segregationist Thought,* edited by I. A. Newby (Homewood, Ill.: Dorsey, 1970), 34.

80. Robert Bennett Bean, "Negro Brain," *Century Magazine,* Oct. 1906, 778–84.

81. Nathaniel S. Shaler, "The Nature of the Negro," *Arena* 3 (Dec. 1990): 23–55.

82. Newby, 1–2.

83. Martin Kane, "An Assessment of 'Black Is Best,' " *Sports Illustrated,* Jan. 18, 1971, 74. See comments by David K. Wiggins, *Glory Bound: Black Athletes in a White America* (Syracuse, N.Y.: Syracuse Univ. Press, 1971), 186.

84. J. M. Tanner, *The Physique of the Olympic Athlete* (London: George Allen and Unwin, 1960), cited in Kane, 74.

85. Quoted in Kane, 76.

86. Quoted in ibid., 79.

87. John Hoberman, *Darwin's Athletes: How Sport Has Damaged Black America and Preserved the Myth of Race* (Boston: Houghton Mifflin, 1997), 195, xxi.

88. T. E. Reed, "Caucasian Genes in American Negroes," *Science* 165 (Aug. 22, 1969), 762–68, cited in David W. Hunter, "Race and Athletic Performance: A Psychological Review," *Journal of African American Men* 2 (fall 1996–winter 1997), 27.

89. Claude Bouchard, "Genetic Basis of Racial Differences," *Canadian Journal of Sport Sciences* 13 (1988), 106.

90. Hunter, 27. See also Vinay Harpalani, "The Athletic Dominance of African Americans—Is There a Genetic Basis?" *Journal of African American Men* 2 (fall 1996–winter 1997), 39–56.

91. Harry Edwards, seminar on race and sports at the University of Oklahoma, Norman, 1985.

92. Quoted in Mark Kohn, *The Race Gallery: The Return of Racial Science* (London: Vintage, 1995), 34.

93. Vicky Edwards, "Not So Fast," *Chicago Tribune,* Sept. 21, 2003.

94. *Tennis Week,* May 15, 2001, 4.

95. Brad Wolverton, "Tennis Everyone," *Tennis,* Sept. 2001, 87.

96. J. Heldman, 68.

97. Brief, *World Tennis,* Aug. 1971, 34.

98. David Gray, "Wimbledon: Only the Final Was a Surprise," *World Tennis,* Sept. 1976, 27.

99. See, for example, Michael Arkush, "Venus Williams' Power Proves Too Much for Seles," *New York Times,* Aug. 7, 2000; Doug Smith, "Venus Williams Powers to German Victory," *USA Today,* May 3, 1999; and Mark Shapiro, "Williams Overpowers Hingis, Faces Kournikova in Final," *Chicago Tribune,* Mar. 27, 1998.

100. See brief, *Tennis Week,* Mar. 26, 1998, 20.

101. Leisa Harris, letter to *Tennis Week,* May 7, 1998, 4.

102. Brief, *Sports Illustrated,* June 25, 2001, 34.

103. Author's interview of Aleta Haynes, Dorchester, Mass., Aug. 8, 2000.

104. Author's interview of William Redd, Richmond, Va., June 16, 2000.

105. Bodo, "Yannick Noah," 35.

106. Navratilova and Amelie Mauresmo have also been victims of stereotyping in that their power has been viewed as a result of their sexual orientation or manliness, unlike white heterosexual women athletes.

107. Rex Bellamy, "Noah a Reminder of the Good Old Days," *London Times,* June 6, 1983.

108. Michael Dobbs, "French Cheer as Noah Outlasts Wilander," *Washington Post,* June 6, 1983.

109. Jane Gross, "Wilander Plays Noah in Final," *New York Times,* June 4, 1983.

110. John Madden, NFL telecast, *New York Giants vs. Chicago Bears,* Fox, Sept. 17, 2000.

111. W. E. Hester Jr. was named chairman emeritus, and Winslow M. Blanchard referee emeritus. Of the twenty-four members, only three were women. Dr. Gary E. Lee was the only nonwhite member. See *U.S. Open '91,* program (White Plains, N.Y.: USTA, 1991), 18–19.

112. Linda Pentz, "Racial Disharmony, pt. III," *Tennis Week,* Nov. 20, 1997, 16.

113. Eugene L. Scott, "Vantage Point," *Tennis Week,* May 7, 1998, 8. Scott's comments also responded to charges of racism by William Washington; George Henry, director of the National Urban Youth Tennis Foundation; Tony Womeodo of All Kids with Aspirations; and Cesar Jansen, a black tennis activist.

114. Ibid.

115. Anthony Fox, letter to *Tennis Week,* June 4, 1998, 3.

116. Pat Koger, letter to *Tennis Week,* June 4, 1998, 3.

117. Allen-Selmore, 116.

118. The material in this paragraph and the next two paragraphs comes from Bud Collins, "Longwood Has New Pro: From Broken Glass to Bent Grass," *World Tennis,* June 1982, 13.

119. The material in this paragraph and the next paragraph comes from Clarey, 51.

120. Judith Jackson Fossett and Jeffrey A. Tucker, eds., *Race Consciousness* (New York: New York Univ. Press, 1997), xiv.

121. Jack Carey, "Prairie View Basking in Drought's End," *USA Today*, Sept. 28, 1998.

122. Adams, "The A.T.A.," 44.

123. Linda Pentz, "Watchdog," *Tennis Week*, Sept. 18, 1997, 52.

124. Gibson, 121.

125. Brief, *Tennis*, Mar. 1990, 16.

126. Bud Collins, "Zimbabwe Zeal," *Tennis Week*, June 1982, 10, 11.

127. Ted Robinson, USA telecast of the French Open, May 31, 2001.

128. Price, "London Blitz," 42.

129. Author's interview of Solomon Crenshaw Jr., Birmingham, Ala., May 13, 2000.

9. USTA Minority Participation

1. See Steve Flink, "Where Are the Champions?" *Tennis Week*, Apr. 13, 2000, 22.

2. 1998 U.S. Open, USA Tennis Plan for Growth, asasports.com, Sept. 1998.

3. Mark Winters, "Fountain of Youth: USTA Seeks the New and Improved Player Development Program for the Millennium," *Tennis Week*, Nov. 26, 1998, 20.

4. "Welcome to Camp," *Tennis USA*, July 1989, 3.

5. See brief, *Tennis USTA*, Mar. 1992, 18.

6. Ellen Markowitz and Mitch Rustad, "Tennis in Public Places: The Real Grassroots," in *Tennis in Public Places*, compiled by the United States Tennis Association (USTA) (White Plains, N.Y.: USTA, 1997), 6.

7. Pat Koger, "Minority Participation," *Tennis USTA*, Mar. 1997, 16–17.

8. Andrea Leand, "Junior Juggling Act," *Tennis Week*, Mar. 6, 1997, 10.

9. Ibid., 11.

10. Andre Christopher, "Play Tennis America and Public Parks: A Perfect Match," in *Tennis in Public Places*, 12.

11. Lisa Olney, "USTA/Eastern News: And the Winners Are . . . ," *Tennis Week*, Jan. 21, 1999, 60.

12. William Washington, letter to *Tennis Week*, Aug. 6, 1998, 3–4. Davis's Black Dynamics has been headquartered at Bollettieri Academy, where black youths were taken only after they had proven themselves to be top competitors. The ATA helped in scouting talent.

13. Steve Flink, "Maximizing Minority/Multicultural Participation," *Tennis Week*, July 2, 1998, 29.

14. Roger Williams, "Is Tennis Doing the Right Thing?" *Tennis*, Nov. 1990, 48.

15. Garber.

16. Joanne C. Gerstner, "Minorities Divided," *Detroit News*, Sept. 8, 1999.

17. Ibid.

18. Discussion from CBS broadcast of the 1998 U.S. Open, Sept. 2, 1999.

19. Higdon, "Rodney's Search."

20. "Reaching Out to Players of Color," *Black Enterprise,* Sept. 1997, 150.

21. The material in this paragraph and the next four paragraphs comes from Gerstner.

22. Gerstner.

23. Linda Pentz, "Dealing the 'Race Card,' " *Tennis Week,* Sept. 18, 1998, 26.

24. The transcript appeared in *Tennis Week.* See "Racism in Pro Tennis?" *Tennis Week,* Mar. 25, 1999, 22. Material in the next six paragraphs comes from this source.

25. Steve Shine, letter to *Tennis Week,* Sept. 23, 1999, 3.

26. Gerstner.

27. 1999 U.S. Open interview with James Blake, Aug. 31, 1999, available at: Fastscripts, www.asapsports.com/tennis.

28. Author's interview with William Washington, parent of ATP and WTA players, Oct. 2000.

29. Pentz, "Dealing the 'Race Card,' " 27.

30. Ibid., 26.

31. William Washington, letter to *Tennis Week,* Aug. 6, 1998, 4.

32. Ibid.

33. Steve Milano, letter to *Tennis Week,* Nov. 26, 1998, 4.

34. Pat Koger, letter to *Tennis Week,* June 4, 1998, 3.

35. Flink, "Maximizing Minority/Multicultural Participation," 28.

36. Ibid.

37. Ibid.

38. Ibid., 44.

39. William Washington, letter to *Tennis Week,* Mar. 25, 1999, 5–6. See also the article to which he responded: Winters, "Fountain of Youth."

40. William Washington, letter to *Tennis Week,* Mar. 25, 1999, 5–6.

41. Julianne Malveaux, "Who Will Find Future Tennis Stars?" *USA Today,* Sept. 15, 2000.

Conclusion

1. G. Heldman, 78.

2. Cited in Mike McNulty, "The Venus and Serena Effect," *Tennis,* Nov. 2000, 8.

3. William Washington, letter to *Tennis Week,* Apr. 24, 2001, 3.

Glossary

Association of Tennis Professionals (ATP): This organization was formed in 1990, when players developed their own tour apart from the Men's Tennis Council and the International Tennis Federation.

Challenger Tournaments: The middle level of tournaments, above the satellite/Futures tournaments, but below the Super Nine tournaments. Challenger events are included on the men's and women's tours.

Futures: The lowest level of tournaments, which last one week.

Grand Prix Tournaments: Until 1990, these tournaments formed the highest category of tournaments on the Association of Tennis Professionals (ATP) tour (excluding the Grand Slams). The status of a tournament is determined by the level of prize money.

Grand Slam Cup: A year-end tournament featuring the winners of the four Grand Slam events, plus others who performed best in those four events. This event was created in response to the professional tennis players' forming the ATP and voting the Men's Tennis Council out of existence.

Net Ball: An English sport similar to basketball.

Open Era: In 1968, major tennis tournaments were opened to professional players.

The "Other": This term is an ethnographical construction, based on and created from the early-nineteenth-century European colonialist notion that viewed noncivilized, nonwhite, non-European, and non-Christian groups as the opposite of Europeans.

Post-Soul: Author Nelson George coined this term to discuss black cultural developments after the modern Civil Rights Movement. See Nelson

George, "The Complete History of Post-Soul Culture," *Village Voice*, March 17, 1992.

Qualifying Rounds: These rounds provide a chance for a player with rankings too low to enter the main draw of a tournament. The qualifying rounds usually consist of four groups of eight players each, and the winner of each group gains a spot in the main draw.

"Race" Ranking: Beginning 2000, the ATP began ranking players by points accumulated only in that calendar year, which determined the number 1 player at the end of the year. The old system, based on a running fifty-two weeks, was maintained as an "entry system" to determine seedings.

Satellite Circuit: The lowest level of tournaments on the professional men's circuit. A satellite circuit spans more than four weeks, with three separate tournaments and a final master's event. In the final event, only the players who have achieved the best results during the previous three weeks are allowed to participate.

Seeding: In every tournament, a certain number of the highest-ranked players are placed in certain spots in the draw to ensure that these players do not play each other in the initial rounds of a tournament.

Super Nine Tournaments: When the ATP reorganized the system of tournament classification, the Super Nine tournaments (replacing the Grand Prix events) became the highest category of tournaments, excluding the Grand Slams.

Tie: A term used in national team competition known as the Davis Cup. A Davis Cup tie includes four singles and one doubles match played over three consecutive days.

Wild Card: A free spot in the draw, which tournament organizers give to a player whose ranking otherwise would not have permitted him or her to enter the tournament. Wild cards are given in qualifying rounds and in the main draw.

Bibliography

Unpublished Sources

Theses and Dissertations

Thomas, Damion Lamar. " 'The Good Negroes': African-American Athletes and the Cultural Cold War, 1945–1968." Ph.D. diss., Univ. of California, Los Angeles, 2002.

Watson, Helen Logan. "Project Serve: A Junior Development Project in an Inner City Area." Master's thesis, Northwestern Illinois State College, Dec. 1970.

Unpublished Manuscripts, Articles, and Speeches

"History of Tennis at Tuskegee University." Manuscript. Tuskegee Univ. Sports Information Office, 1997.

Mathis, Judge Greg. Speech at the Rainbow Push Rally, Chicago, Mar. 21, 2001.

Temple, Orlando M., Jr. "The Impact of the MPC." Paper presented at the USPTA World Conference, Phoenix, Ariz., Sept. 20–23, 2000.

Wamuiru-Wilson, Jinaki. "The Plights of Blacks Playing Tennis." Manuscript, Illinois State Univ., Apr. 1989.

Wheeler, Joseph R. "Triple Match Point: The Story of Branch Curington . . . Tennis Pro." Manuscript, Branch Curington Library, Atlanta, Ga.

Interviews by the Author

Adams, Katrina. Former WTA player, Atlanta, Ga., Oct. 6, 2000.

Agenor, Ronald. Professional tennis player, Birmingham, Ala., May 13, 2000.

Allen, Keith. Former top junior player, Atlanta, Ga., June 19, 2000.

Allen-Selmore, Leslie. Former WTA player, New York, Nov. 2, 2000.

Atherton, Annette. Information officer of the Lawn Tennis Association, London, Oct. 26, 2000.

Chalmus, Maurice. Former satellite player and teaching pro, Baltimore, Md., June 15, 1981.

Cheales, Nick. Information Sport England, London, Oct. 18, 2000.

Chung, Sue Fawn. Former UCLA student, Las Vegas, Feb. 18, 2001.

Crenshaw, Solomon, Jr. Sports journalist, Birmingham, Ala., May 13, 2000.

Curington, Branch. Former teaching pro, Atlanta, Ga., Oct. 11, 2000.

Davis, Rick. Former collegiate player, Atlanta, Ga., Nov. 10, 2000.

Dorsey, Chip. Former collegiate player, Baltimore, Nov. 1982.

Harmon, Rodney. Former ATP player, Miami, Oct. 2000.

Haynes, Alveta. Executive director of Sportsmen Tennis Club, Corchester, Mass., Aug. 8, 2000.

Kneebone, Tony. Merseyside, England, Aug. 15, 2001.

Liger, Bertrand. Collegiate tennis player, DeKalb, Ill., Apr. 11, 2001.

Redd, William. Director of Tennis and Things, Richmond, Va., June 16, 2000.

Sadler, Otis. Program director of the Zina Garrison All-Court Foundation, Houston, Aug. 22, 2001.

Temple, Orlando, Jr. Teaching pro, USPTA Texas Division Multicultural Committee chair, Dallas, June 15, 2001.

Vamplew, Wray. Author, London, Oct. 18, 2000.

Washington, MaliVai. Former ATP player and television commentator, Ponte Vedra Beach, Fl., Oct. 2000.

Washington, William. Parent of ATP and WTA players, Oct. 2000.

Documentaries and Televised Programs

Blake, James. CBS telecast of the U.S. Open, 1999.

CBS telecast of the U.S. Open. Sept. 3, 2001.

Lurie, Mike. "Racial Net Gains on Court Come with a Price." *Sportsline: Tennis*, CBS, May 9, 1999.

Sports Century: Zina Garrison. ESPN, 2002.

USA Network telecast of the French Open, May 31, 2001.

Published Sources

Books, Articles, and Other Printed Matter

Abrams, Nathan D. " 'Inhibited but Not Crowded Out': The Strange Fate of Soccer in the United States." *International Journal of the History of Sport,* 12 Dec. 1995.

Adams, Susan B. "The A.T.A.: The Base of the Pyramid." *World Tennis,* Dec. 1975.

"Africa Seeks New Stars." *West Africa,* Apr. 17–23, 2000.

Aggrey, Joe. "The High Hopes of Africa." *West Africa,* Oct. 16–22, 2000.

Alexander, George. *Lawn Tennis: Its Founders and Its Early Days.* Lynn, Mass.: H. O. Zimman, 1974.

Allen, Sarah. "Do the Right Thing." *Tennis,* Apr. 1999.

Allen-Selmore, Leslie. "Althea, Arthur, Then Me." *Tennis,* Sept. 1997.

"Althea's Odyssey." *Life,* July 2, 1956.

Amdur, Neil. "Reflections from the Open." *World Tennis,* Nov. 1985.

Andriotakis, Pamela. "Between the U.S. and Another Davis Cup Stands a Formidable Frenchman Named Yannick Noah." *People,* Nov. 29, 1982.

Arbena, Joseph L., ed. *Sport and Society in Latin America.* New York: Greenwood, 1988.

Armanet, François, and Christine Mital. "Noah, le guerrier pacifique." *Le Nouvel Observateur,* Apr. 10–16, 1997.

"Around the World." *World Tennis,* Dec. 1968.

"An Artiste de Triomphe: Noah Wins the French." *World Tennis,* Aug. 1983.

Ashe, Arthur, Jr. *Arthur Ashe, Portrait in Motion: A Diary.* 1975. Reprint. New York: Carroll and Graf, Richard Gallen, 1993.

———. "Behind the Scenes in Mexico City." *World Tennis,* July 1975.

———. "Catching Connors in the Stretch." *Sports Illustrated,* July 21, 1975.

———. *Days of Grace: A Memoir.* New York: Alfred A. Knopf, 1993.

———. *A Hard Road to Glory: A History of the African American Athlete since 1946.* New York: Warner, 1988.

———. "Life Goes On." *Tennis,* July 1992.

———. "Shifting Gears." *World Tennis,* Sept. 1981.

———. "The Western Australian State Championships." *World Tennis,* Apr. 1966.

"The Ashe Game." *World Tennis,* Dec. 1968.

"Atkinson First Sugar Classic Chairman." *Black Tennis,* spring 1991.

August, Marilyn. "The French Kiss of Fate." *World Tennis,* June 1984.

———. "Noah Faces Stardom." *World Tennis,* Oct. 1983.

Austin, H. W. "Bunny," and Phyllis Konstam. *A Mixed Double.* London: Chatto and Windus, 1969.

"Australia: The Victorian Championships." *World Tennis,* Jan. 1966.

Bamberger, Michael. "Inside the White Lines." *Sports Illustrated,* Nov. 29, 1999.

Bankoil, Dorian. "Trying to Tap New Markets." ABCNews.com, ESPN sports, Aug. 28, 1997.

Bardin, James. *The Psychological Factor in the Southern Race Problems.* New York: Science Press, 1913.

Barker, Bertram. "A Black Tennis Association: Active since 1916." In *American Tennis Association National Rankings 1983–1984,* 60–61. Philadelphia: ATA, 1984.

Bean, Robert Bennett. "The Negro Brain." *Century Magazine,* Oct. 1906.

Bedell, Elaine. "Yannick Noah: Hero of France on the Tennis Courts." *Ebony,* Nov. 1982.

Begag, Azouz. *Le gone du Chaaba.* Paris: Editions du Seuil, 1986.

Bennett, Dianne, and Matthew Jordan Smith. *Sepia Dreams.* New York: St. Martin's, 2001.

Bingham, Walter. "A Waltz at Wimbledon." *Sports Illustrated,* July 12, 1971.

Biracree, Tom. *Althea Gibson.* Los Angeles: Melrose Square, 1990.

Bodo, Peter. "Easy Does It." *Tennis,* Aug. 1996.

———. "Growing Up with Arthur." *Tennis,* June 1992.

———. "Mal's Content." *Tennis,* Oct. 1993.

———. "The Miracle of MacGregor Park." *Tennis,* Aug. 1987.

———. "Motown's Surprise Hit." *Tennis,* July 1998.

———. "Navratilova & Lendl Defend Their Titles." *Tennis,* Nov. 1987.

———. "Stepping Up." *Tennis,* Apr. 2002.

———. "Yannick Noah: A Champion in Turmoil." *Tennis,* June 1984.

Bookman, Ron. "Arthur Ashe: Still Classy after All These Years." *World Tennis,* Aug. 1980.

Bouchard, Claude. "Genetic Basis of Racial Differences." *Canadian Journal of Sport Sciences* 13 (1988): 104–8.

Boyd, Todd. *Am I Black Enough for You? Popular Culture from the 'Hood and Beyond.* Bloomington: Indiana Univ. Press, 1997.

Boyle, Chris. "Noah Changes Face of the Game." *Tennis Week,* Apr. 30, 1987.

Branham, H. A. *Sampras: A Legend in the Works.* Chicago: Bonus Books, 1996.

Bruce, Joan. "Althea the First." *Sports Illustrated,* July 15, 1957.

Cepeda, Raquel. "Courting Destiny." *Essence,* June 2001.

"Champion." *The New Yorker,* May 19, 1986.

Chase, Edward T. "Player's Dilemma: Savor College Education or Go for Pro Dough?" *Tennis Week,* Apr. 15, 1999.

Chaudhary, Vivek. "Asians Can Play Football, Too." *The Guardian,* Sept. 7, 1994.

"Chip Hooper: Black Power." *Tennis,* Sept. 1982.

Clarey, Christopher. "Adventures in Davis Cup Group IV." *Tennis,* Nov. 1997.

———. "Expatriate Games." *Tennis,* Feb. 1993.

Cleary, Brian. "Talking about Chanda Rubin." *Tennis,* Sept. 1995.

Clothier, Bill. "The Pennsylvania State." *World Tennis,* Sept. 1956.

Coakley, Jay. *Sport in Society: Issues and Controversies.* St. Louis: Mosby, 1994.

Coan, Peter M. "Miracle on Hoe Avenue." *World Tennis,* Oct. 1989.

Collins, Bud. "Longwood's New Pro: From Broken Glass to Bent Grass." *World Tennis,* June 1982.

———. "Romancing the Romans." *Tennis Week,* May 21, 1998.

———. "Signorina Tentalcoli." *Tennis Week,* May 27, 1999.

———. "Zimbabwe's Zeal." *Tennis Week,* June 1982.

Conley, Spence. "Arthur Ashe: Becoming a Tennis Player." *Tennis USA,* July 1975.

Constantine-Sims, Delroy, ed. *The Great Taboo: Homosexuality in Black Communities.* Los Angeles: Alyson, 2000.

Couvercelle, Jean, Guy Barbier, Yannick Cochennec, and Patrick Meltz. "Wimbledon: Simple Dames." *Tennis* (France), Aug. 1990.

Cuaz, Bruno. "Balles perdues a New York." *Tennis* (France), Sept. 1992.

Cummings, Parke. *American Tennis: The Story of a Game and Its People.* Boston: Little, Brown, 1957.

Cunningham, Kim. "The French Connection II." *World Tennis,* June 1986.

Curry, Tim. "Home, Sweet Home." *USTA Magazine,* Apr. 2000.

Davis, Bob. "Ashe Is Not the Problem." *Black Tennis,* spring 1991.

———. "A Search for Sanity?" *Tennis Week,* Nov. 20, 1997.

Deford, Frank. "A Momentous Occasion." *Tennis,* Sept. 1993.

————. "Service, but First a Smile." *Sports Illustrated,* Aug. 29, 1966.

————. "An Understudy Takes Charge." *Sports Illustrated,* Aug. 9, 1965.

Dereix, Andre-Jacques. "Chanda, Chere Rubin." *Tennis de France,* June 1996.

Djata, S. "Chip Dorsey: A Crest Wave of Talent." *Black Tennis,* winter 1983.

Doherty, Donna. "Noah: Coach of the Year." *Tennis,* Feb. 1992.

————. "Yannick Noah: Is He Too Laid Back to Become No. 1?" *Tennis,* Nov. 1982.

Drucker, Joel. "Catching Up with Chip Hooper." *Tennis USTA,* Feb. 1988.

————. "Confidence Game." *Tennis,* June 2004.

————. "Creating Champions." *Tennis Week,* Apr. 15, 1999.

————. "Desert Disarray." *Tennis Week,* Apr. 3, 2001.

————. "Playing Her Own Game." *USTA Magazine,* July–Aug. 2000.

————. "Venus Rediscovered." *USTA Magazine,* Nov.–Dec. 2000.

Duckett, Joy. "And the Women Shall Lead Them." *World Tennis,* Mar. 1982.

"Eddie Davis to Direct Tennis Center." *Black Tennis,* winter 1983.

Edwards, Harry. "The Black Athletes: 20th Century Gladiators for White America." *Psychology Today,* Nov. 1973.

————. "The Myth of the Racially Superior Athlete." *Intellectual Digest* (Mar. 2, 1971): 58–70. Reprinted in *The Black Scholar* (Nov. 3, 1971): 16–28.

Evans, Richard. "Ashe in Africa." *World Tennis,* Jan. 1971.

————. "Clay Court Challenge." *Tennis Week,* July 15, 2001.

————. "Roving Eye." *Tennis Week,* Aug. 5, 1999.

————. "Tough Guy." *Tennis Week,* Sept. 20, 2001.

————. "Vive la France." *World Tennis,* June 1981.

————. "Wimbledon: Ashe Authors a Thinking Man's Guide to Victory." *World Tennis,* Sept. 1975.

"Farrow Has Had Fill of Net Losses." *Black Tennis,* spring 1992.

Fein, Paul. "The Invisible Man." *Tennis Week,* Nov. 20, 1997.

————. "20th Century Retrospective." *Tennis Week,* Nov. 18, 1999.

Ferguson, Andrew. "Inside Crazy Culture Kids Sports." *Time,* July 12, 1999.

Festa, Susan. "The Eight-Year Itch." *World Tennis,* May 1990.

Fink, Peter. "Williams' Wimbledon." *Tennis Week,* July 20, 2000.

"First Negro Davis Cupper." *Ebony,* Oct. 1963.

Fitzgerald, Ed, ed. "Round Table Discussion: The Negro in American Sport." *Negro History Bulletin* 24 (Nov. 1960): 27–31, 47.

Flink, Steve. "I've Never Zina Better." *World Tennis,* Sept. 1990.

———. "Maximizing Minority/Multicultural Participation." *Tennis Week,* July 2, 1998.

———. "The 10 Best Men Plus One." *World Tennis,* Feb. 1976.

———. "Where Are the Champions?" *Tennis Week,* Apr. 13, 2000.

Florence, Warren, and Andrea Leand. "The Battle over Wounded Knee." *Tennis,* June 2001.

Fossett, Judith Jackson, and Jeffrey A. Tucker, eds. *Race Consciousness.* New York: New York Univ. Press, 1997.

Friedman, Devin. "Sister Act." *Elle,* Jan. 2001.

Friend, Tom. "Break Point." *ESPN the Magazine,* June 11, 2001.

Fussman, Carl. "Serene Queen." *ESPN the Magazine,* Aug. 19, 2002.

"Future Stars Are Here—Davis Cup Captain." *West Africa,* Apr. 24–30, 2000.

Garber, Greg. "Blake Picks Up Where Ashe, Washington Left Off." ESPN.com, Feb. 29, 2000.

Gibson, Althea. *I Always Wanted to Be Somebody.* New York: Harper and Brothers, 1958.

Gillmeister, Heiner. *Tennis: A Cultural History.* New York: New York Univ. Press, 1998.

Glantz, Michael H. "Tennis in Ethiopia." *World Tennis,* Mar. 1988.

Goolagong-Crawley, Evonne. *Home: The Evonne Goolagong Story.* New South Wales, Australia: Simon and Schuster, 1993.

Gorn, Elliott, and Warren Goldstein. *A Brief History of American Sports.* New York: Hill and Wang, 1993.

Graham, Lawrence Otis. *Member of the Club: Reflections on Life in a Racially Polarized World.* New York: HarperCollins, 1995.

"Grandfather of Tennis Ace Yannick Noah Killed during Recent Cameroon Uprising." *Jet,* Apr. 16, 1984.

Gray, David. "The U.S. National Amateur Championship." *World Tennis,* Oct. 1968.

———. "Wimbledon: Only the Final Was a Surprise." *World Tennis,* Sept. 1976.

Gray, Frances Clayton, and Yanick Rice Lamb. *Born to Win: The Authorized Biography of Althea Gibson.* Hoboken, N.J.: John Wiley and Sons, 2004.

Grigoriadis, Vanessa. "Like a Virgin." *Spin,* Apr. 2001.

Gustafson, John. "Sister Girl: One Win for Cathy Freeman Would Be Worth All the Gold in Sydney." *ESPN the Magazine,* Sept. 18, 2000.

Hackett, Thomas. "The Dream Seekers." *Tennis,* July–Aug. 2000.

Hardwick, Mary. "The Women." *World Tennis,* Aug. 1971.

———. "The Women's Singles." *World Tennis,* Sept. 1956.

Harpalani, Vinay. "The Athletic Dominance of African Americans—Is There a Genetic Basis?" *Journal of African American Men* 2 (fall 1996–winter 1997): 39–56.

Harper-Griffith, Levar. "On the Job Training." *USTA Magazine,* Apr. 2000.

Harris, E. Lynn. *Any Way the Wind Blows.* New York: Doubleday, 2001.

Harwitt, Sandra. "At 30, MaliVai Washington Calls It a Career." *USTA Magazine,* Mar. 2000.

Hayes, Arthur S. "Camille Benjamin: The Jigsaw Girl." *Tennis,* Mar. 1985.

Haynes, Karima A. "Zina Garrison-Jackson: Tennis Star's Battle Against Bulimia." *Ebony,* June 1993.

Heldman, Gladys M. "Rating Yourself." *World Tennis,* Sept. 1981.

Heldman, Julie M. "Distinguished Women on Tennis: Althea Gibson Darben." *World Tennis,* Apr. 1969.

Helsinger, Christy. "Tennis, the Sport of a Lifetime." *Tennis Week,* Apr. 24, 2001.

Higdon, David J. "Meet an Ivy League Tennis Bum." *Tennis,* Jan. 1991.

———. "Rodney's Search for Tennis Harmony." *Tennis Magazine* online, no. 1197, n.d.

———. "Talking about Lori McNeil." *Tennis,* Sept. 1994.

———. "Tennis Husbands Also Serve." *Tennis,* Oct. 1993.

———. "Zina on Her Own." *Tennis,* Mar. 1989.

Hill, Jeff. "Reading the Stars: A Post Modernist Approach to Sports History." *The Sports Historian,* May 1994.

Hill, Jeff, and Jack Williams, eds. *Sport and Identity in the North of England.* Keele, Staffordshire: Keele Univ. Press, 1996.

"Hitting Out." *World Tennis,* Nov. 1985.

Hoberman, John. *Darwin's Athletes: How Sport Has Damaged Black America and Preserved the Myth of Race.* Boston: Houghton Mifflin, 1997.

Hoffman, Melody K. "The Williams Sisters: How They Inspire Each Other to Score in Tennis, Design, & Life." *Jet,* Dec. 20, 2004.

Homsi, Georges. "Mirror, Mirror, on the Wall." *Tennis Week,* June 24, 1994.

hooks, bell. *Black Looks: Race and Representation.* Boston: South End, 1992.

Horner, Peter. "ATA: The Best Kept Secret in Tennis?" *Tennis USTA,* July 1991.

———. "Sharing the Gift." *USTA Magazine,* May 1999.

Hunter, David W. "Race and Athletic Performance: A Physiological Review." *Journal of African American Men* 2 (fall 1996–winter 1997): 23–38.

"I'm Simply Me." *Newsweek,* Sept. 7, 1964.

"Interclub: Le racing encore." *Tennis* (France), July 1990.

Jackson, Leonard. "Juan Farrow, Tennis Champ." *Black Collegian,* Nov.–Dec. 1977.

Janoff, Murray. "In July 1959 a Shy 26-year-old Black Tennis Player Made His First Trip to Forest Hills." *Tennis USA,* July 1975.

Jares, Joe. "Arthur Was King for a Day." *Sports Illustrated,* Sept. 20, 1965.

J. D. H. "The Ashe Game, part I." *World Tennis,* Dec. 1968.

Jones, Carolyn. "McNeil Brings Team Tennis to Austin." *B T Magazine,* fall 1994.

Kahn, Lawrence M. "Discrimination in Professional Sports: A Survey of the Literature." *Industrial and Labor Relations Review* 44 (Apr. 1991): 395.

Kalt, Jeanette Chappell. "The Women's Rankings." *Tennis,* Feb. 1956.

Kalyn, Wayne. "A Tale of Two Champions." *World Tennis,* Apr. 1981.

Kamlet, Ken. "Going It Alone." *Tennis,* Sept. 1999.

Kane, Martin. "An Assessment of Black Is Best." *Sports Illustrated,* Jan. 18, 1971.

Kaplan, Daniel, and Langdon Brockington. "Prime Time for Women's Open Final." *Sports Business Journal,* Mar. 19–25, 2001.

Kennedy, Ray. "The Zing Go the String." *Sports Illustrated,* June 6, 1983.

King, Robert E. "Trendsetter of the Nineties: Boy Ryland." *Black Tennis,* spring 1996.

Koger, Pat. "Minority Participation." *Tennis USTA,* Mar. 1997.

Kohn, Marek. *The Race Gallery: The Return of Racial Science.* London: Vintage, 1995.

"Ladies & Gentlemen. . . ." *Time,* July 17, 1950.

"Lawn Tennis 1872–1972." *World Tennis,* Aug. 1972.

Lawrence, Bishop William. *Memories of a Happy Life.* Boston: Houghton Mifflin, 1926.

Leand, Andrea. "Behind the Lines." *Tennis,* Apr. 2000.

———. "Earth to Venus: What's Up?" *Tennis Week,* Mar. 25, 1999.

———. "Junior Juggling Act." *Tennis Week,* Mar. 6, 1997.

————. "The Price You Pay." *Tennis USTA,* May 1988.

————. "Time to Grow Up." *Tennis Match,* Sept. 1999.

————. "U.S. Dream Team." *Tennis Week,* Aug. 5, 1990.

Lee, Victor. "Atkinson's Light Shines Brightly." *Black Tennis,* 1985 (no season listed).

Leeds Trades Union Council and Anti-Fascist Action. *Racism in Leeds and West Yorkshire.* Leeds, England: Leeds Trades Council, 1987.

"Lloyd Upset by Garrison." *Black Tennis,* 1985 (no season listed).

Lorge, Barry. "Arthur Ashe: In the Right Place." *World Tennis,* Dec. 1976.

————. "Blue Bloods, New Bloods." *World Tennis,* Jan. 1982.

————. "Lessons in Living." *Tennis,* Apr. 1993.

————. "Uneasy Lies the Head That Wears a Crown." *World Tennis,* Jan. 1981.

Love, Darlene. *My Name Is Love: The Darlene Love Story.* New York: William Morrow, 1998.

Marshall, Marilyn. "Zina Garrison: Aiming for the Top in Tennis." *Ebony,* June 1986.

Martin, James. "Choose Your Weapon." *Tennis,* Sept. 2000.

————. "Swing Time." *Tennis,* Sept. 2001.

Mathabane, Mark. *Kaffir Boy: An Autobiography.* New York: Signet, 1989.

————. *Kaffir Boy in America.* New York: Collier, 1989.

McGann, George. "Doc Johnson, Dedicated to Medicine and Junior Tennis, Wins Marlboro Award." *World Tennis,* July 1965.

McNulty, Mike. "The Venus and Serena Effect." *Tennis,* Nov. 2000.

Meadow, Barry. "Jimmie McDaniel: Never Allowed to Be a Legend." *World Tennis,* Oct. 1979.

————. "What's White . . . and White . . . and White . . . and Why?" *World Tennis,* Feb. 1982.

Mel'ody. "Noah sur Blanc." *Afiavi,* May–June 1993.

Middleton, Hayda. *Sport in Britain.* London: Foreign and Commonwealth Office, Sept. 1997.

Miller, M. K. "Cover-Up." *The Source Sports,* Oct. 2000.

Moran, Brian. "The Life of Bryan." *World Tennis,* Jan. 1990.

Morris, Claranelle. "A New Star Arises in Pacific Northwest." *Black Tennis,* winter 1996.

Moseley, Bob. "He Will Grow with History." *Tennis USTA,* Apr. 1993.

Mulloy, Gardner. "Larsen and Gibson Take Colorado State Titles." *World Tennis,* Nov. 1956.

Newby, I. A., ed. *The Development of Segregationist Thought.* Homewood, Ill.: Dorsey, 1970.

"Newcombe Downs Ashe at NSW." *World Tennis,* Jan. 1966.

Nicholas, Betty. "A Yank in Africa Discovers New Friends." *Tennis USA,* July 1989.

Nichols, Rachel. "The Supremes." *Tennis,* Nov. 2001.

"1998 U.S. Open, USA Tennis Plan for Growth." Available at: asapsports.com, Sept. 1998.

Noah, Yannick. "Arthur mon ami." *Afrique Magazine,* July–Aug. 1993.

———. *Secrets, Etc.* Paris: Plon, 1997.

"Noah Scores TOC with Win over Vilas." *ProTennis,* May–June 1986.

Noverr, Douglas A., and Lawrence E. Ziewacz. *The Games They Played: Sports in American History 1865–1980.* Chicago: Nelson Hall, 1983.

"Odizor Scores Upsets at Wimbledon '83." *Black Tennis,* fall 1983.

Okaitey, Sam. "The Future of Tennis in Africa." *West Africa,* May 8–14, 2000.

Oke, Idowu. "Williams' World." *West Africa,* July 17–23, 2000.

Olney, Lisa. "USTA/Eastern News: And the Winners Are. . . ." *Tennis Week,* Jan. 21, 1999.

Olsen, Jack. *The Black Athlete: A Shameful Story.* New York: Time-Life, 1968.

Pentz, Linda. "Dealing the 'Race Card.' " *Tennis Week,* Sept. 18, 1998.

———. "Racial Disharmony, pt. III." *Tennis Week,* Nov. 20, 1997.

———. "Rockin' Rubin." *Tennis Week,* Apr. 4, 1996.

———. "Watchdog." *Tennis Week,* Sept. 18, 1997.

Perry, Alison. "Wimbledon Bright Spots." *West Africa,* July 4, 1983.

Potter, Edward C. "The World's First Tens." *World Tennis,* Nov. 1957.

"The Power Game." *Time,* July 15, 1957.

Price, S. L. "London Blitz; Lori McNeil Shocked Steffi Graf to Start an Explosive Week of Wimbledon Upsets." *Sports Illustrated,* July 4, 1994.

———. "Simply Super." *Sports Illustrated for Women,* Nov.–Dec. 2000.

"Professor Arthur Ashe: Tennis' Class Act Moves into the Classroom." *Ebony,* July 1983.

"Profile: American Tennis Association." *Third Annual Black Enterprise/Pepsi Golf and Tennis Challenge,* special supplement of *Black Enterprise,* Sept. 1996.

Quarles, Benjamin. *The Negro in the Making of America*. New York: Touchstone, 1987.

"Racism in Pro-Tennis?" *Tennis Week,* Mar. 25, 1999.

Rader, Benjamin G. *American Sports: From the Age of Folk Games to the Age of Televised Sports*. Englewood Cliffs, N.J.: Prentice Hall, 1996.

Rampersad, Arnold. *Jackie Robinson: A Biography*. New York: Knopf, 1997.

"La raquette inspiree." *Tennis* (France), July 1997.

"Reaching Out to Players of Color." *Black Enterprise,* Sept. 1997.

Rice, Horace W. "Bryan Shelton's Latest Racket." *Black Tennis,* Jan. 1986.

"Richard Williams: Venus and Serena's Father Whips the Pros and Makes His Family No. 1 in Tennis." *Ebony,* June 2000.

"Rising Tennis Stars Leslie Allen, Yannick Noah Show Promise." *Ebony,* June 1981.

Robertson, Cliff. "Remember the Good Times." *World Tennis,* Oct. 1980.

Robinson, Louie. "Black Athletes—Are There Any Winners?" *The Crisis,* May 1983.

Rosengren, John. "On the Court with Michael Jordan." *Tennis,* Dec. 1999–Jan. 2000.

Rust, Edna, and Art Rust Jr. *Art Rust's Illustrated History of the Black Athlete*. Garden City, N.Y.: Doubleday, 1985.

Rustad, Mitch. [No title]. *Tennis,* June 2004.

Sachs, Adam. "Red, White & Williams." *Tennis,* Sept. 2003.

Sailes, Gary A., ed. *African Americans in Sport*. New Brunswick, N.J.: Transaction, 1998.

Samuels, Allison. "Life with Father." *Newsweek,* July 2, 2001.

Schoenfeld, Bruce. *The Match: Althea Gibson and Angela Buxton*. New York: Amistad, 2004.

———. "The Venus Trap." *Tennis,* July 2003.

———. "Who Is Jamea Jackson?" *Tennis Match,* Apr.–May 1998.

Scott, Eugene L. "Vantage Point." *Tennis Week,* May 7, 1998.

Sebbar, Leila. *Sherazade*. Translated by Dorothy Blair. London: Quartet Books, 1999.

"Serena Williams: Wins at U.S. Open; First Black Female Champion since 1958." *Jet,* Sept. 27, 1999.

Shaler, Nathaniel S. "The Nature of the Negro." *Arena* 3 (Dec. 1890): 23–55.

Shmerler, Cindy. "Alexandra the Great?" *Tennis,* July–Aug. 2000.

———. "Luck Be a Lady." *World Tennis,* Sept. 1990.

———. "Under Control." *World Tennis,* Sept. 1985.

Silverstein, Paul A. *Algeria in France: Transpolitics, Race, and Nation.* Bloomington: Indiana Univ. Press, 2004.

Simpson, Larry. "A Royal Tennis Presence in New Orleans." *Tennis USTA,* Apr. 1997.

Smith, Doug. *Whirlwind, the Godfather of Black Tennis: The Life and Times of Dr. Robert Walter Johnson.* Washington, D.C.: Blue Eagle, 2004.

Sommers, Irene. "Who Brought Tennis to America?" *Tennis,* Sept. 1994.

Stein, Joel. "The Power Game." *Time,* Sept. 3, 2001.

———. "Williams Wins!" *Time,* Sept. 17, 2001.

St. John, Allen. "Father Knows Best." *Tennis,* May 2003.

Summerhayes, Martha. *Vanished Arizona: Recollections of My Army Life.* 1908. Reprint. Chicago: Lakeside, 1939.

Talbert, Billy. "The Serve." *World Tennis,* June 1958.

"Talent Scout." *World Tennis,* July 1989.

Taylor, Quintard. *In Search of the Racial Frontier: African Americans in the American West 1528–1990.* New York: W. W. Norton, 1998.

"Tennis: A Sport on the Move." *West Africa,* Apr. 23–29, 2001.

"Tennis, the Sport of a Life Time." *Tennis Week,* Apr. 24, 2001.

Thompson, Tommy. "This Pro Turns Out a Professional Product." *Texas Tennis,* Mar. 1987.

Thorpe, David. "Changing the Game." *Bullseye,* spring–summer 2003.

The Tiger. Texas Southern Univ. yearbook, vol. 27. Houston: Texas Southern Univ., 1975.

Tignor, Stephen. "A Mal-Function." *Tennis,* June 1999.

"The Top Ten." *World Tennis,* Feb. 1965.

Toure. "Mister Smith." *Tennis,* Feb. 2000.

"Tribute: Althea Gibson." *Tennis,* Nov.–Dec. 2003.

Trotter, Joe, Jr. *The African American Experience.* Boston: Houghton Mifflin, 2001.

———. *Black Milwaukee: The Making of an Industrial Proletariat, 1915–1945.* Urbana: Univ. of Illinois Press, 1985.

Tucker, Steven M. "Against All Odds." *Racquet,* fall 1991.

Twine, France Winddance, and Jonathan W. Warren, eds. *Race: Researching Race in Critical Race Studies.* New York: New York Univ. Press, 2000.

Tym, Alice. "The Kenya Nationals." *World Tennis,* May 1970.

U.S. Bureau of the Census. "Occupation by States." In *Population,* vol. 4 of *Fifteenth Census of the United States, 1930.* Washington, D.C.: Government Printing Office, 1933.

U.S. Open '91. Program. White Plains, N.Y.: USTA, 1991.

U.S. Tennis Association (USTA), comp. *Tennis in Public Places.* White Plains, N.Y.: USTA, 1997.

———. Circuit Office. *2000 Eddleman USTA Challenger Program.* Lynn, Mass.: H. O. Zimman, May 2000.

"Venus and Serena Come to DC." *Sister 2 Sister,* July 2001.

"Venus and Serena Williams Live Up to the Hype." *Tennis Week,* Sept. 20, 2001.

Virginia Slims Legends Tour 1996. Program. St. Petersurg, Fla.: WTA, 1996.

"A Visit to Richmond." *World Tennis,* July 1968.

Wagner, Eric A. *Sport in Asia and Africa: A Comparative Handbook.* Westport, Conn.: Greenwood, 1989.

Walker, Juliet E. K. *Encyclopedia of African Business History.* Westport, Conn.: Greenwood, 1999.

"Washington Continues to Improve." *Black Tennis,* spring 1991.

"Welcome to Camp." *Tennis USA,* July 1989.

Wertheim, L. Jon. "The Serena Show." *Sports Illustrated,* May 26, 2001.

———. *Venus Envy: Power Games, Teenage Vixens, and Million-Dollar Egos on the Women's Tennis Tour.* New York: Perennial, 2002.

Wheeler, Joseph R. "Triple Match Point: The Story of Branch Curington . . . Tennis Pro." *Black Tennis,* summer 1983.

"Where Are They Now?" *Newsweek,* Sept. 1, 1969.

Whitsitt, Sam. "Soccer: The Game America Refuses to Play." *Raritan: A Quarterly Review* 14 (summer 1994): 58–69.

Wiggins, David K. *Glory Bound: Black Athletes in a White America.* Syracuse, N.Y.: Syracuse Univ. Press, 1977.

Williams, Roger. "Is Tennis Doing the Right Thing for Blacks?" *Tennis,* Nov. 1990.

———. "Lori McNeil." *Tennis,* Sept. 1994.

Winters, Mark. "Fountain of Youth: USTA Seeks the New and Improved Player Development Program for the Millennium." *Tennis Week,* Nov. 16, 1998.

———. "Grassroots Start." *Tennis USA,* Dec. 1997.

———. "Hawk Lands on a Different Court." *Tennis USTA,* May 1998.

Witherall, Mary. "Winning Is Only Half the Battle." *World Tennis,* May 1987.

Wolverton, Brad. "Tennis, Everyone." *Tennis,* Sept. 2001.

"XL Bermuda Open." *Tennis Week,* Apr. 23, 1998.

Published Interviews

Amdur, Neil. "Conversations with Lt. Arthur Ashe." *World Tennis,* June–July 1968.

"A Cut Above." Interview with James Blake by Eddie Taylor. *Deuce,* 2002 (no season or month listed).

Entretien avec Chanda Rubin par Yannick Cochennec. *Tennis* (France), Aug. 2003.

Entrevue avec Guy Forget avec Bruno Cruz. *Tennis* (France), Dec. 1990.

Interview with Beverly Coleman. *B T Magazine,* spring 2001.

Interview with Nick Bollettieri. *Tennis Week,* Jan. 15, 1998.

"J'aimerais gagner un Grand Tournoi, et me tirer en douce." Entretien avec Yannick Noah par Guy Barbier et Jean Couvercelle. *Tennis* (France), Dec. 1989.

"Je serai pret pour Roland Garros." Entrevue avec Yannich Noah par Jean Catuffe. *Le Monde de Tennis,* June 1990.

"King Richard." Interview with Richard Williams by Paul Fein. *Tennis Week,* Nov. 20, 1997.

"Sister Slam." Interview with Serena Williams by Roy S. Johnson. *Savoy,* Nov. 2002.

Newspapers

Atlanta Journal-Constitution
Baltimore Sun
Brooklyn Daily Eagle
Chicago Defender
Chicago Sun-Times
Chicago Tribune
Dallas Morning News
Dallas Times Herald
Detroit News
Florida Times-Union

London Times
New York Herald Tribune
New York Times
USA Today
Washington Post

Index

Italic page number denotes photograph.